Options of Command

OPTIONS OF COMMAND

by

Colonel Trevor N. Dupuy
U.S. ARMY, RET.

Hippocrene Books
NEW YORK

53GP

For information, address: Hippocrene Books, Inc.,
171 Madison Avenue, New York, N.Y. 10016.

Published in the UK by Antony Bird Publications Ltd.,
Strettington House, Strettington, Chichester, West Sussex.
ISBN 0907319 09 2.

Printed in the United States of America.

Library of Congress Cataloging in Publication Data

Dupuy, Trevor Nevitt, 1916–
   Options of command.

   1. World War, 1939–1945—Campaigns.   2. Strategy.
3. Tactics.   4. War games.   I. Title.
D743.D82   1984   940.54'1   84-9014
ISBN 0-88254-993-6

Contents

List of Maps

Introduction

WORLD WAR II was by far the most titanic struggle of world history. It can be conveniently, and without excessive over-simplification, broken down into four major sub-wars, each a tremendous military conflict in its own right: (1) Japan against China, Britain, and the United States in Asia; (2) Germany (and Italy) against the Western Allies (Britain, France, the United States, and some smaller nations in Europe and North Africa); (3) Germany against Russia in Eastern Europe in the most gigantic single land war ever fought between two nations; and (4) Japan against the United States (and some allies) in the greatest maritime war of history. Figure 1 shows the interrelationship of these wars, and the periods of involvement of the major participants.

Had some of the important decisions in the great battles of these interrelated wars been made differently, not only would the course of the sub-war have been changed and possibly its outcome affected as well—the courses of all the other sub-wars would to some extent have been affected. In some instances the change in the course of the war and the sub-wars could have altered the course of subsequent history, even without a substantial change in the overall outcome; if only simply by affecting the disposition of forces at the conclusion of conflict. In other instances, both the outcome and subsequent history might have been totally different.

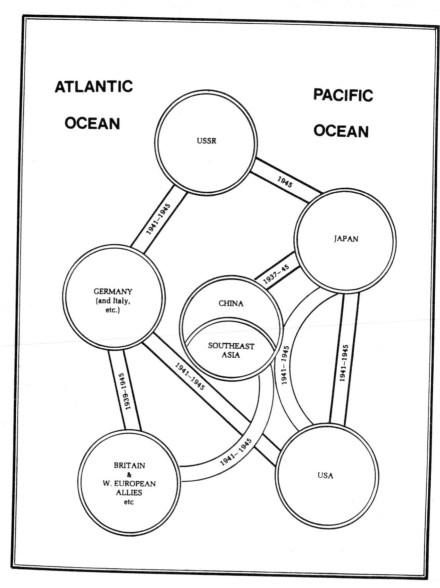

FIGURE 1
INTERRELATIONSHIP OF MAJOR SUB-WARS OF WORLD WAR II

Commanders, both field commanders at all levels and senior commanders in their headquarters or oval offices, must constantly decide among options, whether they be related to strategic planning well in advance or to tactics on the battlefield. History shows that reasonably well-trained, responsible, military professionals usually have selected wisely, or at least selected an option that did not result in a totally unexpected or disastrous outcome. In some instances exceptional commanders have been inspired to select an option not obvious as available to them, and through such inspiration have won battles that should have been lost. Sometimes, however, even good commanders have made "bad choices," providing their opponents with an opportunity to change the course of the operation and gain a result quite different from that which the commander sought. It matters not whether the wrong decision was based on faulty information, or was influenced by enemy guile, or was simply an egregious blunder. If a wrong decision was exploited by the enemy, the results were just as devastating to the general who was the victim of chance or circumstances as they were to the stupid blunderer.

Sometimes the random effects of chance, luck, or coincidence can provide the opportunity for a dramatically unexpected outcome, but even in this case there is an option for the commander who sees the opportunity and exploits, or fails to exploit it.

The historian, and the non-professional as well, can readily think of numerous examples where a commander's choice of option influenced much more than the situation he faced. Had Xerxes not allowed himself to be enticed by Themistocles into dividing his fleet at Salamis, for example, ours might have been a Persian rather than a Greco-Roman heritage. Had it not been for the happy inspiration of Robert Bruce to use his camp-followers to feign an attack at Bannockburn, four centuries of British history would have been totally changed. Had the Duke of Normandy not made one last effort, combined with a deceptive maneuver, at Hastings, proud Englishmen might trace their heritage back to Harold the Savior rather than William the Conqueror.

It seemed to me and some of my colleagues of the Historical Evaluation and Research Organization that we might sharpen our historical perspectives, and at the same time have some fun, if we were to see what might have happened if some options of command in World War II had been chosen differently. This book is the result.

We have selected ten campaigns of World War II that were important for a variety of reasons, and in which a principal commander, under slightly different circumstances, might have made a different decision, and set in motion an operation with a different ending and, in some cases, a significant effect on subsequent developments. In each case we have laid the background for the decision as it actually happened, altered only enough to make the different decision feasible and reasonable, and we have then carried the operation to a reasonable conclusion. We have tried to make the decisions appropriate to the character of the men who "made" them as well as to the circumstances under which they were made. We've enjoyed doing it. We hope you will enjoy reading what might have been.

As principal author I have been involved in selecting the options in all of the chapters and discussing the repercussions of each selection. I have drafted some of the chapters, and I have commented in detail on them all, suggesting and making revisions. My colleagues in turn have commented in detail on mine. In the end, the responsibility is mine, but I am greatly indebted to Dr. John E. Jessup, Mr. Paul Martell, Mr. C. Curtiss Johnson, and Mrs. Grace P. Hayes, without whom these "might-have-beens" might not have been.

Options of Command

Prologue

BETWEEN 1937 AND 1945 some or all of the major nations of the world were fighting one another, on battlefields and oceans that covered a large portion of the surface of the earth. This world war, that was really several wars, changed the entire world and its people in ways that are still being felt forty years later. Wars are fought by people, and the course of their development is in the hands, and the minds, of a few men. What happens on a battlefield, what happens in a whole theater, what happens for years, even centuries, to come, hinges often on a choice of options. In World War II those choices were made, and the results are recorded for all time. But what if some of the choices had been different? What would have happened?

What if Hitler had knuckled under at Munich? What if Chiang Kai-shek had rallied his forces and driven the Japanese off the mainland? What if the Germans had pushed across Asia to the Pacific Coast? What if they had developed an atomic bomb and used it on England? These are flights of fancy beyond credibility. But what if the Japanese approach to Pearl had been detected? And what if Hitler had believed those who told him the Allies would land in Normandy? Or what if Stalin had believed that the Germans were about to attack his western frontier and had prepared to resist them? These are reasonable options that might have happened.

Remember, if you will, what actually happened, but

follow these tales, which start with what was and—through a few plausible, even though sometimes chancy, choices that each commander might reasonably have made—come out in a different way.

Let's look at the early general course of the war and its major sub-wars, as a basis for subsequent review of those battles where the results might have been changed by different command decisions.

The Early War between Japan and China

Most historians believe that World War II began when Japanese troops based in Manchuria (which Japan had been consolidating since 1931) moved south into China proper, and had their first clash with troops of Nationalist China at the Marco Polo Bridge near Peking on July 7, 1937. In the next three years Japan occupied great areas of mainland China, and drove the National Government from its capital in Nanking to a temporary capital at Chungking in west-central China. But though the Chinese were not able to offer very effective military opposition to the Japanese, they did not give up, and followed a "scorched earth" policy as they withdrew in front of the invaders. Thus, as the area of Japanese control widened, the pace of the Japanese advance, and of the war, slowed down.

The Japanese invasion came at a time when China was in the throes of a great civil war between President Chiang Kai-shek's National Government and Mao Tse-tung's Communists. The Japanese, of course, were taking advantage of this internal struggle. However, the Chinese warring factions patched up a partial, de facto, truce, and cooperated to a limited degree in opposition to the invasion.

One reason China was able to maintain its resistance (despite the fact that its seacoast was occupied or blockaded) was a trickle of military supplies which it received from Britain and the United States through Rangoon and the Burma Road to Kunming in southern China. This provision of support to China from presumably neutral nations was as greatly resented by Japan as the cruel and ruthless aggression against China was resented by the West, particularly the United States. By early 1940 relations between Japan and the United States had become extremely strained.

The Early War between Germany and the European Allies

Under the Nazi regime of Adolf Hitler, a resurgent and expansionist Germany absorbed independent Austria in early 1938, took much of independent Czechoslovakia after the Munich Conference of September 1938, and occupied the remainder of Czechoslovakia in March 1939. The obvious next victim of Hitler's program of "peaceful" conquest and *drang nach osten* (drive to the east) was Poland. Britain and France recognized after their humiliation at Munich that Germany's course of aggression could be stopped only by force. Thus they decided to guarantee Poland's independence, as a warning to Hitler, and when his troops invaded Poland on September 1, 1939, Britain and France honored their commitment to declare war on Germany.

Just prior to the German invasion of Poland, the previously hostile dictatorships of Hitler's Nazi Germany and Stalin's Communist Soviet Union had unexpectedly signed a non-aggression treaty. After Germany's newly-developed and overwhelming *blitzkrieg* had crushed the desperate but futile resistance of the Poles, Soviet troops also invaded Poland and annexed the eastern portion of that country in accordance with a secret protocol signed at the same time the Nazi-Soviet non-aggression treaty was instigated.

Meanwhile, in the West, the hastily-mobilizing Western Allies—Great Britain and France—had been helpless, as far as providing assistance to Poland was concerned. They had neither the capability nor the inclination to undertake any offensive actions against western Germany, where a handful of German troops garrisoned the formidable Westwall (or Siegfried Line) along Germany's western frontiers. The result was an inactive stalemate in western Europe, dubbed the "phony war" by Western journalists. The phony war continued through the winter of 1939–1940, as both sides assembled forces behind their respective lines of fortifications—the Westwall in Germany, and the Maginot Line which covered France's northeastern frontier with Germany, from Belgium to the Rhine River and the Swiss border.

At sea there had been somewhat more action. Although German merchant shipping immediately disappeared from the high seas, German submarine activity was intense and effective against British merchant vessels and warships. Also, some German raiders caused brief problems for the British Admiralty. The most dramatic occurrence at sea, up to this time, was the Battle of the River Plate, off the coast of South America, between the German pocket battleship *Graf Spee* and three smaller British cruisers. Although seriously damaging the British vessels, the *Graf Spee* also was crippled. She took refuge in the Uruguayan port of Montevideo, where she was destroyed by her crew. By the end of the year British mastery of the surface of the seas was secure, but it was evident that German submarines continued to pose a serious threat to that mastery.

Late in November, 1939, Soviet forces invaded Finland. This was the beginning of a series of moves by Stalin to extend the rest of the Soviet frontiers further west, toward Central Europe, to match the gains already made in Poland. But this first Soviet move met an unexpected rebuff. The Finns repulsed the initial Soviet attacks, inflicting great losses on the attackers. The Finnish cause was hopeless, however. During the winter the USSR massed overwhelming forces against tiny Finland and, despite horrible losses inflicted by the highly efficient Finnish Army, overwhelmed Finn defenses, and Finland capitulated on March 12, 1940.

Thus, in the early months of 1940 there was a stalemate

along the two major fighting fronts of the two wars which—up until this time—remained completely unrelated to each other. But while there was not likely to be much further dramatic activity for some time to come along the extended battlelines in China, the massing of German forces in western Germany, and of Anglo-French forces in northeastern France, promised an imminent, furious revival of active warfare.

CHAPTER I

Ardennes, 1940:
Forests and Fortifications

ALTHOUGH IT IS IMPOSSIBLE to deny the significance of the superb military performances of such Allied commanders as Marshal Weygand, General De Gaulle, and Field Marshal Lord Gort—or the indomitable contribution of the new British Prime Minister, Winston Churchill—beyond a doubt the man primarily responsible for the Allied victory which ended the evil of Nazism in 1940, was French Premier Paul Reynaud. He made the crucial decision, without which the campaign of 1940 would probably have been lost by the Allies. That decision: recall General Maxime Weygand from retirement to replace General Maurice G. Gamelin as Commander in Chief of Allied forces in France, and promote Colonel Charles De Gaulle to général de brigade and to serve as Weygand's chief of staff.

Reynaud and Gamelin

Reynaud had become Prime Minister on September 14, 1939 the day after former Premier Édouard Daladier had created a War Cabinet, and then had suffered a heart attack. Like Daladier before him, Prime Minister Reynaud also took the portfolio of National Defense. His momentous decision was several days in formulating in the new

Premier's mind, but it appears that it became inevitable on October 1, 1939, one month after the war began. Reynaud had been intently studying reports prepared for him by Gamelin's headquarters on the progress of the war in Poland. He had called Gamelin to the Ministry to discuss the implications of these reports. The two men sat beside a coffee table in the Premier's large office. "It seems that De Gaulle and Fuller have been on the right track all along." The little Prime Minister lit a cigarette, leaned back, and blew a long, thin stream of smoke up into the air, then suddenly lowered his eyes to meet Gamelin's. The general shrugged. "Not necessarily," he replied. "There were too many Germans for the Poles, they were too well trained, they had air superiority, they had too many items of modern materiel. Poland is a technologically inferior nation, and the Poles were surprised."

"I agree with your first four points," responded the Prime Minister. "But these alone were not enough to cause the collapse of a substantial nation and its army in a mere three to four weeks." Again the Premier looked searchingly at the general. "And I totally reject your last two points. Poland is not as industrialized as Germany or France, but the Poles are teaching us a thing or two about the technology of cryptology." Gamelin nodded, a bit uncomfortably. "And there was no surprise; the Poles were as ready as they could be." The General squirmed. "Would we have fared better than the Poles?" Gamelin was silent.

"I want De Gaulle promoted to *general dé brigadé*, and placed at the head of a special staff section on modern warfare directly under you. And if the British are not smart enough to recall Fuller to active duty, let's get him over here as a consultant to De Gaulle."

General Gamelin quietly rose from his chair.

"*M. le Président*,"* he said, "you are injecting yourself into purely military affairs in a fashion that I do not be-

---

*It was proper to refer to the Prime Minister as "President du Conseil de Ministres."

lieve is appropriate for the civilian head of the government. My staff and I are intently studying the results of the Polish Campaign. We believe we are learning what is necessary. If you are not satisfied with my performance, I serve at your pleasure. But so long as I am commander in chief, I insist upon my right to perform my duties in the professional manner which appears to me to be most appropriate."

Reynaud, never known as a tiger in decision-making, decided not to accept the challenge.

"I am sorry if I have offended you, my dear General. May I suggest that we both think further about this conversation, and perhaps meet and talk again about it in a few days." After a few polite pleasantries, the meeting ended.

Reynaud and Weygand

Twenty-four hours later Reynaud was sitting at the same coffee table, talking to another general; this one, however, was in civilian clothes. He was retired General Maxime Weygand, who had won fame as Marshal Foch's chief of staff during the final months of World War I, and who had later helped Marshal Pilsudski stop the Russian invasion of Poland in the decisive Battle of Warsaw, in 1921. Weygand, spruce as usual, seemed to Reynaud much younger than his seventy-two years. But Weygand had always looked younger than his years.

After a few brief comments about the war in general, and the Polish Campaign in particular, Reynaud got right to the point in the same words that had started his critical exchange with Gamelin the day before: "It seems that De Gaulle and Fuller have been on the right track all along."

"Yes," responded Weygand, "so it seems. I do not of course have access to intelligence reports. But from what I read in the newspapers, and hear elsewhere, on the fashion in which the Germans employed their tanks, the operations could have been planned by the brilliant young 'Charlie' De Gaulle or the very peculiar 'Boney' Fuller."

"Don't you think we ought to do something about that, immediately?" asked the Premier.

"Of course," responded the General. "I trust that Gamelin and his staff are in the process right now. Of course Maurice doesn't consult me—no reason why he should."

There was a long pause. Weygand, long accustomed to the ways of heads of state, who had to weigh policy matters with which he was not concerned, sat quietly. Suddenly Reynaud spoke.

"General Weygand, if I were to recall you to active duty, would you accept the post of Allied Commander in Chief, *vice* Gamelin? There is only one condition."

"*Monsieur le Président*," responded the general, "if that condition does not touch an old soldier's honor, I would welcome the opportunity to serve my country again in war."

"I would want you to appoint De Gaulle, promoted to brigadier general, as chief of a special planning staff directly under you. In effect he would be your chief of staff, just as you were that of Foch."

"An interesting comparison. I was the typical, self-effacing staff officer; Charlie is not. It might be a very difficult relationship. Yet the stakes are great, and the need is urgent. I accept."

De Gaulle's Appreciation

Six months later to the day, Saturday, March 2, 1940, there was another meeting in Mr. Reynaud's office, now filled with several rows of chairs. It was a large and very distinguished group. The entire French Cabinet was there. There were five Englishmen in civilian clothes; Prime Minister Chamberlain of Great Britain, War Minister Sir Leslie Hore-Belisha, First Lord of the Admiralty Winston Churchill, Air Minister Sir Archibald Sinclair, and retired Major General J.F.C. Fuller. In addition to General Weygand, now back in uniform, there was General A.J. Georges, the overall field commander for northern France under Weygand, and his three principal sub-ordinates: General Gaston Billotte, whose First Army Group was assembled behind France's border with Belgium, from the English Channel to Montmédy; General André Gaston Prételat, the commander of Second Army Group, which was deployed behind the Maginot Line from Montmédy to Epinal; and General Antoine Besson, whose Third Army Group (actually only one army, composed largely of fortress troops) occupied the fortifications of the Line. Also present were the nine subordinate army commanders, one of whom was General John Vereker, Lord Gort, commander of the British Expeditionary Force.

The group was being addressed by a young, pencil-thin, tall (6'4") brigadier general.

"Gentlemen," said Brigadier General Charles De Gaulle. "My study group has finished its appreciation, or estimate of the situation along the German frontier, and we have submitted our recommendations to the Commander in Chief. With some changes, he has approved our recommendations (Weygand smiled; the arguments had been intense), and he has asked me to present his approved plan to you at this meeting.

"You will note that in the assessments I am about to present, I discount the possible contributions of the Belgians and the Dutch. If there is a contribution, it will be a welcome bonus; if not, we shall not be disappointed. As you know, neither country has permitted joint planning, in the event the Germans invade their territories. That the Germans will so invade Holland and Belgium I have no doubt; they will *not* want to go through the meatgrinder of the Maginot Line. But whether we will have time to arrange any sort of effective coordination with the Dutch or Belgians must remain very much in doubt.

"But before going further into operational concepts, let me make general comparisons of the opposing forces—again, discounting the Dutch and Belgians.

"The Germans have 123 divisions—about two and one

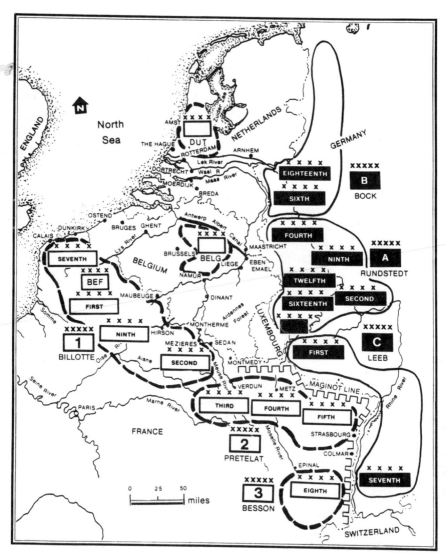

Deployment of Allied and German Forces Prior to German
Invasion, May 10

half million men—deployed from the North Sea to Switzerland, as shown on this map. Ten of these divisions are armored divisions, with experience in Poland; nine are motorized divisions, of which four have been created in the last six months. The Germans have about 2,500 tanks—an average of 250 tanks per armored division. Note that the Germans have all of their tanks in armored divisions, and note that most of these are concentrated in the rather narrow sector of Army Group A, of General von Rundstedt. This massing of armor is very significant, as we shall see.

"The Allies have 103 divisions: nine are British, one Polish, and thirteen are fortress troops in *la Ligne Maginot*. Of these 103 divisions, eight can be called armored divisions, but they are not to be compared in experience, doctrine, or morale with the German divisions.

"On the other hand, we have a tremendous superiority over the Germans in tanks—both in numbers and quality. We have over 3,600 tanks, and tank for tank ours are better than theirs. But we have fewer than 2,000 in our armored divisions; the rest are scattered among the infantry divisions, to be employed in what our British allies call 'penny packets.' So our tank superiority, in my considered judgment, is illusory.

"In the air, they will be able to employ about 3,500 combat aircraft; we have only about half that number, although again the superiority might appear to be on our side if we were able to count the British Bomber and Fighter Commands. (I am not privy to the strength of those commands, though I can guess.) But without greater assurance of British cooperation, we can count only on the 300 British aircraft in France, added to our own pitiful force of 1,400.

"In addition to quantity and quality of tanks, we have some other advantages. As Clausewitz so truly wrote, 'Defense is the stronger form of combat.' As I said earlier, the German deployment reveals very clearly that they have no intention of getting bogged down in the Maginot Line.

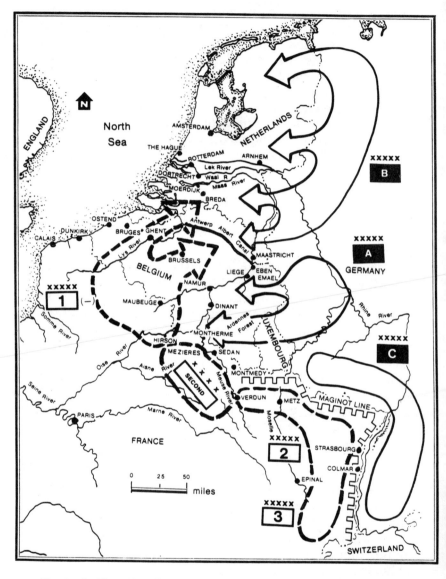

Strategic Situation D + 2 − D + 4 as Predicted by De Gaulle
without French Redeployment

(I must say that I am baffled by our own deployment; with half our manpower committed behind the Maginot Line. What benefit are we deriving from it?) They have so concentrated forces in the north that they obviously are thinking—or want us to believe they are thinking—in terms of an updated Schlieffen Plan.

"My colleagues and I have done a rather intensive, if relatively crude, wargaming of the options open to the Germans. We have been greatly aided in this by the participation of General Fuller, who has kindly applied his own very sophisticated doctrinal ideas about the employment of armor to the opportunities and problems from the German point of view." "Boney" Fuller gravely nodded, without a smile.

"When they attack, Army Group B will drive rapidly into Holland and Belgium. They anticipate that we will not allow the Schlieffen Plan to have a second chance. They visualize this as the graceful wave of the toreador's red cape in front of the Allied bull. The five armies of our Army Group One will rush north to anchor secure positions in the lower Meuse, Waal, and Rhine Valleys. (Presumably the Germans know something about our plans.) Within two to four days, our deployments will be roughly as shown on this map: a concentration of four armies in Flanders and the Low Countries; a concentration of four more armies in and behind the Maginot Line, linked together by a very narrow, vulnerable waist in the Montmédy-Sedan region by the French Second Army.

"We believe that as this situation crystallizes, von Rundstedt's Army Group A will drive due west, toward that vulnerable waist. And unless we have prepared plans against such a contingency, I believe they will be able to penetrate and will isolate the Allied armies into two groups, to be dealt with in detail. Does anyone have any doubts as to how that will end? It will be Poland again!"

De Gaulle paused, and looked around the room. He had the rapt attention of his audience.

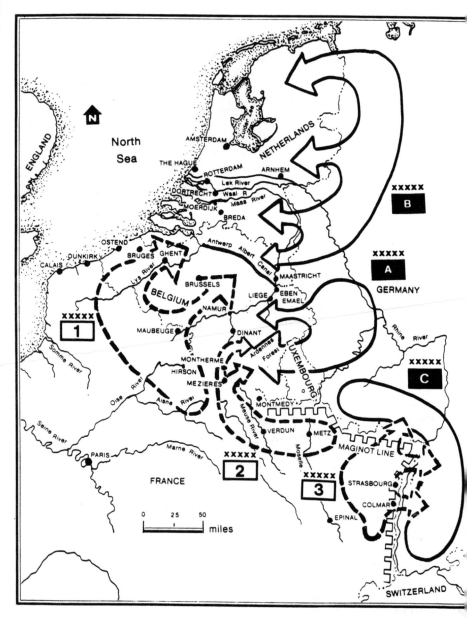

De Gaulle's Proposed Redeployment

De Gaulle's Plan

"What can we do about it? It is easy. Be ready for *les sales boches*, and defeat them! Here's how.

"General Billotte's Army Group must still advance northward into the dangerous German trap, but perhaps with a bit less *élan* and verve than the present plans suggest. General Prétélat's Army Group Two must also shift northward promptly, to form a blocking position along the Meuse River, with outposts as far forward as they can be pushed into the Ardennes. And the non-fortress units of General Besson's Army Group must also shift west and north of Strasbourg, and begin immediate demonstrations—*real* demonstrations, not those play actions which caused the Western press to speak of a 'phony war' five and six months ago—against German troops to their front. Does this include raids across the Rhine? Of course it does! I show our proposed redeployment on this map.

"If we are ready, the Germans will be repeating October of 1914; and we shall be repeating October of 1918. It can be a glorious victory!

"Orders will be issued to the Army Group commanders tomorrow. For reasons of security, however, details of the plan must not go below the level of army staffs. *Vive la France!*"

But De Gaulle was not allowed to end his presentation so easily. In his fluent but atrocious French, Mr. Churchill asked when De Gaulle expected the German attack.

"We must be ready as soon as possible. Certainly by April 1. Undoubtedly before June 1. If I had to guess, I would pick early May. And may I in turn ask you a question, M. Churchill? Although I know it is not your department, can you tell me when we can expect the British 1st Armored Division?"

Churchill mumbled, and did not reply. War Minister Hore-Belisha spoke up. "It should be before June 1."

"Let's hope the Germans attack late," replied De Gaulle.

One French general asked why the shift in deployments would not be made until after the German attack began.

"Very simple, *mon général*. We think we know what the German course of action is likely to be with current deployments. If we were to start suddenly shifting our armies around, they would begin to wonder what we were doing, and why. It could lead to a very significant change in German plans. Let it be we who surprise them, and not the other way around. We must exercise the tightest security. As I said, until movement orders are actually issued, not a word about this plan or concept must go below the army headquarters."

Finally the questions ceased. Weygand got up, looked around the room and strode to the podium where De Gaulle had been standing.

"We seem to have exhausted them, Charles," he said. "Please take my seat while I say a few final words." Weygand paused, and looked around the room.

"General De Gaulle has not given us a blueprint for victory. That will have to be won on the battlefield with the sweat and blood of our brave young officers and men. And in the days and weeks that remain to us it is our task—that of those of us in this room—to provide the inspiration, the confidence, the professional competence they will need as they prepare for the battle. During the time that remains, and in the days and weeks of the battle, we must endeavor to impart to those young men everything which we greybeards have learned so painfully over so many years.

"But what General De Gaulle *has* given us—certainly he has given it to me—is the underpinning for the essential ingredient of confidence. Certainly the Germans will not act exactly in the way that he has predicted. But logic, *his* logic, makes it clear that they will do something *like* his prediction. And we shall be ready! No matter what they do, his is a positive plan which will permit us to seize the initiative from a surprised and shaken foe, and win the war on *his* soil; where it should be won. It is our French tradition. It is the British tradition. *Vive la France! Vive la Royaume Unie!*"

As De Gaulle had promised, the orders were issued to the army groups the next day. Orders to armies were issued on March 4.

The German Offensive

The German plan, in fact, was essentially that which had been predicted by De Gaulle, emerging from the same kind of process of military logic by brilliant young military intellectuals. But the German offensive began in the early morning hours of Friday, May 10, 1940, with a fury that in itself surprised the Allies, and surprised the Dutch and Belgians—who immediately opened their frontiers to the Allies.

Following overwhelming predawn bombardments of all major Dutch and Belgian airfields, German Army Groups A and B crossed the Belgian and Dutch frontiers. Initially the main effort was on the right, by Army Group B, in Holland. Paratroop drops in the vicinity of Rotterdam, The Hague, Moerdijk, and Dortrecht quickly paralyzed the interior of the Netherlands

In the neutral Low Countries, Belgium nominally had some 600,000 men in twenty-two divisions, under the command of King Leopold III. The Dutch Army theoretically comprised some 400,000 men, under the command of General Henri G. Winkelman. Neither was assembled in full strength. Both countries had elaborate defensive systems, made more formidable by canal networks, with further arrangements for flooding great stretches of country by opening dikes. The troops, however, were not very well trained, and their equipment was less modern and less complete than that of the French and British. The most serious deficiency, however, was the lack of adequate defensive plans. In hopes that they could remain neutral, neither Belgium nor the Netherlands had dared to discuss joint defensive plans with the French or British, and had rebuffed every Allied effort to carry on even informal discussions.

Early in the day, glider and parachute units landed on the top of powerful Fort Eban Emael, northern anchor of the main Belgian defense line, neutralizing it, while other German troops crossed the Albert Canal, which should have been defended by Eban Emael's guns. The violence and success of the initial German attacks, combined with terror bombings of the interior regions of both countries, threw their populaces into confusion and panic.

Fall of the Netherlands

News of the early German successes aroused great alarm in Paris and London. Prime Minister Chamberlain, whose government had been tottering because of failures in Norway and general lack of popular support, resigned to permit lionhearted Winston S. Churchill to lead a coalition British government in the face of the German avalanche.

Pressing its initial advantage, German Army Group B drove steadily forward, despite frantic Dutch flooding of much of the countryside. By May 13, German main elements had begun to force their way into the so-called Fortress of Holland, joining up with most of the paratroops, who had seized and held the key bridges over the Rhine estuary. At the same time, German spearheads met advance elements of General Henri Giraud's French Seventh Army near Breda, and drove them back toward Antwerp. The Queen of the Netherlands and her government escaped by ship to England from the Hague. On May 14, Germany demanded complete surrender, on pain of the destruction of all Dutch cities by aerial bombardment. As proof of its intentions, the Luftwaffe brutally destroyed the entire business section of Rotterdam while negotiations were in process. Winkelman surrendered.

The Defense of Belgium

Things were far less one-sided in Belgium.

A small liaison team under Major General Jean de Lattre de Tassigny, had arrived in Brussels from Weygand's headquarters before dawn on the 10th. (In fact, a similar team had been sent to the Hague, at the same time; it had been less successful than the Brussels team, and was withdrawn on the 14th.) King Leopold and the senior members of the Belgian Operations Staff had immediately met with De Lattre and his group. They were pleased with the Allied plans, which involved a far stronger commitment of forces than they had anticipated.

"*Votre Majesté*," said De Lattre, "Army Group One, with the cooperation of your border officials, is already crossing the frontier on a broad front from the North Sea to Dinant. The Second Army Group is beginning to advance in multiple columns northward through the Ardennes Forest, alert to their right for the anticipated German drive through the Forest, and with special tank-antitank groups hastening to seize critical road junctions and terrain features in the Forest. If the Belgian Army will stand, most of your kingdom can be saved from the flood."

"We will stand," responded the King. He reached across the table to shake De Lattre's hand, then with his staff hastened to complete the Belgian plans.

The Ardennes

De Gaulle had predicted that the German hammer blow—Rundstedt's Army Group A—would wait for two or three days before moving into the Ardennes. But the Germans had anticipated that the difficulty of the terrain would prevent them from reaching the Meuse before May 12 at the earliest, even if they began to move on the 10th. So before noon that day German units were already streaming across the Ardennes.

But, in fact, German progress was even slower than had been anticipated by General Halder and his General Staff. The French cavalry, and Belgian chasseurs, whom the Germans had expected they could sweep aside with ease, were quickly reinforced by small teams of French armor and infantry, which held the vital junctions and links in the rocky wooded countryside. But the roads were plentiful, even if undulating, and by combining maneuver and overwhelming strength, the five armored and three motorized divisions in General Paul L.E. von Kleist's Panzer Group pushed ahead. By evening of the 13th, elements of General Heinz Guderian's XIX Panzer Corps had reached the Meuse at Sedan, and spearheads of General Georg-Hans Reinhardt's Panzer Corps were at Montherme and Mézières. During the next day both corps concentrated in the deep river valley.

German intelligence reports were sounding an alarm, however. They had expected to be opposed by units of General André-Georges Corap's French Ninth Army, and units of General Huntziger's Second Army. Instead they were facing elements of the Fifth Army—under General Bourret—near Sedan and Mézières, and elements of General Édouard Requin's Fourth Army near Montherme. Where were Corap and Huntziger?

The Battle of the Meuse River

It soon became evident that they and their armies were at Namur and Dinant, respectively, and that the French First and Seventh Armies, and the BEF, had integrated themselves with the Belgians to provide a firm and unyielding arc behind the Meuse River from Namur to Eban Emael, and along the Albert Canal north and west of Eban Emael. That fortress was tightly invested; their spectacular initial success here on the 10th had little practical value for the Germans.

The critical days of the Flanders Campaign were May 15–17, along the Meuse River, from Sedan to Montherme. De Gaulle had thought it would probably be a little further north, near Dinant, and so he had assembled a new and secret French Sixth Army, commanded by General Touchon, just east of Maubeuge. De Gaulle merely sent an order for Touchon to slip to the south about fifty kilometers, to be in a blocking position in case the Germans broke through. It was a wise precaution.

Early in the morning of the 15th the Germans launched an all-out assault across the river, supported by devastating dive-bombing attacks, which soon silenced the accurate French artillery. By evening both of Kleist's corps had succeeded in establishing substantial bridgeheads on the west bank of the river, and part of Rommel's 7th Panzer Division of Hoth's Corps was also across, north of Montherme. The Germans had suffered severe losses in their assaults, probably greater than they had inflicted. And the French lines, though driven back, were still intact. More serious for the Germans, after dark—with German aircraft departed from over the battlefields—French artillery resumed accurate, devastating fire. This made it very difficult for the Germans to reinforce and resupply their battered units in the bridgeheads.

The story was the same the following day. With the support of swarms of aircraft the Germans again silenced the French artillery, and inched ahead in all three bridgeheads. A tenuous junction was made on the Aisne-Meuse Canal, west of Sedan and Mézières. But darkness again ended German aerial dominance of the battlefield. French artillery reasserted its superiority, and retained it for the ensuing eight hours of darkness.

On the 17th, both Guderian and Reinhardt were stopped completely in their efforts to expand their bridgeheads. The German air support effort was markedly smaller than it had been the two previous days, and the unexpected appearance of Spitfires and Hurricanes of Air Chief Marshal Dowding's Fighter Command, not only reduced the effectiveness of the smaller German effort, it sent up their losses. The British War Cabinet, apparently satisfied that the line would be held in Flanders, loosened the reins on Dowding.

North of Montherme however, there was an unexpected development. Despite French artillery interdiction during the night, somehow or other Major General Erwin Rommel's 7th Panzer Division got about fifty tanks across the river. Shortly before dawn the French were

surprised by a slashing armored attack toward the head-
waters of the Oise River, near Hirson. Rommel was unaware, of course, that this was the headquarters of General Touchon's Sixth Army, in reserve, just waiting to
deal with such a development as his incipient breakthrough.

In fact, although alerted, Touchon's men did not get
into the fight that day. General Requin's Fourth Army still
had an uncommitted division in reserve. Requin now
launched that division, supported by two independent
tank battalions, in counterattack. Near the ancient field of
Rocroi the French and Germans met each other in what
was essentially the first battle of modern armor. It was a
draw. But for the Germans, anything short of a breakthrough was a failure. Their "Plan Yellow," launched
with such vigor and high hopes just one week before, had
now clearly failed.

The Allied Counteroffensive

Weygand, remembering the success of Marshal Foch's
Aisne-Marne Offensive, in July 1918, immediately after a
similar German failure, had been waiting for this moment. Somewhat to De Gaulle's annoyance, Weygand had
reorganized the three field army groups. Billotte now had
the French First and Seventh Armies, and the BEF, none
of which had yet been seriously tested in combat. Prétélat
had the Ninth, Second, and Third Armies, also having
seen little action. Besson—now completely divorced
from the Maginot Line—had Touchon's Sixth, and General Garchery's Eighth Army, neither of which had fired a
shot, save at aircraft overhead. The Fourth and Fifth Armies, which had borne the brunt of the German attack,
were to remain in position, falling into GHQ Reserve after
Besson's Third Army Group had pushed sufficiently far
east of the Meuse. H-Hour was to be 4:30 on May 18, eight
hours after the German defeat was clear.

The psychological impact of the counterattack was

everything that Weygand had hoped for. The despondent Germans were completely surprised, and for two days a state of near panic pervaded the German Army. But the Germans were too good for this situation to continue indefinitely, and the French were not good enough to exploit it adequately. Nevertheless by the evening of the 20th, when the lines began to stabilize, the Allies were in possession of Maestricht, and had units across the German frontier near Aachen; they had recovered Eben Emael, and held at least ten kilometers east of the Meuse River in the Liége area. They held the line of the Ourthe River, and approached the Luxembourg frontier west of Bastogne. Thence the line ran generally south to Montmédy and the Maginot Line.

"*La Ligne Maginot*," said De Gaulle expansively to Weygand, as they had dinner alone together in GHQ—a chateau near Vervins—"has proven decisive! Some day historians will report that the proof of the value of the horribly expensive Maginot Line is that not one shot has been fired from it or at it—perhaps a slight exaggeration, but not much—while it has permitted France to assemble overwhelming combat power superiority elsewhere on the battlefield, and thus to be successful!"

"Don't be premature, Charles," cautioned Weygand, holding up his napkin. "We have had only ten days of war so far; how long did World War I last?"

"The psychology is different this time, *mon général*," responded De Gaulle. "*Nous verrons*—We shall see."

Five hours later—3:00 A.M. May 21, a telephone rang in Weygand's bedroom office. The groggy general picked up the phone of a private line to the Prime Minister, Paul Reynaud.

"Have you heard the news, *mon général*?" Still slightly confused, and only half awake, Weygand replied quite truthfully. "No, *M. le Président*."

"The *Boche* General Staff has killed Hitler. Halder was also killed in the exchange of fire with Hitler's bodyguards. But Brauchitsch, calling himself Temporary

Führer of the Fourth Reich, has offered to negotiate. He says: "All issues between Germany and the Allies are negotiable."

"Please meet me in my office at 10:00 in the morning, Marshal Weygand. Bring with you *Général de division* De Gaulle."

Afterword

The above presentation of the Flanders Campaign of 1940 is remarkably close to the actual course of events, with one significant exception. This presentation assumes that the elimination of the dead, unimaginative hand of Édouard Daladier from the position of Prime Minister and Defense Minister of France would have resulted in a new and logical Allied professional military estimate of the situation in Northwest Europe in 1939–40. It is hard to see how such a new look at the situation by qualified French professionals, under the stimulus of a sharp, intelligent political leader like Reynaud, could have reached any other conclusion regarding the German plans, and the logical Allied response to those plans, than is suggested in the preceding paragraphs. Such a reassessment, no matter who the generals responsible, would almost certainly have reached the conclusions drawn in this presentation by De Gaulle and Weygand.

Without a De Gaulle and a Weygand, the result would likely have been a stalemate in northwestern Europe, not unlike that of 1915–18. But with men of imagination and ability, an Allied victory such as is suggested here, was certainly well within the bounds of reasonable possibility.

CHAPTER II

Battle of Britain

Planned Invasion of Britain

As GERMAN TANKS rumbled across the Low Countries and France in May 1940, it seemed to Adolf Hitler that the end of the war in the West was at hand. For the Low Countries, prostrate under the occupying Germans, and for France, whose government gave up on June 21, the war was indeed over. And, as the British withdrew to Dunkirk and departed in boatloads for their island, it looked as if they too would soon sue for peace. Then, Hitler thought, he could attack Russia and gain in the east the *Lebensraum* he needed for his people.

But the British would not see reason. So, on July 2, Hitler ordered his generals and admirals to proceed with plans to invade England; the operation was known as "Sea Lion."

As long as the Royal Air Force was flying in strength, however, attempting to cross the English Channel in force would be extremely hazardous, and so the first step in preparation for Sea Lion must be the elimination of the RAF. Gaining an advantage in the air, Reichsmarschall Hermann Goering told Hitler with confidence, would take only four days; in four weeks the whole RAF could be destroyed. And with the RAF out of the skies, Goering believed, a token landing would suffice to bring the British to surrender. On August 2 he issued his "General

Direction for the Operation of the Luftwaffe against England," setting as primary targets the ground installations of the RAF and the industries feeding it. British shipping and important ports also would be attacked.

Luftwaffe Attackers

Ready to undertake the job of destroying the RAF were three German *Luftflotten*, or air fleets. *Luftflotte* 2 had headquarters in Brussels and an operational area that included northern France east of the Seine River and north of Paris, and all of Belgium, the Netherlands, and northwestern Germany. Its commander, Field Marshal Albert Kesselring, a 54-year-old former artillery officer, had made his name as an administrator when he served on the German Army General Staff in World War I. He learned to fly at the age of forty-eight and had commanded Luftwaffe units in the Polish campaign that started World War II, and in the battle for France.

Headquarters for *Luftflotte* 3 was at St. Cloud, on the outskirts of Paris, in an area that included all of France west and south of the area of *Luftflotte* 2. Its commander, Field Marshal Hugo Sperrle, a few months older than Kesselring, had transferred from the infantry to the flying service in his early thirties and had been in command of the German air contingent that fought in the Spanish Civil War.

In the occupied area of Scandinavia, north of the area of *Luftflotte* 2, *Luftflotte* 5 had headquarters at Stavenger, Norway. Its commander, General Hans Juergen Stumpff, had led an air corps when German forces occupied Norway in the spring. *Luftflotte* 5 was to participate in the blockade of Britain by attacking shipping along the coast of Scotland and as far south in England as the Humber River. To accomplish this Stumpff had about 150 long-range bombers, in two incomplete *Geschwaden* (wings), plus 37 Me-110 fighters.

Luftflotten 2 and 3 between them had approximately 3,000 aircraft, of which roughly 1,300 were bombers, and

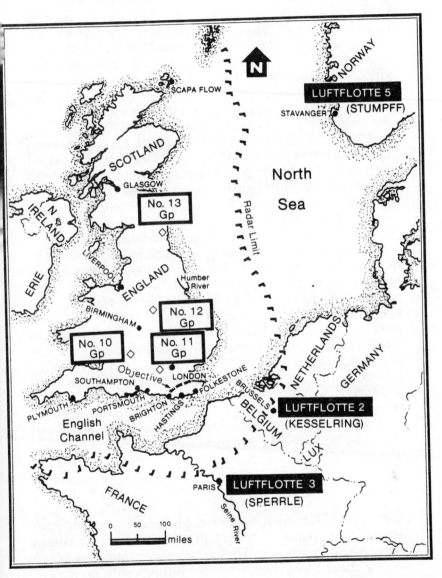

Strategic Situation, Battle of Britain and Operation Sea Lion, Summer/Fall 1940

almost a third of these were the fastest and best German bomber, the Ju-88. The rest of the bombers were the older He-111 and Do-17. There were also 300 slow and vulnerable Ju-87 Stukas, the dive bombers that had performed so effectively in the Polish campaign, and in the invasion of France, where they had had no opposition. The bombers were organized in twelve complete and three incomplete *Geschwadern* and four independent *Gruppen* (groups). There were in addition about 800 short-range Me-109s, eight complete *Geschwadern* of fighters, and parts of two more. The long-range fighter force comprised fewer than 300 Me-110s, whose performance against the British Spitfires and Hurricanes in the Battle of Flanders had been unsatisfactory. In addition to these, the two air fleets had a number of reconnaissance aircraft and minelaying seaplanes, and a few night fighters.

The German Air Minister, and Commander in Chief of the Luftwaffe, Reichsmarschall Hermann Goering, had been an outstanding fighter pilot in World War I. As leader of the famous Richtofen *Geschwader* he was awarded his country's highest award for valor, the *Orden pour le Mérite* (the Blue Max). He had joined the Nazi Party in 1922 and took part in the "Beer Hall *Putsch*" the next year, in which he was severely wounded. This proved to be tragic for Goering, for he was given morphine to ease the pain, and he never overcame the addiction he acquired. Goering was completely loyal to Hitler and rose with him to be second in command of the Nazi Party, and thus the second most influential person in Germany.

RAF Defenders

Across the Channel, there were four groups of the RAF Fighter Command to defend Britain. Number 11 Group was charged with the defense of London and southeastern England from Hampshire to Suffolk, with headquarters at Uxbridge. Since it was closest to the German bases in France and the Low Countries, 11 Group was to bear the brunt of the attack, suffer the heaviest losses, and gain prestige by recording the most victories. Commanding the group was a New Zealander, Air Vice Marshal Keith Park, probably the best fighter tactician in the RAF. Park was a veteran of World War I, who had fought as a ground soldier at Gallipoli and been wounded at the Somme. By managing to lose his medical records he transferred to the Royal Flying Corps and succeeded in shooting down 20 German aircraft. Between the wars most of his assignments had been in the fighter branch.

North of the 11 Group area, Number 12 Group was responsible for air defense of the eastern counties and the Midlands. Its commander, Air Vice Marshal Trafford Leigh-Mallory, also a veteran of World War I, had had specialized assignments involving cooperation with the Army during the years between the wars. Number 13 Group, headquartered at Newcastle, covered the north of England, all of Scotland, and as far west as Northern Ireland. Air Vice Marshal Richard Saul, commander of the group, had commanded an air squadron in World War I.

South of the area of 12 Group and west of 11, Number 10 Group covered the West Country. It was under the command of Air Vice Marshal Quintin Brand, with headquarters at Rudloe, near Bath. A South African, and also a veteran of World War I, Brand had devoted considerable effort to developing night fighter tactics. Between the wars he established a record for a flight from England to the Cape of Good Hope.

To face the attacking Germans the RAF Fighter Command had a strength of about 900 fighters. Most of them were Hurricanes and Spitfires, organized in 50 squadrons with about 600 aircraft ready to fly. In addition, there were some Blenheims—night fighters that had been converted from light bombers—and some two-seater Defiants. There were 22 squadrons in 11 Group, 15 in 12 Group, and the rest were divided between 10 and 13 Groups.

Air Officer Commander in Chief of Fighter Command since July 14, 1936, was Air Chief Marshal Hugh Dowding. As his nickname, "Stuffy", might suggest, he was cold, formal, and aloof; he was never a popular man. Dowding had been commissioned in the Royal Artillery in 1900 at the age of eighteen, after graduation from the Royal Military Academy at Woolwich. Thirteen years later, while attending the Staff College at Camberley, he took flying lessons early each morning, before classes at the college began, and so qualified for transfer to the Royal Flying Corps. His subsequent extensive and impressive combat experience in World War I gave him a permanent place in the RAF, when it was formed in 1918.

Standard fighter aircraft in the First World War were often cockpit biplanes, built with wooden frames covered with fabric. In the years after the war aircraft designers began building part metal or all metal monoplanes, highly streamlined, with plexiglass canopies enclosing the cockpit. Dowding, serving in a research and development assignment on the Air Staff in the 1920s, recommended that this type of aircraft, which was winning the annual Schneider Cup trophies, should be developed into fighters for the RAF. From this recommendation came the Hurricane and the Spitfire.

Nearly ten years later Dowding, now a senior officer in the RAF, was serving on the Air Council, responsible for RAF research. He became interested in the work of a young scientist, Robert Watson-Watt, who was experimenting with radio waves. Watson-Watt had discovered that it was possible to observe the reflection of radio waves from distant objects. With Dowding's encouragement he pressed ahead with his work on Radio Direction Finding. As a result, when World War II started, Radio Detection and Ranging—soon called RDF, and later RADAR—had become an invaluable device for detecting distant aircraft, day or night, in clear weather or foul. Dowding deserves to share the credit with Watson-Watt.

A strong-minded, stubborn, and imaginative man, as head of Fighter Command, Dowding soon found himself in disputes with colleagues and superiors. His recommendation that his fighters be built with bullet-proof windshields, for instance, was considered ludicrous by many senior Air Staff officers. The Air Staff also disapproved his idea of building hard-surfaced runways for his fighter airbases; instead they accepted the advice of an Army engineer, that hard surfaces could not be properly camouflaged. In May of 1940 Dowding found himself in a serious disagreement not only with the Air Staff but also with the new Prime Minister, Winston Churchill. Recognizing that the defeat of France was inevitable, he objected to Churchill's willingness to respond to desperate French requests for more air support. He wanted to save every precious British fighter aircraft for the inevitable battle for the control of the skies over Britain.

British Aircraft Production

The existence and size of Britain's Fighter Command owed much to the efforts of Sir Thomas Inskip, who since 1936 had been Minister for the Coordination of Defense. The British Air Staff had been asking for more and more bombers, believing that proper air strategy was to strike at an enemy's war-making potential. Since it was assumed that there was no defense against bombers, the Air Ministry believed that it would be a waste of resources to build up a large force of defensive fighters. But Inskip, strongly supported by Dowding, pointed out that the Germans had an unapproachable lead in building bombers. He reasoned that if the RAF could hold off German attempts to gain control of the skies over Britain long enough, a blockade of Germany by the Royal Navy, combined with Allied help, could bring victory. Inskip agreed with Dowding that British fighter aircraft, assisted by Robert Watson-Watt's radar with its ability to give warning of approaching bombers, should be able to fight off German bombing attacks. Since fighters cost considerably less than bombers, the public and the Cabinet were impressed by these arguments. They accepted Inskip's recommendations that the hasty build-up of the RAF should focus on fighters. There were strong protests from many air marshals, including Lord Trenchard, who had been the first commander of the RAF, who declared in the House of Lords that building up fighter strength instead of bombers "might well lose us the war!"

Thanks to the work of Lord Beaverbrook, Minister of Aircraft Production, by the end of the Battle of Britain Fighter Command had more aircraft than it had had at the beginning. Having been told to "produce aircraft as quickly as possible without regard to established procedure," Beaverbrook cut through red tape and got the job done. Unfortunately he could do nothing about replacing experienced pilots.

British Tactical Doctrine

In Dowding's concept, as we have seen, his fighter force should be used only for the mission for which it had been intended—to defend Britain. Thus he strongly protested against proposals to send squadrons to aid the French or to attack German shipping in the Channel. Reluctantly, Churchill acceded to Dowding's views.

Radar was a critical—and perhaps the crucial—factor in the defensive doctrine developed by Dowding and his staff for Fighter Command. While German raiders were still assembling over the Pas de Calais they were visible on British radar screens. Dowding's controllers could therefore send RAF fighters to the most advantageous spot to meet the attackers. Since this was often over British territory, British pilots who bailed out unhurt could usually return to action almost immediately. German pilots who survived being shot down became prisoners of war.

It was Dowding's view—and he insisted on it—that a minimum number of aircraft, preferably a single squadron, should be sent up when a flicker on the radar indicated enemy intruders. Reinforcements would be sent aloft as needed. But he had opposition from within his own ranks regarding this doctrine. Most vocal among his protesting subordinates were the commander of Number

12 Group, Air Vice Marshal Leigh-Mallory, and Squadron Leader Douglas Bader, also of Number 12 Group. Leigh-Mallory and Bader advocated the so-called Big Wing response, sending up a large number of fighters as soon as the Germans were detected, on the theory that the more defensive fighters there were the better they could accomplish the mission of driving off or shooting down hostile bombers. In retrospect it is clear that Dowding's concept was the correct one, and assured flexibility in response to the German attacks.

With a few exceptions the British fighter squadrons were using a tight V—or "Vic"—formation in 1940. In this formation the twelve fighters of a squadron were formed into four Vics, each of three aircraft, with the Vics flying one behind the other. However, this required the pilots to put much concentration on holding formation, and it was somewhat difficult to do this and also to watch for enemy aircraft at the same time, particularly when enemy fighters approached from the rear. In some squadrons the formation was altered to three Vics, with a fourth plane in each Vic weaving behind the formation to cover against attacks from the rear. These fourth planes were called "Tail-end Charlies," but, unsupported by other aircraft, they were often shot down. By mid-summer of 1941 the British had modified their four-ship formation to one which they called the "finger four," because the aircraft flew in positions that could be likened to outstretched fingertips.

The British Spitfires and Hurricanes generally endeavored to avoid the high performance German Me-109s and go directly for the German bombers. The Spitfire—Britain's best fighter—was slightly slower than the Me-109 and could not fly quite as high, but a good British Spitfire pilot could hold his own against the German airplane. The Hurricane, was more outclassed by the Me-109, although it was far better than the German long-range fighter, the Me-110.

British fighters were more heavily armed than the Germans, having eight free-firing .303 caliber machine guns in their wings. The Me-109 had two 7.62mm machine guns in the wings and a 20mm cannon firing through the propeller hub.

German Tactical Doctrine

German pilots had gained experience with modern high performance aircraft during the Spanish Civil War, and as a result the Luftwaffe had a loose four-ship formation of fighter aircraft called a *Schwarm*, further subdivided into two pairs of aircraft called *Rotten*. The two planes of a *Rotte* worked closely together, one as leader, the other as wing man. While the leader of the *Rotte* attacked an enemy aircraft, the wing man provided protection to the rear by watching for enemy attacking from behind. Similarly, when one of the *Rotten* was engaged, it was protected by the other.

Experience in Spain had also taught the Luftwaffe that the most effective escort technique was for fighters to fly ahead of the bombers and attempt to destroy enemy defensive fighters before they could engage the bombers. Although bomber crews tended to feel insecure if they could not see their escorts, German fighters nevertheless often ranged ahead far out of sight.

The Luftwaffe at first used the Ju-87 *Stuka* against targets in Britain, on the theory that the divebomber could bomb with greater accuracy than high altitude level bombers. They even equipped some of the other bombers—including the Ju-88 and Do-17—with dive brakes so that they could dive bomb as well. However, all of these aircraft were slow in comparison with the British fighters, and many of them were shot down. Goering, convinced that offensive bombing was the only way to win an air battle, blamed the bomber losses on lack of courage on the part of the escorting fighters and failure to provide adequate protection. This was due, he believed, to the practice of the fighters of ranging ahead of the bombers. Consequently he issued orders that fighters should provide only close escort. The veterans of Spain, young fighter commanders like Adolph Galland and Werner Moelders, were both offended and frustrated by these criticisms and orders.

The Battle; First Phase

On July 19, 1940, German aircraft started striking at British convoys in the English Channel. Attacks were repeated almost daily for a month, and in that time 150 of the RAF fighters that went up to drive the Germans off were lost, but they shot down 286 Germans. This was a prelude to the big campaign by which Goering planned to destroy the Royal Air Force. Scheduled to start on August 10, *Adler Tag* (Eagle Day), the campaign would concentrate attacks on Fighter Command's airfields, to destroy the installation, the radars, and any aircraft that might be on the ground. However, August 10 came and went, with weather so poor that the attacks were cancelled and rescheduled for the 12th. But the weather remained bad, and only a few raids were flown.

It was on August 13 that the real Battle of Britain began. Nearly 500 bomber sorties and 1,000 fighter sorties took off for England on that day. They were met by 700 Fighter Command sorties. Thirteen British aircraft were lost, but six of the pilots survived. The Germans lost 45 aircraft. Not all of these were shot down, however. Cloudy weather and confusion in the German orders contributed to a number of accidental German losses.

Weather continued to interfere with German plans, but nevertheless the weeks that followed saw repeated heavy raids on British targets. August 14 was unflyable, but on the 15th the Luftwaffe flew 1,786 sorties, and lost 75 airplanes, including one-sixth of Stumpff's *Luftflotte* 5. The RAF sent 974 fighters up, and lost 34, a loss that could be covered by reserves.

Goering was highly distressed. It was at this point that he issued orders, in spite of firm objections from his fighter commanders, that the fighters must provide close escort and stop deserting the bombers to range ahead.

On the third day of operations, August 16, the Luftwaffe flew 1,715 sorties, Fighter Command 776. German strikes against Fighter Command's installations caused much damage, and Luftwaffe losses were a little lower, 45 aircraft, while the RAF lost 21 fighters in the air, plus an unknown but probably substantial number on the ground. Although many RAF pilots landed safely, nevertheless losses of trained fighter pilots were becoming critical. The Air Ministry approved the transfer of a number of pilots who had been flying Fairey Battle light bombers, considered obsolete by this time, from Bomber Command to Fighter Command.

On August 17 there were no Luftwaffe attacks. The following day, however, was an active one, marking the end of the first phase of the Battle of Britain. Four groups of Ju-87 *Stukas* destroyed the radar station at Poling. Two British squadrons, one of Spitfires, and one of Hurricanes, rose to attack. One group of *Stukas* lost 12 of 28 aircraft, and six more were so badly damaged they were scarcely able to limp back to France. In all 71 German airplanes were lost, compared to 27 of Fighter Command. The total losses for these first four days of major operations were 95 for Fighter Command and 236 for the Luftwaffe. This was shocking to the German leaders; clearly a heavy price was being paid for results that were not spectacular.

New tactics seemed to be called for. Accordingly Goering issued new orders on August 19. Since the blips on a radar screen could not distinguish fighters from bombers, the number of German fighters in proportion to bombers was to be greatly increased. In this way, Goering hoped to entice Dowding into sending large formations of the best of his force, primarily 11 Group, against vastly superior numbers of German fighters. Kesselring's *Luftflotte* 2 was to make the main attacks, on Fighter Command installations and radar sites. At night, or when there was daytime cloud cover, Sperrle's *Luftflotte* 3 would primarily attack aircraft factories. Goering told Sperrle to make plans for an attack on Liverpool, and ordered Stumpff of *Luftflotte* 5 to prepare for a similar night attack on Glasgow. But until Goering himself gave the word the cities were not to be hit.

While weather postponed the start of the next phase of the Battle of Britain, Park issued new instructions to his pilots of 11 Group. They were to bypass attacking German fighters and concentrate on the bombers. Moreover, whenever possible they were to engage the Germans over the English countryside and at least stay close enough to the coast so that if they had to crash land or bail out they could do so over southern England and thus be available to fight again.

The Battle; Second Phase

On August 24 Kesselring's aircraft struck aerodromes in Kent and Sussex. Fighter Command's 11 Group shot down 38 attackers, but lost 22 of their own. Sperrle's bombers missed the dockyards at Portsmouth and hit the town, and also missed aircraft factories outside London and hit that city. This was the first bombing London had experienced since the Zeppelin raids of World War I.

The following day Sperrle sent 45 bombers to attack the Fighter Command aerodrome at Warmwell in Dorset. The bombers were escorted by over 200 fighters, far outnumbering the defending fighters of 10 and 11 Groups, which could not evade the German fighters in order to concentrate on the bombers as Park had ordered. The airfield was badly damaged in the raid, and 20 German and 30 British aircraft were lost. That night German bombers struck targets in the Birmingham area. Also that night RAF Bomber Command attacked Berlin in retaliation for the bombing of London on the 24th, unaware that the German attack on London had been unintentional.

Sperrle hit Fighter Command's field at Goodwood on August 26, while Kesselring's bombers were striking aerodromes in Kent, Essex, and Suffolk, badly damaging one of 11 Group's fields. German losses were 41 aircraft, the greatest single day loss since August 18. Fighter Command lost 50, also their greatest.

After a day off on the 27th, Kesselring's bombers again struck a number of airfields in southern England on the morning of the 28th. That afternoon he followed up with a formation entirely of fighters, no bombers at all. Park scrambled his fighters to meet them. Total losses for the day were 30 German and 20 British aircraft. Sperrle's bombers struck Liverpool that night with more than 600 bomber sorties. British night fighters were not yet adequately equipped for night operations, nor were the pilots highly skilled, and they were able to shoot down only seven of the German bombers.

British Doctrinal Debate

The fact that German aircraft continued to strike day after day, and night after night, in spite of Fighter Command's efforts and heavy losses, seemed to confirm the views of the proponents of the Big Wing tactics. The argument over whether to send small forces or large to meet attacking Germans had become bitter. Instead of being resolved within Fighter Command the tactical controversy had become a political issue involving the government as well as the highest levels of command.

The squadrons of Fighter Command, charged with defense of the whole of England and Scotland, were widely dispersed over Great Britain, so that they could meet German bombers wherever they might appear. Under Dowding's doctrine an incoming raid of 30 or 40 bombers escorted by 50 or 60 fighters might be met by a British squadron of 12 fighters. As German formations grew to hundreds of aircraft, the odds against the RAF grew even higher.

Dowding, ever suspicious that the Germans would send a small formation to draw up RAF fighters, then follow it with a larger raid against a different area, had refused to send up all of his fighters at once lest they be out of fuel and on the ground when a second, more deadly, formation appeared. Park, commanding 11 Group, understood this, and handled his squadrons accordingly. But Leigh-Mallory, commanding 12 Group, disagreed, arguing that scrambling several squadrons would give the British better odds.

Leigh-Mallory's views were strongly supported by Douglas Bader, the legless fighter, who commanded Number 242 Hurricane Squadron of 12 Group, at Coltishall. Looking at the question from the viewpoint of a constantly outnumbered fighter pilot, he suggested that three squadrons at a time would be about right.

Since 12 Group's bases were farther Group from the German fighter bases than were those of 11, 12 Group's squadrons had time to put up more units and have them properly positioned before the Germans arrived. But they were supposed to provide protection for 11 Group's home fields while 11 Group was up, and if the squadrons of 12 Group went up as the Big Wing tactics called for, those fields would be unprotected.

The disagreement was complicated by Leigh-Mallory's belief that he should have been placed in command of 11 Group, where the main action was likely to be. Park and Leigh-Mallory also squabbled over responsibility for air cover over fighter bases, and "poaching" by squadrons that strayed from their own territory while chasing German raiders. Dowding, assuming that his orders were being followed, stayed out of these disputes, although it would probably have been better if he had not.

Bader's adjutant, Peter MacDonald, had been a Member of Parliament for fourteen years, and he saw to it that the politicians in the Air Ministry and other government offices were properly "educated" in the Big Wing theory. The Under Secretary of State for Air, Lord Harold Balfour, and other civilians thus became concerned in a tactical matter that never should have been their problem. The result was a decision from the Air Ministry that Fighter Command should adopt the Big Wing tactic. Reluctantly, Dowding complied. So on August 30, 1,000 RAF fighter sorties greeted the Germans when they arrived to bomb an aircraft factory at Luton and installations at Biggin Hill.

The Pendulum Swings to the Luftwaffe

From August 31 through September 6, Kesselring's bombers hit aircraft factories and oil refineries in Britain, and crippled Park's sector control stations. Park, following the Big Wing tactic, still continued to try to avoid the all-out fighter-to-fighter battle that Kesselring wanted. But he lost 161 aircraft in that period to the Germans' 189, and it was becoming difficult to continue to send the large numbers aloft.

Determined to force a decision, Goering at this point issued orders for the next phase of the battle. Kesselring would continue attacks on RAF Fighter Command aerodromes by day, and Sperrle would bomb them by night, in a concentrated effort to drive British fighters from the air.

On September 7 there was a fierce air battle over London. Kesselring sent more than 300 bombers, with an escort of 600 fighters, to bomb airfields in the London area. Although 21 British fighter squadrons rose to meet them, none were at full strength. There simply were not enough pilots to fly available aircraft, nor enough airfields still operable to handle them. The result was still more damage to fields, more stray bombing of London itself, and a loss of 56 British aircraft against 41 German losses.

Two days later 200 bombers raided London area airfields by daylight. Twenty-eight British pilots and 38 British aircraft were lost, and the Luftwaffe lost 28 of its airplanes. On the 11th, 100 bombers attacked Tangmere aerodrome, while others were hitting an aircraft factory near Southampton. The Germans lost 29 aircraft, and Fighter Command lost 25.

German intelligence officers had been studying the operations reports of Luftwaffe bomber and fighter squadrons, particularly of the *Stukas*, counting aircraft shot down, and crossing off RAF airfields and squadrons reported hit and destroyed. Hitler, carefully watching these reports, debated whether to go ahead with his plans for Operation Sea Lion, the amphibious invasion of southern

England. At lunch with his staff on September 13, he was optimistic. The chances of defeating Britain solely from the air looked so good, he said, that he had no immediate intention of risking the hazards of an invasion attempt. But the next day Goering assured him that with four or five days of good weather his Luftwaffe would have the air superiority necessary to cover the invasion. Since there had been no sign of a British bid for peace, Hitler now decided to go ahead with the invasion.

Preparations for Operation Sea Lion

Preparations for Sea Lion had been in progress for months with a variety of craft, including Rhine River barges, assembling in the Channel and North Sea ports. Meanwhile army units were moving into position near the coast. British intelligence was picking up reports of these movements, and German agents captured in Britain also yielded bits of information that pointed to an imminent cross-Channel move. As early as September 7 the British Chiefs of Staff had approved bringing the Home Forces to a state of instant readiness. The Royal Navy's plan for resisting an attempted invasion was put in motion. The battleships *Nelson* and *Rodney* sailed from Scapa Flow to join the battle cruiser *Hood* at Rosyth, while cruiser and destroyer forces at Portsmouth and Sheerness, flanking the likely invasion area, were strengthened. The battleship *Revenge* was at Plymouth, within range, while the battle cruiser *Repulse* and aircraft carrier *Furious* remained at Scapa Flow.

The German bombing of airfields continued on September 14, at a cost to the RAF of 28 more aircraft and to the Luftwaffe of 14. On the 15th Kesselring threw every available bomber and fighter into two daylight raids on Fighter Command's airfields, destroying 52 aircraft and losing 60. By this time, with new pilots sent up as rapidly as they arrived at their first bases, Fighter Command was really in poor shape, although German intelligence estimates that for all practical purposes Fighter Command had ceased to exist were exaggerated. All of 11 Group's airfields had been damaged, and several were completely useless. So many pilots had been lost that training programs had not been able to keep the available cockpits filled.

On September 17 Hitler decided that the RAF was no longer a threat to his invasion plans, and he gave orders for Operation Sea Lion to proceed. Preliminaries would start on October 7, with the first landings scheduled for October 8.

The invasion fleet continued to assemble in the ports of northwestern Europe. By October 7 over 150 landing barges of various sizes and capabilities and ships from the merchant marine were standing by on the French coast from Calais to Dieppe to carry German soldiers and their equipment across the Channel.

Three of the best German infantry divisions, trained in landing operations in the preceding months, had been moved to the coastal area and stood ready to board the vessels and land in the first wave. Behind them were three more, which would cross the Channel as soon as a beachhead was secured. They were prepared to exploit the initial success and proceed inland. Ten more divisions were ready to cross the channel behind the first six divisions. Landing beaches had been carefully selected, close to the ports of Brighton, Hastings, and Folkestone.

The plan was for the troops to board their transports late on October 7, and to land on the British beaches by dawn on October 8. Once ashore they would push toward the first objective line, roughly twenty miles from the coast, Brighton-Uckfield-Tenterden-Ashford-Canterbury. Luftwaffe units would fly almost continuous cover. Destroyers and torpedo boats would accompany the transports, and coming down from the North Sea, the battleships *Scharnhorst* and *Gneisenau*, with their 11-inch guns, the pocket battleship *Admiral Scheer*, also with 11-inch guns, and the heavy cruiser *Admiral Hipper*, with 8-inch guns, would be providing support, and warding off British naval vessels. They would be accompanied by destroyers, while a pack of U-boats prowled as close as they dared to British ports. The naval task force was commanded by Admiral Otto von Schrader, sailing on the *Scharnhorst*.

German intelligence, partially fed by British counterintelligence, predicted that resistance ashore would be light. Equipment that had been abandoned at Dunkirk in June had not yet been replaced, and units that had returned were assumed by German intelligence to be still in the process of reorganization and training. Civilian morale, the Germans speculated, had been so shattered by the repeated losses on the continent, the spectacle of hurried evacuation from Dunkirk, and the losses suffered by Fighter Command, that those living in the invasion areas would be willing to help the Germans once they got ashore. On this they misjudged, for the setbacks and the Luftwaffe attacks had in fact brought the British people together in a determination to hold out against all odds.

The German preparations had been impossible to conceal, and as they intensified in the first days of October, British preparations also intensified in expectation of an attempt within a few days. The *Furious* and *Repulse* steamed south from Scapa Flow, and rendezvoused with the *Nelson*, *Rodney*, *Revenge*, and *Hood*, off Rosyth. Admiral Sir James Somerville, Commander in Chief of the Home Fleet, was assigned the responsibility for protecting the coastal waters of Britain. *Furious* was carrying her full complement of Swordfish torpedo bombers, about 24 aircraft. These antiquated biplanes, nicknamed "Stringbags" by their pilots, still could launch a 21-inch torpedo at an enemy ship. Guarded by destroyers and a dozen submarines, the capital ships headed toward the area where invasion was threatening. A group of light cruisers, destroyers, and submarines gathered at Plymouth, prepared to attack the invasion flotilla from the west. Ashore, work was rushed on barbed wire and fixed defenses, and minefields were laid along the coast in the threatened area. The nation was warned of the possibility of an attack, and civilians were given instructions on how to prepare for it.

The Invasion

October 7 was cloudy, with a wind from the southwest at ten to fifteen knots that increased slowly to about twenty-five by midnight. By the time darkness fell the German troops were aboard their odd fleet—barges brought from the smooth waters of the Rhine to a totally alien sea, coastal steamers that in peacetime carried passengers or cargo from port to port, fishing vessels still smelling strongly of their catches. Crowded aboard with their weapons, the soldiers progressed from discomfort to misery as the seas built up in mid-Channel, tossing the vessels about, and washing over the sides of the barges.

Word of the departure of the fleet was radioed from France by agents in the developing French underground, and from Plymouth, Portsmouth, and Sheerness, British destroyers and cruisers and a swarm of motor torpedo boats put to sea, while the capital ships increased their speed as they steamed southward along the coast.

The assorted German attackers were scarcely beyond mid-Channel when they found themselves under fire from British naval guns. The smaller defending ships moved in to attack the slowly moving transports, while the larger ones and the submarines concentrated on their naval escorts. Already hampered by the cloud cover, the Luftwaffe aircraft could not distinguish friend from foe in the confusion and the darkness; their protection proved of little use.

Through all obstacles many barges and other craft ploughed on toward the British coast, and disaster. Although minesweepers preceded them, and cleared part of the area, the wind and sea had moved some mines into shallow water, where a number of the shallow draft barges came to grief. Others foundered when they broached to in the surf that rolled in on the beaches. Coastal artillery and some field artillery opened up as the landing parties came within range.

Naval Battle of the Broad Fourteens

Meanwhile the big ships of the two main fleets had encountered each other in the North Sea. The clouds had thinned by dawn, and British reconnaissance aircraft had spotted the German fleet as it approached the Broad Fourteens* from the northeast. At about the same time German aircraft returning from an attack on airfields spotted *Repulse*. Both alerted their forces, and *Furious* promptly launched her Swordfish.

The British ships were about fifty miles from the Germans, on a course south by east, the *Repulse* and *Hood* and their covering destroyers in the lead, followed by the battleships *Nelson* and *Rodney*, with *Furious* between and slightly behind them. Admiral Somerville's flag was on the *Nelson*. The German ships were proceeding in line ahead, with *Admiral Hipper* in the lead, followed by *Admiral Scheer*, *Gneisenau*, and *Scharnhorst*.

Upon realizing that the British fleet was out in force Admiral von Schrader ordered the German fleet to reverse course to try to avoid an encounter, Schrader had recognized this possibility, and was prepared. At his call German *Stukas* and other aircraft equipped for dive bombing took to the air, and German U-boats were alerted to close with the British ships.

Swordfish planes from *Furious* made the first contact, flying through heavy antiaircraft fire from the covering German cruisers and destroyers as well as the capital ships, to launch their torpedoes. They scored two hits on *Scharnhorst*, stopping her dead in the water. A third torpedo glanced off *Gneisenau*, causing some damage. A destroyer transferred Schrader and his staff from the *Scharnhorst* to the *Gneisenau*.

Luftwaffe *Stukas* and other dive bombers struck at the British ships shortly after this, seriously damaging *Hood* and slightly damaging *Rodney* and *Furious* before being

*North Sea west of the Hools of Holland, so called because the flat sea bottom in the region is almost uniformly fourteen fathoms below the surface.

driven off by antiaircraft fire and by 11 Group fighters that Dowding had sent out to assist the naval vessels.

Altering course to east southeast, Somerville's fleet came within range of the retiring Germans by midday. In the running battle that followed, the long range naval guns of both sides landed damaging rounds. A torpedo from a British destroyer finished off *Scharnhorst*. *Stukas* and Me-109s constantly harassed the British ships, causing more damage than did gunfire. A British submarine scored a hit on *Admiral Hipper*, and she was soon listing badly to port as she continued on her way. A destroyer on each side hit undetected mines, and the German vessel went quickly to the bottom. The British destroyer was able to make it back to port.

The German fleet moved in under cover of coastal guns on the Dutch coast, and Somerville, unwilling to expose his fleet to the fixed gunfire, broke off and turned back toward the British coast. Shortly thereafter a German U-boat, undetected, crept within range of *Hood* and with a single torpedo damaged her so badly she ultimately sank.

The engagement was costly for both sides. None of the capital ships escaped damage, and *Hood* and *Scharnhorst* had been sunk. The British lost two destroyers besides, with three others and a light cruiser seriously damaged. Only one German destroyer was lost, although two had heavy damage. The damage to *Admiral Hipper* proved too severe to control, and the next day she was abandoned shortly before she sank.

The End of Sea Lion

Meanwhile, at the other end of the landing area, *Revenge* and her escorts had put to sea and were shelling the landing craft as they crossed the Channel, fighting off constant attack from German aircraft. A direct bomb hit on *Revenge* damaged her badly enough so that she was forced to return to Plymouth. But the smaller vessels continued to wreak havoc on the German craft.

Instead of the three divisions that were expected to land on the first day, only about the equivalent of half of one division managed to get ashore, in three areas. Three small beachheads were secured, and British troops rushed to oppose them, preventing the Germans from exploiting inland, or linking the beachheads. The German troops defended the beachheads against British attacks for two days, but when it became apparent that no one was coming either to reinforce or evacuate them, and having run out of food and ammunition, they surrendered.

Thus ended Sea Lion. More than half of the craft involved in taking the landing force across the Channel had been lost, most of them with few or no survivors. It had been a disaster, Hitler's first serious setback. But the Battle of Britain did not end immediately.

Furious at the failure of his invasion plan, Hitler ordered the Luftwaffe to bomb British cities. Then it was that even Goering realized the British could not be defeated from the air, and that without a successful invasion there would be no surrender. British production was still providing more aircraft than were lost, and training schools were turning out more pilots than the Luftwaffe, itself diminished by its activity in the preceding months, could destroy. British antiaircraft batteries, capitalizing on advance knowledge gained from intelligence sources and radar, became more deadly, until Goering finally admitted that bombing alone was not enough and convinced Hitler that the results were not worth the cost in airplanes and pilots. The Battle of Britain was halted, and Hitler turned his eyes to the east and started planning for the invasion of the Soviet Union. The Sea Lion fiasco had cost him a large part of three divisions of the Wehrmacht's best men, a loss that would be felt in subsequent years of war.

Afterword

This narrative of the Battle of Britain faithfully reflects history through August and the first week of September, 1940. It departs from the facts when it describes the German attacks against the RAF bases continuing after September 7. It is debatable whether Hitler and Goering made their decision to shift from attacking the bases to attacking London because of an enraged reaction to the British air raids on Berlin in late August, or whether it was because Goering did not realize how close he and his Luftwaffe had come to success in their earlier attacks against the Fighter Command bases. Whatever the reason, the shift of target gave a breathing spell to Fighter Command, which was—in large part due to its shift to the Big Wing tactics—very close to collapse.

Both the Germans and the British made serious errors in judgment in the Battle of Britain. The Germans in their objective, the British in their tactics. But if the Germans had stuck to their original plans, history might have unfolded as our narrative describes, whether or not the British adopted the Big Wing doctrine. As it was, the British change in tactics, which might otherwise have assured German victory, had relatively minor consequences when the Germans shifted their attacks from the RAF bases to London. This shift of objective, which assured the survival of the RAF, was the main reason that the German plans to invade Britain were frustrated and that Operation Sea Lion was never begun.

The effects of the decision to adopt the Big Wing tactics were those expected by the experienced fighter commanders, Park and Dowding. From August 31 through September 6 Park lost 161 aircraft to the German's 189. On September 7 while his group was losing 56 aircraft to 41 German losses, Park's aerodromes were severely damaged when all of his 21 fighter squadrons were committed and unable to protect the airbases. And four days later, the airplanes of 12 Group, which had been scrambled in conformity with the Big Wing tactics, were unavailable for the defense of Tangmere when 100 German bombers attacked, causing more serious damage. However, once the thrust of the German attack had shifted away from the airfields, the RAF could effectively apply Big Wing theory/doctrine to drive off enemy bombers approaching the cities.

It is ironic that Germany's blitz on London thus actually saved Britain and the RAF. This fact is often overshadowed by the remarkable way in which the British people endured the severe punishment of the daily bombings of their cities. Having braced themselves for the seemingly inevitable invasion attempt, the British were able to carry on daily routines and to protect their island nation despite the abnormal conditions imposed by the German raids. Productivity had been maintained so that by the end of the Battle of Britain, Fighter Command had more aircraft and equipment—but not pilots—available than there had been at the start of the attacks. This resilience of the British was greatly underestimated by the German High Command and was perhaps another crucial error in German judgment. Even in our hypothetical narrative, where the Germans had so weakened the RAF and felt confident in launching Sea Lion, we believe that the British Royal Navy and coastal fortifications would have been able to repel the invasion and prevent the conquest of Britain so necessary in Hitler's vision of German expansion.

CHAPTER III

Barbarossa:
The Plan That Boomeranged

THERE WAS NEVER any question in Hitler's mind that the Soviet Union had to be destroyed. From the time he wrote *Mein Kampf* in 1932, the one unwavering conviction held by the future German dictator was that the Slavic people—hence its most numerous component, the USSR—needed to be annihilated to make way for the new order.

For the Soviet leadership, the rise of Nazi Germany—in place of the Marxist socialist Germany the Bolshevik leaders had all hoped for since the October Revolution—could only be viewed with alarm. Hitler and his philosophy encompassed everything that was anathema to the communists and thereby created an even greater threat to the revolution than the spectre of capitalist oppression. The main difference between the two national perceptions in the mid- and late-1930's, as apparently seen in both capitals, was that Germany was on the move, while the USSR was still recovering from the period of international isolation that followed upon the chaos and destruction of the Russian Civil War and the ensuing socio-political upheaval that had drained the nation of its manpower and so had colored its outlook.

Thus, while both Germany and the Soviet Union were totalitarian, and both were expansionist by tendency and tradition, Germany was clearly on the offensive, while the Soviet Union was, albeit unwillingly, just as clearly on the defensive. With Germany apparently eyeing the Balkans and Poland to the east, the security of the Soviet state was threatened. It became clear to the Soviet leadership, therefore, that it must continue its programs of building the new socialist state while using whatever means were available to gain time in which to prepare for an apparently inevitable Germanic onslaught.

The real concern began after the Munich Crisis in 1938, when Stalin recognized that the dismemberment of Czechoslovakia, and the apparent incapacity of the European powers to agree on a policy other than appeasement, left the Soviet Union to its own devices. A plan was required to provide the time necessary to prepare, without drawing too much attention to what was really going on.

The Dictators Play for Time

The Soviets needed an environment in which they could gain time and strengthen their strategic position. The opportunity came in 1939, when Poland refused Hitler's demands for territory. With England and France declaring that they would take up arms if Poland was attacked, Hitler put out feelers to the Soviet Union, designed to reduce tensions between the two nations, in order to neutralize the USSR at a critical point in the Nazi timetable while giving the Soviets only what could be easily recovered when it suited Hitler to move against the Soviet Union. Since such a delay suited Stalin, on August 27, 1939 a ten-year non-aggression agreement was signed, whereby each side pledged to remain neutral should the other be attacked by a third power. For Hitler, this constituted the neutralization he desired. For the Soviets, it meant nothing, except for the time it gained. However, the secret protocol assured to the Soviets the eastern part of Poland and gave them vital bases in Lithuania, Latvia, and Estonia that provided protection for northwest Russia, especially Leningrad, while, at the same time, giving the Soviets better access to the Baltic. To the Germans, these concessions were simply a means of mollifying Stalin; all would be recovered when the Soviet Union was conquered.

At the very time that final terms of the agreement were being worked out, senior military representatives of the United Kingdom and France were in Moscow for consultations. On August 15, 1939, Marshal Klimenti Voroshilov—giving no hint of ongoing negotiations with Germany—pretending to brief the Allies on Soviet plans, stipulated a number of conditions for active Soviet participation against any further German expansion, while at the same time making a series of arbitrary demands to which the Allies would be hesitant to agree.

What Voroshilov did not tell the Allies when he explained that the USSR could mobilize approximately 175 divisions, and that its first echelon could be ready in ten days, was that since the beginning of 1939 the Soviet Union had been assembling a secret army.

The Soviet Secret Army

In the spring of 1939 there was a small scale war with Japan in progress along the border of Manchuria and Soviet-dominated Mongolia, where Japanese raids had become frequent and increasingly serious. Stalin grasped at this as a welcome opportunity to increase the ready strength of the Red Army and modernize its structure, training, and weaponry in anticipation of what seemed an inevitable conflict with the expansionist programs of Adolph Hitler.

At the Eighteenth Party Congress, held in March 1939, Stalin laid the basis. Outside pressure aimed at destroying the great socialist experiment had intensified, he told the members, and since Britain and France had refused to join in a collective security agreement, the Soviet Union would have to go it alone. Because of the threat of further Japanese aggression in the east the armed forces must be at least partially mobilized. Units would be called from all military districts and shipped to the Far East for duty along the border.

Stalin did not bother to mention to his comrades that what he had said was not necessarily the complete truth. Some units would indeed be sent to Mongolia, but not all. The rest would be secretly sequestered and turned into the most modern army in Europe.

Stalin did not intend to get into a guns or butter debate over what he perceived as a specific threat to the Soviet Union. Nor did he intend to involve any more of the top leadership than was necessary in the decision to build a secret army. If he was right he would take the credit. If, however, he was wrong, then figuratively few would know.

To create an army was one thing, to hide it, another. The USSR is vast, and the distance to the Far East where the mobilized units were ostensibly to go contains many areas that were literally uninhabited and yet were within easy distance of the Trans-Siberian and other east-west rail lines. The location had to be secure from prying eyes and capable of being closed off to all save those who would be there for training. The area east of the Urals and west of the Ob river was the final selection, even though it was nearly two thousand miles from the most likely point of utilization along the Polish-Russian border.

The total state control of communications made it relatively simple, not only to seal off the training area from the outside world but, also, to put into effect a massive deception plan, to direct attention elsewhere or at least to confound the Germans as to what was under way in western Siberia.

In essence, there were two Red Armies, one in the field on the eastern and western borders of the Soviet Union and the other deep in the interior of the country. The first army knew little if anything of the second; and, if any wondered, in the Soviet Union one asked no questions.

There was little said, therefore, when a number of Red Army units disappeared somewhere between their home stations and the Far East. What correspondence was permitted between the troops involved and their homes was very carefully censored. And, although many of the troops involved in the special training obviously realized that something strange was going on, severe discipline and equally severe reaction to asking too many questions simply obviated any conjecture.

Drafting troops to fill the ranks of the secret army was easy. Finding enough qualified senior officers to train and lead them was something else, particularly so because Stalin had seen fit to purge the officer corps of a large percentage of its best men only the year before. To meet the problem, officer training was speeded up, and the entire class of 1939 at the Frunze Academy "disappeared" just before graduation, its members sent directly to the secret army, east of the Urals.

Code-named *Skifoi*, and officially designated the Mobile Front, it was planned that by early 1941, the secret army would consist of eight mechanized corps, each with two tank divisions and one motorized rifle division, plus normal support organizations. To provide modern, efficient weapons for the new force as well as for the visible Red Army, production was speeded up on airplanes, tanks, and guns. The MiG-3, Yak-1, and LaGG-3, already in prototype, began to roll off newly-constructed assembly lines. Production of KV and T-34 tanks was multiplied, and new artillery and antiaircraft weapons were developed and built in great numbers. When the Finnish War impressed Stalin with the need for a bomber command with aircraft capable of striking medium range targets at least as deep into Poland as the Pila-Poznan-Breslau line, the Pe-2 and an advanced version of the Il-4, designated Il-6, were rushed into production.

On September 1, 1939, German panzers pushed through the flimsy defenses on the western Polish border, and when Great Britain and France declared war in accordance with their treaties with Poland, World War II had begun. On September 17, with western Poland in German hands, Soviet forces crossed Poland's eastern border in accordance with the secret protocol of the Soviet-Nazi Pact and incorporated the area as far west as Bialystok into the Soviet Union. Work on constructing fortifications on the new border began soon thereafter.

Building and training the secret force was well under way by this time, and Major General A.I. Antonov assembled a staff at Berezovo in western Siberia, about 200 kilometers north of the Mobile Front headquarters at Oktyabrskoye, to make plans for using the force in a comprehensive defense of the western frontier. This planning group of brilliant Soviet officers started work in May 1940. Although they were told to plan for an augmentation of about 30 divisions, it was three months before they were fully briefed on the Mobile Front.

In its initial form, the plan (code-named *Manerka*—Mess Kit), which was prepared by the *Skifoi* planning group, contemplated meeting the enemy attack at the frontier, either holding him off there or fighting a series of retrograde actions to already prepared secondary defensive lines. Then contact would be broken and the defending troops would fall back behind another prepared defensive position generally along the Dvina-Dnieper line where the secret army would be deployed. The plan was predicated on delaying the enemy until his timetable became useless and he was faced with the knowledge that he would have to fight a winter campaign, in the open, in Russia. In the meantime, of course, the Red Army would have become fully mobilized and would thereafter move to eject the intruder from Soviet territory. The planning of the counteroffensive was not a part of the *Skifoi* Planning Group's charter. For planning purposes, the 30 divisions were formed into five armies: First, Fifteenth, Seventeenth, Twenty-fourth, and Twenty-fifth. These units were to move on order to occupy the Dvina-Dnieper line, code-named *Stameska* (Chisel). There they were to be reinforced with at least twelve additional divisions from the reserve, which by that time would be mobilized. Only in the most dire circumstances was this force to move forward of Line *Stameska*.

The German Plan for Barbarossa

German planning for an attack on the Soviet Union began in earnest in July 1940. At Hitler's order the German Army General Staff concluded that an attack on the Soviet Union to remove it as a potential threat on Germany's east was feasible, and General Major Erich Marcks, Chief of Staff of the Eighteenth Army, was brought from East Prussia to German Army Headquarters in Berlin (*Oberkommando des Heeres*—OKH) to develop an attack plan for Operation *Barbarossa*.

On the same day, the Chief of the *Oberkommando der Wehrmacht* (OKW), the Armed Forces High Command, Field Marshal Wilhelm Keitel, directed the Chief of the OKW Operations Staff (*Wehrmachtführungsstab*), *General der Artillerie* Alfred Jodl, to undertake similar planning for an all-out invasion of the Soviet Union. Although the OKH possessed the real planning talent and the OKW was merely a personal military headquarters for Hitler, the dual planning demonstrated once again both the brilliance and conceptual uniformity of German General Staff officers.

After months of discussion and planning, OKH completed Plan *Barbarossa*. It was approved by Hitler, and signed by Field Marshal von Brauchitsch, Commander in Chief of the German Army, on February 3, 1941. In general terms the plan called for three army groups: North, Center, and South, to attack along generally parallel axes, North and Center north of the Pripyet Marshes, while Army Group South advanced south of the marshes. The key to success lay in surprise and speed. The main element was to be the speed with which the panzers and motorized infantry could move, disrupting any Soviet ability to organize along continuous defensive lines.

At Hitler's insistence the plan called for the taking of Leningrad before Moscow. Only if the Red Army should totally collapse could both cities be attacked simultaneously. Although this meant that whatever benefit Moscow served as a strategic communications center would continue to exist even if the route to Leningrad was blocked, most senior German officers were confident that the campaign at most would last only a few weeks. The Red Army was to be destroyed west of the Dvina-Dnieper line, in an area where it was thought by some, though not all, of the German planners that the Soviets would have to stand and fight.

Meanwhile several events took place that put the whole plan in jeopardy. The first was Mussolini's vainglorious decision in October,1940—without consulting Hitler—to attack Greece, and the near disaster that followed. The second was the coup d'etat that took place on March 26, 1941 in Yugoslavia. To prevent Britain from exploiting these events and raising the Balkans against Germany, prompt action was necessary. Troops had to be diverted from the Russian front for duty in the Balkans, and Hitler ordered a four week delay in the execution of *Barbarossa*. He raged, and swore even more terrible vengeance on the Slavs, but, this may have been Hitler's most costly decision. However, his army performed magnificently, and in a few weeks the Balkans were pacified.

By the beginning of June 1941, to carry out *Barbarossa*, the Germans had readied the most formidable fighting force ever assembled. Some 154 divisions plus Finnish and Romanian units were massed along the frontier with at least 3,000 tanks and 2,000 aircraft, poised to strike into Russian territory. Most of the men involved in this massive force had had at least one year's training and had already fought in at least one campaign. Although there were some doctrinal deficiencies, this force was in every way superior to the Red Army. However, the Germans did not fully appreciate the Soviet potential nor did they know anything about the secret army.

Soviet Preparations

The buildup of German forces in East Prussia and Poland had not gone undetected by the Soviets. The probability of an attack eastward was recognized as German intelligence activities were observed. Beginning in February 1941, German photoreconnaissance aircraft flew over key installations along the Baltic coast and into White Russia and the Ukraine almost daily. They were trying to pin down the location of every Soviet military unit, every supply dump, every airfield. Soviet protests were brushed aside; the intrusions were explained by the Germans as "pilot errors," but this fooled no one.

Only once did Soviet security lapse sufficiently to permit the Germans to deduce what was going on behind the Soviet frontier. In an unexplained event, a group of Luftwaffe officers was allowed to visit a Soviet aircraft plant. They reported an unusual amount of activity that appeared to be directed toward production of a new type of aircraft, but no such planes were observed in the western provinces, and no other source confirmed their existence. So the report was ignored in Berlin. Certainly there were other security breaches, but those involved were treated so harshly that there was no disclosure of the activity east of the Urals.

As time went by many of the flaws in organization, manning, and equipping of the regular Red Army that had been dramatically demonstrated in the Finnish campaign were corrected. By the spring of 1941 it was expected that the Red Army units on the German frontier and their immediate reserves could hold against the first German thrusts and conduct a retrograde movement of sufficient skill and sophistication to allow the Mobile Front to use its mobility and firepower more effectively than in a static defense on the *Stameska* line. Consequently changes were made in the *Manerka* plan.

In the new concept the Red Army was charged with maintaining defensive integrity during a protracted delaying action, using previously prepared defensive position along continuous phase lines. While there was a risk in this, the Soviet High Command felt confident that the much improved Red Army could carry out this mission, thereby leaving the *Skifoi* force free to deliver one or more counteroffensive blows that would expose either or both of the German flanks. The German attack would be blunted at the frontier, provided sufficiently early warning was received, and the German advance would be sufficiently slowed by the Soviet occupation and defense of successive delaying positions so that the Mobile Front could be brought forward from its assembly areas to the rear of the *Stameska* line. There it would be committed, probably near the flanks or on the shoulders of a salient, to deliver a crippling, if not lethal, blow to the Nazi advance.

To accomplish this scheme the Mobile Front planning group was divided into two elements: one that dealt specifically with the northern sector and the other with the south. The north was felt to be the more important area. Two plans were developed that would allow for pinching off any movement toward Leningrad, or attacking the left flank of a German drive toward Moscow, if that should develop as the principal German objective. Under no circumstances was the Mobile Front to be broken down lower than army elements because of the inherent problems of trying to mesh the new communications systems with the older ones found in the regular Red Army units, and because of equally difficult logistical and coordination problems as well.

As for the regular Red Army, the *Stavka* of the Soviet High Command had been as busy as the *Skifoi* planning group in revising its plans for the defense of the western frontiers. Specifically, by the end of July 1940, the "Defense Plan for the State Frontiers 1941," had been drafted and, although not yet sanctioned by Stalin in explicit terms, had become the basis of some immediate activities in the border provinces. A defense construction program was initiated, including elements that were beyond what available military district troops could possibly use. Just behind the 1938 western boundary, for instance, airfields were constructed, then covered with a layer of topsoil. These caused comment among those who witnessed or participated in the work, not about the camouflage, but about the location and the unusually long runways, designed for the new aircraft, of which they knew nothing.

The single most important element of the planning for the employment of the regular Red Army was the acceptance, in 1940, of Marshal Shaposhnikov's philosophy for the defense of the frontiers. The bulk of the military forces available in the military districts stretching from the Baltic to the Black Sea were to be held in covered concentration areas to the rear of the old 1938 boundaries, while only small, well-organized and equipped forces would be stationed along the new border in Poland. While this would expose the newly acquired Baltic States, western White Russia, Volynia, and Moldavia to possible German occupation, it would also allow for sufficient warning under almost all circumstances as to the actual directions of the German attack. The main elements of the Red Army, when the attack began, would occupy the main delay position, designated P1, while the covering force would fight a delaying action back to that line, then pass through the P1 and occupy the P2 line to the rear. There it would be reinforced with newly mobilized units and those gathered from military districts in the rear. Line P1 would be held or abandoned as the situation developed. But line P2 would be held until or unless a general withdrawal was ordered. A complicated delay timetable was sketched out to accomplish all of this, which almost became the plan's undoing, but, even though Stalin was not overly impressed by the plan—his notion was to stop the attack at the frontiers—he accepted the Shaposhnikov plan.

By April 1941 the Red Army High Command and the military district commanders were fully aware of the strength of the German forces arrayed before them. Since the end of February all manner of information about the German threat had been flowing into the Kremlin. On March 1, for example, the United States Ambassador in Moscow informed Molotov that American sources had uncovered the German attack plan. Almost simultaneously, Under Secretary of State Sumner Welles warned the Soviet Ambassador in Washington that confirmation of the pending German attack had come from such disparate locations as Stockholm, Bucharest, and Athens. Stalin was confronted in April with information from Winston Churchill that, indeed, a German attack was to be expected momentarily, although the originally established German timetable had been delayed because of the situation in the Balkans. Under these circumstances, the British Prime Minister warned, the Soviets should expect the attack no later than the end of the third week in June.

Stalin went out of his way to convey to the Americans and to the British his serious doubts as to the authenticity of their information about the German plans. And he spoke contemptuously to his colleagues in the Politbureau of his belief that the Western Allies were trying to encourage a German-Soviet war so that the two dictatorships would destroy each other. (As he expected, word of these conversations got back to Berlin.) Secretly, however, to the handful of senior Soviet officials who were familiar with the existence of the Mobile Front *Skifoi* Plan and the Shaposhnikov Defense Plan, the Soviet dictator commented that the British and American intelligence information was confirming the wisdom of those secret plans.

In light of the growing number of high-level warnings and a similarly ominous number of tactical indications, in May, Stalin ordered the *Skifoi* plan implemented. The Mobile Front began to move secretly and quietly to its forward positions during the last week in May. Preparations were not complete, but there was little else that could be done.

The regular Red Army too began its final preparations. Units were placed in an advanced state of readiness, all commanders down to division were briefed on the delay plans and the schedule, but nothing was said about the Mobile Front. Nothing was done to expose the newly constructed installations and those that had been refurbished and upgraded, so as not to tip the plan and cause a German reaction any earlier than expected.

To facilitate control of the regular Red Army forces, and in anticipation of utilization of the Mobile Front, a number of changes and additions were made in the structure of the ground forces. General Georgi Zhukov was given command of the Mobile Front, and General A. M. Vasilevsky replaced him as Chief of the Soviet General Staff. The Red Army forces north of Vitebsk and in the Baltic provinces, with the Twenty-seventh Army from the reserves, were organized into the Northwest Front. Forces south to the Pripyat River became the West Front. The Southwest Front comprised the forces south of there to the Odessa Military District. The Twenty-first Army was attached to the West Front, and the Twenty-sixth to the Southwest. Four more armies were in various stages of mobilization, but not expected to be ready for duty much before July 1.

Although much had been done toward upgrading equipment and organization for defense of ground forces, and the Soviet Union itself, against air attack, there was still a shortage of radar sets and heavier caliber guns. An intricate system of communications to report intruder aircraft, installed in early 1941, actually broke down in the first days of the war. It was left to field commanders to establish air defense protection as best they could. The secrets surrounding the new aircraft unfortunately included a failure to publish recognition guides. As a result many of them were attacked by friendly groundfire when they first appeared, with the most unfortunate results.

The Soviet activity east of the frontier was duly noted by the Germans, but their assessment of the condition of the Red Army continued to indicate that it was in no condition to render more than token resistance.

By the end of May 1941, all of the elements of Soviet "State Frontier Defense Plan 1941" had been initiated. This included distributing to all commanders so-called "Red Packets" of implementing instructions. Border units were placed in an advanced state of alert, much-improved communications nets were activated—but only the landlines not the radios. Air defense units were ordered to attack any German aircraft that attempted to penetrate deeper than 50 kilometers into Soviet territory and specifically to attack any attempted overflights of the critical areas of Riga and Memel (Telsiai) along the Baltic. The bridges around Vyborg and Lake Ladoga were prepared for demolition, and the rather extensive barrier plan at Petrozavodsk was implemented. In the meantime, the 25 Mobile Front divisions were being moved by rail—almost all other rail operations in the Soviet Union were halted as a result—from the security area to their forward positions. The five armies were all equipped with the newest weapons and equipment available. Three armies, the First, Seventeenth, and Twenty-fourth, were concentrated in three assembly areas generally along a line Pskov-Velikiye Luki-Smolensk. The two remaining armies were situated in the general areas of Novgorod-Severski and Mirgorod. Two additional mechanized brigades were attached to the Fifteenth Army at Mirgorod with the mission of screening the left flank of the Stameska Line. Tables 1 and 2 show how the German and the Soviet forces were organized as they prepared for the approaching clash.

0300 Hours, June 22, 1941

The attack caught the Soviets by surprise, not because it was unexpected—almost everyone was waiting for it—but rather by its ferocity. Up until the very moment of the attack, Radio Moscow had continued to assure the people that all was well and that *rapprochement* with the "enemies of the proletarian revolution" was still a possibility. As the German preparations for the attack had intensified, even to the extent of practicing bombing runs over actual targets close to the border, the Soviets had delighted in acting the fool for their German observers. Red aircraft would scramble to meet the Germans, only to

TABLE 1

Organization of the German Wehrmacht for the Execution of *Fall Barbarossa*

Army Group North (Field Marshal Wilhelm Ritter von Leeb)

Sixteenth Army (Busch)
Eighteenth Army (von Kuechler
Fourth Panzer Group (Hoepner)
First Air Force (Keller) (Attached)

Total: 21 Infantry Divisions
3 Panzer Divisions
3 Motorized Infantry Divisions
The Finnish Army consisted of:
16 Infantry Divisions
4 German Infantry Divisions

Army Group Center (Field Marshal Fedor von Bock)

Fourth Army (von Kluge)
Ninth Army (Strauss)
Second Panzer Group (Guderian)
Third Panzer Group (Hoth)
Second Air Force (Kesselring) (Attached)

Total: 30 Infantry Divisions
9 Panzer Divisions
7 Motorized Infantry Divisions
1 Cavalry Division

Army Group South (Field Marshal Rudolf Gerd von Rundstedt)

Sixty-sixth Army (von Reichenau)
Seventeenth Army (von Stuelpnagel)
Italian Corps

Total: 25 Infantry Divisions
5 Panzer Divisions
3 Motorized Infantry Divisions
4 Mountain Infantry Divisions
7 Romanian Divisions

TABLE 1 (continued)

Hungarian Corps
Slovak Division
Croatian Regiment
Eleventh German-
  Romanian Army
  (von Schobert)
Third Romanian
  Army
Fifth Romanian
  Army
Fourth Air Force
  (Loehr)
  (Attached)

Recapitulation

Personnel Assembled	3,050,000
Horses	625,000
Motor Vehicles	600,000
Tanks	3,350
Artillery Pieces	7,184
Bombers and Dive Bombers	1,160
Fighter Planes	720
Reconnaissance Aircraft	120

OKH Reserve

AG South	4 Infantry Divisions
AG Center	6 Infantry Divisions
AG North	2 Infantry Divisions
Unassigned	2 Panzer Divisions
	1 Motorized Infantry Division
	9 Infantry Divisions

TABLE 2

The Organization of the Red Army on the Eve of the Invasion

Northwestern Front *(Baltic Military District)*
(Col. General F.I. Kuznetsov)

    Eighth Army (Sobennikov)
    Eleventh Army (Morozov)
    Twenty-seventh Army (Berzarin)
    XI Mechanized Corps (Atchd) (Mostovenko)

Western Front *(Army General D. G. Pavlov)*
(Western Military District)

    Third Army (Kuznetzov)
    Fourth Army (Korobzov)
    Tenth Army (Golubev)
    VI Mechanized Corps (Atchd)
    Thirteenth Army (Filatov)
    XXI Corps (Yershakov)
    XIII Mechanized Corps
    XIV Mechanized Corps
    Mechanized Corps (Front Reserve)
    VI Cavalry Corps

Southwestern Front *(Kiev Military District)*
(Colonel General M. P. Kirponos)

    Twelfth Army (Ponedelin)
    Fifth Army (Potapov)
    Sixth Army (Muzychenko)
    Twenty-sixth Army (Kostenko)
    VIII Mechanized Corps
    VI Mechanized Corps
    XXII Mechanized Corps
    XV Mechanized Corps

TABLE 2 (continued)

XIX Mechanized Corps
IX Mechanized Corps

Northern Front *(Leningrad Military District)*
(Lt. General M. M. Popov)

Seventh Army (Gorelenko)
Fourteenth Army (Frolov)
Twenty-third Army (Pshennikov)
X Mechanized Corps

Southern Front *(Col. General Ya. T. Cherevichenuo)*

Ninth Army
Eighteenth Army
XLVII Rifle Corps
XXXV Rifle Corps
II Rifle Corps
XVI Mechanized Corps
XVIII Mechanized Corps
II Mechanized Corps

Mobile Front *(General G. Zhukov)*

(North Group) (Yeremenko)
First Special Army (Karbyshev)
Seventeenth Special Army (Sobennikov)
Twenty-fourth Special Army (Bogdanov)

(South Group) (Ryabyshev)
Fifteenth Special Army (Zakharov)
Twenty-fifth Special Army (Chuikov)
Brigade Group (Konev)

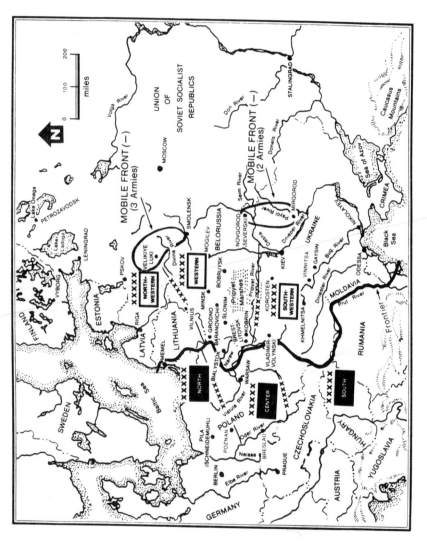

Strategic Situation, Beginning of Operation Barbarossa, June 22

stall on the runways. Antiaircraft fire would be sporadic and almost totally inaccurate. How much of this was truly inefficiency and how much was feigned confusion was never clearly delineated.

Throughout all of this preparation, the civilian population had remained totally unaware of the feverish preparations under way to defend the homeland. The conscious decision had been made at the Kremlin that the citizenry of the far western regions would be sacrificed for the salvation of Great Russia and the heartland of the Soviet State. Special NKVD units were assigned the task of keeping the road networks free of refugees so as to facilitate military movements.

The attack of German Army Group North proceeded on June 22 according to plan. Under cover of a heavy aerial bombardment all along the front, the leading assault elements of Leeb's command began moving forward to locate and fix the Soviet frontier detachments for the shock forces that were to follow. Kuechler's Eighteenth Army had as its primary objective the suspected Red Army armor concentration around the Lithuanian city of Kaunis, while Hoepner's Fourth Panzer Group was aimed at a similar concentration between Grodno and Vilnius (Vilna). Both units reported only sporadic resistance as they crossed the frontier.

Just to the south, the Third Panzer Group (Hoth) reported similar light resistance in its initial report to Army Group Center, but by noon it was becoming obvious that Hoth was not going to be able to maintain the expected momentum through the Augustov Forest that covered both sides of the frontier. At 11:00 A.M. Hoth reported that he had lost contact with his right assault division and that all areas reported extremely stiff resistance. Because of the density of the Augustov Forest in that area, Kuznetzov, the Third Red Army commander, who was facing Hoth, had decided to use the woods for channelling the Germans into extremely difficult terrain, where they would become bogged down. With his main force he had dug in along a line west of Vilnius-Baranovichi, and it was there that Hoth was stopped. The lost German division had simply been shunted off to the south where it was badly mauled in the woods west of Slonim. The success at Slonim was reported all the way back to Moscow, where it was received with great jubilation.

The rejoicing was short-lived, however, as reports from the Kobrin-Vladimir Volynski sector and from the area south of Lutsk were less than encouraging. Even though most of the bridges over the Bug had been destroyed in time, some remained standing, and for some reason the defenses around these critical points had not been effective. Guderian's Second Panzer Group was crossing the Bug in sufficient numbers to create fear that the three forward armies in the Western Front were in danger of being encircled.

Still farther to the south, the Germans were making slow but deliberate progress, although every turn in the road offered a new obstacle to the advance. When Rundstedt reported that the advance of Army Group South was not up to expectations, OKW reacted by suggesting that Rundstedt's purpose was to conceal his inability to control the situation. The Army Group South headquarters thereafter remained silent, and not until two weeks later would it report that it had been stopped in its tracks all along the lower Bug.

Something Had Gone Wrong

By that time, OKW and Hitler were becoming more and more aware that something had gone wrong, and although copious amounts of blame had been passed to OKH for its ineffectiveness, there was no one to blame except Hitler and Goering for what happened in the air. German fighters and fighter bombers performed well in support of the ground operations, but the miscalculation as to the potential of the Red Army Air Force caused a great deal of embarrassment and concern, especially when Soviet bombers appeared over the headquarters of Army Group North at the very moment that Leeb was

briefing Goering and his protege, Erich Koch, the Gaulei-
ter of East Prussia. In the ensuing melee, a number of
senior staff officers were killed, and both Goering and
Koch were seriously wounded. What was more
significant to Leeb, the commander, who survived unscathed, was that about thirty percent of his fuel supply
and a number of other critical items sitting on railcars
were destroyed because he had been assured that the
Soviets did not have any appreciable bomber force. He
now found himself without sufficient fuel to last out the
week, without sufficient fighter units to protect his almost
totally exposed supply system, and with little or no sym-
pathy from either OKW or Luftwaffe headquarters.

No less could be said about the results of the bombing
raid on Warsaw that destroyed the railyards and crippled
Army Group Center's resupply capability. Ironically,
Bock, the Army Group Center commander, had reported
to OKW that there was no appreciable enemy air activity,
and that he was convinced that his air support had destroyed every Soviet airfield in his sector. When asked
later, he could not say where the bombers came from,
except to indicate that they had penetrated German airspace without difficulty as they were of a type never seen
before. Bock was convinced that they would return, and
was requesting aircraft capable of protecting his rear area,
lest he have to divert aircraft from their close support
ground missions to fly air cover. Almost as an
afterthought, Bock added that he had already lost over
100 aircraft to hostile antiaircraft fire.

Moscow was suffering from an anxiety reaction to the
news that was coming in from all sides, especially from
the reports of frightful casualties, for the "no retreat until
ordered" directions quite often left Red Army units in
exposed and fatal positions. A lack of planning for adequate communications exposed the entire Soviet venture
to excessive risk. The destruction of a communications
center simply meant no communications, and some
Soviet units were literally left behind when the next local
withdrawal was ordered. Also, by July 1 a number of the

new aircraft had been shot down, and the Germans were no doubt studying them with extreme interest.

By mid-July, although both sides had suffered grievously, the die was already cast. The Soviet army had not been defeated, and, except for two relatively small penetrations, the Germans had not been able to prevent the Red Army from maintaining a continuous defensive posture from the Baltic south to the Ukraine. What had been touted as a lightning war by the Germans was rapidly turning into a war of attrition, generally along the pre-1939 Russian frontiers. This did not sit well with either the OKW or the commanders in the field. The long-smoldering rivalry between Guderian and Kluge, for instance, broke into the open when Guderian was unable to reduce the Soviet-held fortress at Brest-Litovsk. This set up a chain reaction that spread all the way to the OKH, where staff officers now spent much of their time issuing written confirmation to orders that were being more and more questioned in the field.

It was obvious by the end of July, even in Berlin, that the timetable was in a shambles. Army Group North had advanced only to a line running from a point 60 kilometers west of Riga, to Minsk-Korosten-Vinnitsa. The southern end of the line was anchored at Nikolayev, Odessa having fallen to the Germans on July 24. On D + 40 the German advance had not reached the line it was to have crossed on D + 21, and it was, of course, nowhere near as far into Soviet territory as it was supposed to be. The Red Army had held, and the Germans had yet to meet the Mobile Front, yet the first five days in August almost spelled the doom of the entire Soviet enterprise.

On August 1, the *Stavka* made the determination that the P2 line had held as long as was possible and that the *Stameska* line was almost ready. Without regard for the fact that communications between the front headquarters and the armies had been marred by numerous breakdowns, the Soviet High Command ordered the execution of the final withdrawal to the *Stameska* line. When the Red Army units began to break contact, the Germans, sensing the movement all along the line, moved to capitalize on their opportunity. By the night of the 4th of August, what had started as a now familiar routine withdrawal had turned into a near rout, as German motorized infantry and panzer units pursued the fleeing Soviet troops. In the center of the line, where communications had broken down completely, the Soviet Third and Eleventh Armies were largely destroyed, thereby threatening the possibility of a major Wehrmacht penetration.

For the Germans, this breakdown in Soviet cohesion was felt to be a godsend. There was some hesitation, before the full impact of the success in the center was realized, that allowed more Soviet troops to escape, but this condition was brief, as the German advance in pursuit of the fleeing Soviets gained speed. The sudden turn of events was accepted with disquiet at OKH headquarters. OKW and Hitler's personal *coterie*, on the other hand, were ecstatic over the fact that the Red Army appeared to be in full flight before the Wehrmacht. Never mind the fact that there was hardly any movement in the north around Riga and never mind the fact that a number of conflicting reports had been received in German headquarters via Sweden that something was going on behind the Dvina river. The Red Army was on the run and could be overtaken and defeated by the panzer groups.

Driving ahead, along the Brest-Minsk-Smolensk axis, for example, Heinz Guderian's troops were like hounds after the fox. By August 16, after several sharp engagements by Red Army units that apparently had not been informed of the withdrawal order, they had advanced to a point between Minsk and Bobruysk. Cutting south of the White Russian capital, Guderian had hoped to trap the fleeing Red troops in the gap between the Dvina and the Dnieper. Instead he had created a salient, with both his flanks exposed at the same time he had outdistanced his supply trains. At this juncture he recommended to Bock that he be allowed to halt to enable his flank units to catch up and his panzers to refuel. Before he received an answer, he was struck on his left shoulder by the Mobile Front.

Within hours of the ill-fated order to withdraw to the *Stameska* line, the *Stavka* realized that the Germans were not to be so easily shaken off. While the Soviet forces were learning the finesse of breaking contact, the Germans were learning how to identify the signs of such a movement and how to react to these signs. The results had been near disastrous for the Red Army. For the Russians, the delay plan had worked well, almost too well. The forward units were on the verge of exhaustion when the order to withdraw came and small errors in judgment at the lower levels of command grew into major problems at the higher echelons, control was lost, and the Red Army appeared to be in retreat.

Even so, the benefits available to the Soviets in this situation were greater than those available to the Germans, if they could capitalize on them. The Soviets were withdrawing toward their most strongly fortified positions, while the Germans were spreading themselves laterally over a much wider front, and at the same time they were extending their supply lines. Not only had Guderian's Second Panzer Group created a salient in the center, but so had Hoepner (Fourth Panzer Group) in the north and Kliest's First Panzer Group in the south. One of the unsolved mysteries of the war is how the Second Panzer Group was allowed to become mired in the Pripyet Marshes, but there it was, and its loss of effectiveness, more than any other single factor, may have been responsible for what was to happen.

The Secret Army Counterattack

Within four hours of the counterattack on Guderian's left flank, the German Seventeenth Army came under murderous attack from Khmelnitsa to Gaysin. The German Army Group South was about to meet the Mobile Front. The two armies in the Mobile Front's southern group came at the Seventeenth Army abreast, following a tremendous artillery preparation by masses of artillery whose existence was not even suspected by the Germans. The Seventeenth Army was in full retreat by dark, its commander and most of its staff officers dead from a surprise attack by Sturmovik fighter-bombers. The Soviets held their advance west of the Bug to allow the Forty-third and Fiftieth armies on their flanks to catch up, lest they too find themselves being flanked.

At approximately 6:00 A.M. the following morning, the Mobile Front (South) reopened its advance at the same time that the Soviet Sixty-first Army passed through the defended position at the south of the Soviet line, hitting the German Allied Eleventh Army.

Within 48 hours the Seventeenth German Army ceased to exist, grouped up as it was under the treads of the previously secret new Red Army tanks. The Eleventh Army, on the other hand, without specific orders to do anything, stood and fought, making the Soviets pay dearly for every inch of ground they liberated. When the German and Allied forces did withdraw, they carried out the most brutal mistreatment of the western Ukrainian people, many of whom had welcomed the coming of the Germans as a sign that they might yet be free of the Great Russian yoke. As word spread of the atrocities committed, especially by the Hungarian and Romanian Waffen-SS units, the Ukrainian populace rose up—as did the Moldavians—and helped drive the Nazis from their land.

Guderian's plight was no better. Between the initial blow from the Mobile Front (North) and the exhortations from Hitler to ignore the Soviets' attempt to cloud the issue of ultimate German victory and to press on to Moscow, Guderian was bedeviled by the thought of ultimate disaster or disgrace. Both came upon him at the same time. At approximately 7:00 A.M. on August 17, all contact was lost with the Ninth Army on his left flank, and sporadic gunfire was heard to the rear of the Panzer Group command post. Guderian had been surrounded, but he was not able to confirm the fact until late in the day. Confusion reigned everywhere, and Soviet attack bombers appeared on the horizon. By midnight the famed panzer leader was convinced that at least three armies, equipped with remarkably modern equipment, plus elements of at least two more armies were around him. By 6:00, Kluge's Fourth Army, with whom Guderian maintained the most tenuous of contact, reported that it was faced by two armies, instead of the suspected one, and large numbers of reports were being received about "Mongolian troops" among the attackers.

The Soviets had chosen exactly the right moment to strike. Most of the forward Red Army forces had managed to withdraw behind the *Stameska* line, and those that had remained in the forward areas afforded just the right amount of delay to permit the Mobile Front to move into position. The superior mobility of these wholly mechanized units made this a relatively simple task, compared to what would have been faced if the counteroffensive had not been launched at exactly the moment that the German pursuit had begun to slow. The arrival of numbers of reserve units and those shifted from the Far East also helped stem the German tide and reinforce the Mobile Front's capability to an inestimable degree. Of no little assistance were the numerous partisan groups that had sprung up all through the occupied zone. Although the Soviets would claim after the war that this was the result of Party activity, the real reason appears to lie more in the realm of self-preservation against the depredations of the Germans, both those in the SS units and those in the Wehrmacht itself. When the Germans were forced to retreat after the annihilation of the Seventeenth Army in the Ukraine, the retribution visited upon German wounded and stragglers was as severe and as blood-curdling as the actions of the Germans had been against the Soviet populace.

The well-planned counteroffensive rolled forward inexorably. The territory of the Soviet Union was all but cleared of German invaders by the end of September. In the south, where the Second Panzer Group had been shifted to replace the destroyed Seventeenth Army, a pocket of resistance still held out around the Lvov-Kubno area. In the center and north, however, the Red Army had already crossed into the old Polish territory, and was threatening Warsaw where a major popular uprising was taking place. Soviet bombers were over German territory almost every night.

The World Was Stunned

The world was stunned by the magnitude and swiftness of the campaign. Almost overnight, Stalin had emerged as one of the great military geniuses of modern times. What was not reported, of course, was the enormous sacrifice in manpower that he had willingly suffered to gain this prestige. Leaders in the Allied capitals and in the United States began, albeit not without reluctance, to look upon Stalin as a man who had beaten Hitler and as the natural leader of the coalition against Nazi Germany; Communist parties around the world were treated to a long period of legitimacy that enabled them to reach unexpected heights of political power.

As for Germany, it still held Europe by the throat, but that grip was slipping. In all occupied areas resistance grew, and finally, to stave off what now seemed an inevitable debacle in the east, the OKW began the difficult planning necessary to bring Rommel and his forces back from Africa. Hitler, of course, blamed everyone but himself for the failure of *Barbarossa,* and his fits and rages now reached such levels of offensiveness that he made his most fateful mistake.

At a combined meeting of the principal officers of the OKW and OKH staffs, Hitler flew into a frenzy when he was informed that sending the Home Army to the Eastern Front would not redress the situation and that the only course was to seek peace with Stalin. In his rage, Hitler struck Brauchitsch and called him a "Prussian pig." Two days later in a bunker in East Prussia Brauchitsch and Halder met with General Erich Fromm, the commander of the Home Army, and one of his staff officers, Major Count

Klaus von Stauffenberg. Also present were Colonel General von Witzleben, Lieutenant General Heinrich von Stuelpnagel, and a "liaison officer" from the headquarters of Rommel's Afrika Korps. Within two hours, the decision was made: Hitler had to go. The plan was carried out, after one almost disastrous false start, on November 15, 1941.

Within 24 hours after the death of Hitler, Field Marshal Gerd von Rundstedt, officially designated Head of State of the Fourth Reich, summoned the American *chargé d'affaires* to the Reichs Chancellory. *Chargé* Leland B. Morris was asked to inform his government and, through Washington, the governments of the United Kingdom and the Soviet Union, that within 48 hours he would unilaterally order German forces on all fronts to observe a ceasefire. Marshal Rundstedt further requested the United States Government to convene a peace conference, which Germany would be willing to attend without prior conditions.

That evening the Japanese ambassador in Tokyo notified his government that Germany was leaving the war. A few hours later American radio monitoring stations in Hawaii, the Philippines, and Guam noted an unexpectedly heavy flurry of Japanese naval radio traffic. The messages were soon decoded in Washington. Japan was cancelling hitherto unsuspected plans for a series of major offensives in the Pacific. Japanese negotiators in Washington were ordered to accept President Roosevelt's terms for peace in Asia.

The rest is history.

•

Afterword

Despite the plausibility of the events described above, in fact, Stalin in 1941 refused to believe that Hitler was planning to invade Russia. He did not accept the warnings reaching him from British, American, and other sources, including some of his own, and felt secure in the belief that the German dictator would not undertake to open an eastern front that would divide his forces, at least until England had been eliminated from the war. Work proceeded on fortifications along the post-1939 western frontier, but those that had been completed were inadequately manned, or not manned at all, and few new weapons were added to the Soviet inventory.

But Hitler *was* planning to attack to the east, and the description of the German preparations in the preceding narrative is completely historical.

Stalin, having convinced himself that the warnings were false, that they were in fact a Western scheme to try to provoke a disastrous Russo-German war, made none of the preparations that are described in this story. But they were all feasible, and they could have been made, had planning begun soon enough. There was no secret army, and no new weapons and equipment in 1941, although these things were on drawing boards or in prototype models. The germ of a plan for stopping, then throwing back, the German offensive had been proposed to Stalin, but he had turned it aside, and no such operational plan was developed.

In the actual event, the German attack was an almost complete surprise. In spite of the lack of warning, the ensuing chaos, and the incomplete defenses, the Soviet troops fought stubbornly and (with some unanticipated assistance provided by Hitler's strategic blunders) were finally successful in slowing the German timetable and stretching what Hitler had hoped would be a quick win into a protracted war. Had the Soviets had men, equipment, and an operational plan such as they are given in this story, the situation on the Eastern Front—and elsewhere in the world—might have been very different.

CHAPTER IV

The Battle for Moscow

IT WAS DAWN on June 22, 1941, exactly one day after the 129th anniversary of Napoleon's ill-fated invasion of Russia, when German armies crossed the Soviet border from the Baltic to the Black Sea, launching a war on a scale hitherto unknown in recorded history. The Soviets, unprepared, found themselves facing a seemingly hopeless situation.

The Drive Into Russia

The Germans achieved complete surprise. With immense strength they struck against Soviet ground forces, airfields, railroad systems, rear bases, and other military and civilian installations. In the frontier battles numerous Soviet armies were encircled and destroyed. During the first day of war the Soviet Air Force lost over 1,200 aircraft—38% of its strength. In the Bialystok-Minsk pocket alone 30 infantry and 8 tank divisions were surrounded. Some 350,000 men were taken prisoner, over 3,000 tanks and 2,000 artillery pieces were captured or destroyed.

In view of the severe Soviet losses and the speedy German advance—on the average 40 miles per day between the border and Minsk—a German victory seemed assured. On July 4, General Franz Halder, Chief of the Army General Staff (*Oberkommando des Heeres*, OKH), expressed justifiable optimism, shared by most of his colleagues, that the mission of destroying the Red Army west of the Dvina and Dnieper rivers was accomplished, and that for all practical purposes the Russian campaign had been won, in less than two weeks. Of course he did not imply that operations were already terminated. OKH knew that it would take many more weeks to occupy vast areas of the Soviet Union and to overcome the fierce resistance of the remaining Soviet forces. But German victory was believed to be irreversible.

Hitler was equally optimistic. "It is a good thing that we destroyed the Russians' panzers and their air force right at the start," he said to General Alfred Jodl, Chief of Operations of the High Command Staff (Oberkommando der Wehrmacht, OKW). "The Russians will be unable to replace them."

In the first month of the war the most decisive battles took place near the center of the Soviet-German front in Byelorussia. Here, pointed directly toward Moscow, Army Group Center advanced, under Field Marshal Fedor von Bock, a highly regarded 61-year-old officer, victorious veteran of the Polish and French campaigns.

With two panzer groups spearheading the advance, the offensive progressed, seemingly almost without effort. The crucial problem confronting Bock was to keep his infantry from falling too far behind the armor. The army group had only a few motorized infantry divisions, and this proved to be a handicap. It was difficult to retain contact between the onrushing armor and the slow-moving infantry; Bock knew this was courting danger. But the infantry divisions could not help being delayed whenever they were engaged in completing an encirclement initiated by the panzer groups, or in mopping up pockets of bypassed Soviet troops.

Facing the onslaught of Army Group Center was the Soviet Western Army Group, at the outset under General D. G. Pavlov. But after the German victories in June, Pavlov was arrested, accused of treason and negligence, and executed. On July 2 Marshal S. Timoshenko assumed command of the Western Army Group. Soon Soviet resistance stiffened and the battle gained in intensity. By tremendous efforts, the Red Army slowed the German advance and, in some areas, was even able to stabilize the front for brief periods.

It took Army Group Center two weeks, from July 3 to 16, to advance 150 miles from Minsk to Smolensk, at an average of about 11 miles per day. And when it reached the outskirts of the city it was met by the fiercest resistance yet encountered and was unable to close the encirclement ring. The battle raged until July 26, by which time large numbers of Soviet troops had either withdrawn or escaped eastward. Nevertheless, when the Germans finally closed and then liquidated the Smolensk pocket, they captured over 300,000 prisoners and destroyed or captured nearly 300 tanks and 3,200 artillery pieces.

By the end of July, grim combat developed at the tactically important Yelnya salient, which Guderian's Second Panzer Group had expected to occupy around July 20. The Soviets stood fast and inflicted heavy losses on the attackers. Faced with stubborn Soviet resistance and several setbacks, Bock concluded that it was essential to stop temporarily to regroup and rest. He halted offensive operations, assumed a defensive posture, and regrouped.

Meanwhile in the southern and northern areas of the huge Soviet-German front, the offensive, despite stunning successes, was also behind schedule, failing to meet the original German expectations.

Army Group South was commanded by Field Marshal Gerd von Rundstedt. In his sector the Soviet Southwestern Army Group under General M.P. Kirponos continued to fight a stubborn and skillful delaying action, avoiding most German enveloping maneuvers. On the left flank of Army Group South the pressure exerted by the Soviet Fifth Army from the Pripyet Marshes diverted more and more German divisions from their primary mission. The thrust of the First Panzer Group, however, finally succeeded in breaking through the Soviet lines not far from Berdichev, and the group continued to drive toward Pervomaysk and deeper into the Dnieper River bend to establish a bridgehead south of Kiev. However, further north, the Sixth Army was stalled some 30 miles west of Kiev.

In the sector of Army Group North, German forces under Field Marshal Wilhelm von Leeb had fought their way eastward over difficult ground and against spotty resistance offered by the Soviet Northwestern Army Group, commanded first by General F. I. Kuznetzov and later, after July 4, by General P.O. Sobennikov.

After three weeks of good progress, on July 12 Army Group North met stubborn resistance along the Luga River. An attack on Novgorod (south of Leningrad) also was beaten off. In other sectors of the front, as well, in Latvia and Estonia, the German advance was slowed.

Leeb had the same problem Bock had encountered in keeping his infantry up with the armor. On July 19, surprised by Soviet toughness, he halted his offensive some 60 miles from Leningrad so that the main forces of his army group could reach the Luga.

Change in Campaign Plan

Against this background of substantial, but less than complete, success, Hitler decided to change the original campaign plan. He shifted the main weight of the German effort from the center of the front, where it had been directed toward Moscow, to the flanks. In the south the new objectives would be Kiev, the Crimea, the Donets industrial region, and the Caucasus. In the north the objective would remain Leningrad. Army Group Center was to switch to the defense so that its two panzer groups (Second and Third) could be attached temporarily to Army groups South and North respectively, to carry out the encirclement of exposed Soviet forces. After fulfilling these missions, the two panzer groups would regroup, return to Army Group Center, and take part in a renewed offensive toward Moscow.

Hitler's directive horrified German army leaders, who

were aware of the far-reaching consequences of such a move. The efficiency of the German army had suffered from the rigors of the campaign. In the first five weeks of the war the invading army had suffered some 215,000 casualties—15% of its strength—and lost over 815 tanks. Replacements were slow in arriving, and the logistical situation was critical. The idea of turning away from Moscow, which was a complete change in the fundamental strategy, infuriated the military commanders, who did not wish to sacrifice the major objective of the campaign for local tactical victories. They feared that the new strategy would force them to fight a protracted war for which they were unprepared. OKH believed that capture of Moscow—communications and political center of the USSR—was the key to a blitz victory, and that with the fall of the city the Soviet state would crumble and fall. Thus, in order to reach the Volga River and achieve victory, any moves that reduced the tempo of the operation toward the Soviet capital by failing to capitalize on the drive and shock of panzer formations should be rejected.

The urgency for capturing Moscow was increased by intelligence reports signaling large scale mobilization and concentration of fresh Soviet troops at the western approaches to the city. In addition, new field fortifications were being constructed west of Moscow, and their completion would enable the Red Army to offer much stronger resistance, which would surely slow the German advance further.

Field Marshal Walther von Brauchitsch, German Army Commander in Chief, with firm support from General Halder, tried to change Hitler's mind, but to no avail. Even Jodl, normally a yes-man, joined in the effort to convince the Führer of the dire consequences of his decision. It was of no use. Hitler was adamant. In fact, this postponement of the advance toward Moscow was really a reversion to his own original idea. When the *Barbarossa* plan was formulated Hitler had insisted that first priority be given to the Ukraine, with its industrial potential, and to the capture of Leningrad, the cradle of the communist revolution and by itself also an important industrial center. He believed that the advance on Moscow should continue only after the objectives in the Ukraine were attained, and Leningrad had fallen. He had only reluctantly approved the OKH plan for a main effort toward Moscow.

Now, since the Russians had succeeded in slowing down the OKH offensive, Hitler concluded that the only way to defeat the Red Army and annihilate the Soviet state was by encircling and destroying Soviet forces piecemeal. This of course meant a series of less spectacular successes, and the advance would not be as rapid as that of June and July. Nevertheless, he believed it would eliminate all tactical risks and enable the Germans to close gaps between armies and army groups.

Brauchitsch, trying to avoid a serious confrontation with Hitler, refused Halder's suggestion that they both continue to exert a maximum effort to force Hitler to change his decision. However, Bock would not give up so easily. In addition to firm belief that the collapse of Moscow would end the war in total German victory, he wanted to be the one to enter the Soviet capital at the head of his triumphant troops and to be known in history as the conqueror of Moscow, a distinction that even Napoleon could not seriously claim. Bock could count on the unqualified support of his army commanders, especially of the dashing Guderian, who hoped that his tanks would be the first to reach the Kremlin's walls.

True, Rundstedt, in the south, did not share Bock's optimistic enthusiasm for a Moscow strategy. Stalled in the Ukraine, Rundstedt saw the situation quite differently. To him Hitler's ideas made sense, and he was not much concerned with the change of plans. To defeat the Soviet forces in front of him he badly needed Bock's Second Army and the Second Panzer Group. And if he could get them only at the expense of an advance toward Moscow, so be it.

In the north, Leeb wanted to capture Leningrad as soon

as possible. So he, too, was happy with the redeployment of some panzer and infantry formations from Army Group Center to his command.

Confrontation at Borisov

The critical confrontation between the Moscow-first advocates and Hitler came to a head on August 4, when Hitler, on urgent invitation from Bock, visited the headquarters of Army Group Center at Borisov. Hitler arrived almost two hours late in a very bad mood. His recurrent stomach pains made him uncomfortable. He still had not fully recovered from dysentery and a cold that had struck him down a few days earlier at his *Wolfsschanze* (Wolf's lair) headquarters. His personal physician, Dr. Theo Morrell, was at his side with a supply of antacid pills and other drugs.

With his hands trembling, Hitler exchanged handshakes with Bock, Halder, and the army commanders, and nodded to the remaining commanders and staff officers. Without uttering a word he took a place at the head of the table, waved to the officers to sit down, and gestured to Bock to start.

The army group commander opened the conference by reporting briefly on the situation at the front, and on personnel and equipment matters. But as soon as he started to put forward his reasons why an immediate attack on Moscow was necessary, Hitler leaped to his feet and shouted, "I forbid you to mention the attack on Moscow! The offensive in the south has been decided and ordered, and it is no use talking any more. I know your ideas, and I regard them as totally unacceptable! The advance toward Moscow will begin only after the fall of Leningrad and after the Soviet Fifth Army in the South has been destroyed and Kiev is in our hands."

Then with fury and venom, gesturing wildly, Hitler gave a stern lecture to the assembled generals and senior staff officers on the strategic importance of his decision. It was an exceptional scene. The Führer of the German

Reich, the dictator whose military experience was limited to the duties of a corporal in World War I, was teaching the finest brains in the German Army how to conduct military operations. He guaranteed that only his plan would facilitate the capture of Leningrad, annihilate the Soviet forces in the Ukraine, and open the door to the Crimea and the Caucasus. These areas, he noted, were more important than Moscow, and their capture would assure the Reich's final victory. Occupation of the Ukraine was vital not only because of its industry and grain, but also because it would eliminate the Crimea as an unsinkable Soviet aircraft carrier for bombing airfields in Romania, the most important source of fuel for the Wehrmacht.

Then Hitler talked at length of his plans to make the Ukraine the granary for Germany, and how to bring the Nazi New Order to the conquered lands. With anger and indignation he ended the tirade, accusing the assembled generals of *naiveté*, lack of understanding of grand strategy, and even of sabotaging his, the Führer's, war effort. They were all too low and mean to understand his purpose, he said.

Hitler slumped into his seat, exhausted, his forehead and face shining with perspiration. "I will make no concessions over the matter," he murmured. "I have had enough!" He pressed both hands on his abdomen at the spot that seemed to pain him, and sat motionless, staring at the audience, his blue eyes watery and distant, his lips tight.

Dead silence blanketed the room. As Hitler talked the atmosphere had grown increasingly tense. The officers were stunned. Hitler seemed to be touching the very nerve of their professional pride. Never had they been so humiliated. The Führer had created a solid wall of antagonism.

Bock got up slowly. With all eyes on him he straightened his field marshal's uniform, coldly glanced at the generals around him, turned to Hitler, and with voice firm but full of emotion he submitted his resignation. "If a German field marshal cannot express his views freely to the Führer, then his service to the Reich is of no value," he said. "I trust that you will find someone who views these things differently from me to take my place, but I doubt that it will be anyone present here. I and my army commanders fully believe that the quickest road to victory is through Moscow, and that we must start the offensive while the weather is still favorable. And now, my Führer, I ask your permission to leave."

Hitler was dumbfounded. He barely controlled himself. But before Bock reached the door he regained a degree of composure and stopped him. "*Herr Feldmarschall*, you have chosen an easy path. With difficulties mounting, you have resigned. I am not in so fortunate a position. I don't have anyone to turn to. Calm down, *Herr Feldmarschall*, I refuse to accept your resignation. Please return and continue your report. No harm can be done by listening to what you have to say."

A sigh of relief filled the conference room. Suddenly everyone was struck by the feeling that somewhere hidden deep inside him Hitler feared his professional generals. Bock hesitated a moment. Then, without showing any emotion, he went directly to the huge map hanging on the wall, picked up his ivory-tipped pointer from the table, and, with one hand folded behind his back, continued the briefing.

Expertly using the map to emphasize the tactical and strategic importance of his reasoning, Bock began by pointing out that the Soviets had already started to build a defense line between the Baltic and the Black Sea, along which they would attempt to stop the German advance before the outbreak of winter. "No doubt the Russians want to protect their major industrial centers, to increase their war-waging capabilities," he said. "If the mobile war degenerates into static warfare, the Soviets, with their immense manpower potential, will be able to organize and train many new armies by spring. This in turn will force us to divert more forces and effort to the Eastern

Front, which would contradict the objectives of the blitzkrieg."

To prevent the Russians from accomplishing their aims, Bock continued, the Germans would have to keep the Red Army off balance. This could best be achieved by a direct thrust on Moscow. Since the defense of their capital was vital to the Soviets militarily, economically, and especially politically, the communist leaders would commit all available forces to defend it. Thus, by attacking Moscow, Army Group Center could destroy the bulk of the enemy forces, split the war theater in two, destroy the enemy communications network, seriously impair any future organized resistance, and eventually bring about the collapse of the Soviet empire.

During the advance on Moscow all other operations, being secondary in importance, should be stopped, unless they could be integrated into the overall plan for the powerful offensive against Moscow. The offensive would meet with success only if the forces of Army Group Center were properly massed, and logistically supported, with main efforts by strong panzer forces made at the southern and northern flanks of the army group.

The time element was extremely important, said Bock. Because of weather conditions the offensive would have to be carried out as soon as possible. The objectives would have to be reached by the second half of October. In view of the distance to be covered, and expected Soviet resistance, at least six to eight weeks would be required to accomplish the operation. Taking into account the need to rehabilitate some of the panzer elements and the motorized infantry, and time required for regrouping, the offensive could not start sooner than August 20–25.

Apologizing for not having a detailed operational plan ready, Bock offered several suggestions. Two field armies might launch a frontal attack toward Moscow, one in the south along the Roslav-Kaluga axis, and the other in the north via Rzhev and Dmitrov. The Second Panzer Group, deployed on the right flank, would envelop Moscow from the south and east and cut all the railroads and highways leading to the capital. One field army would move behind the Second Panzer Group to secure the flank of the army group from the south, thus preventing any possible Soviet counterattacks from that direction.

On the left, the Third Panzer Group would thrust toward and capture Kalinin, cut the Moscow-Leningrad railroad, and continue toward the southeast. The panzer groups would meet east of Moscow, encircling the city. Moscow could not survive. With the fall of Moscow, Army Group Center would take up a defensive posture some 100 miles east of the city, between Vladimir and Ryazan.

The tall and stately army group commander reiterated once more his certainty that his was the only realistic plan for winning the war before the onset of the grim Russian winter. He returned to his seat.

Hitler was indignant, irritated, and bitter. With sarcasm approaching rudeness he made it clear that he would have to think twice before taking advice so profoundly different from his own ideas. His purpose was to liquidate the enemy forces in the Ukraine and Leningrad first, so that the forthcoming advance on Moscow would not be endangered. He could not understand why German general officers would be opposed to such a simple and foolproof plan.

Hitler continued his monologue for a few minutes. Finally, fatigued, he calmed down a bit. "For the time being," he said, "I shall not change any of my directives. But I am willing to review *Herr Feldmarschall*'s proposal and consider its benefits. I should like to have a specific operation plan submitted to me the day after tomorrow. I can promise you that I will be open-minded and consider all options. And now there is no point in continuing our discussion." With that he nodded slightly to the gathered generals and senior officers and walked out, with Halder, Bock, and Dr. Morrell at his heels. They passed silently down the long corridor leading out of the building to the waiting cars. Half an hour later Hitler was in the air, flying back to East Prussia to his *Wolfsschanze* headquarters.

Far from being happy with the results of the conference, Bock and his staff nevertheless saw a ray of hope in Hitler's indecisiveness. As ordered, they quickly prepared a detailed operational plan for an immediate advance on Moscow and on August 6 dispatched it to OKH to be presented by Brauchitsch and Halder to the Fuehrer. But Hitler did not wish to meet with the Commander in Chief of the Army and instead asked the Chief of Staff of the Armed Forces (*Oberkommando der Wehrmacht*, OKW), Field Marshal Wilhelm Keitel, to review the plan and make his recommendation.

Aware of the far reaching consequences of this plan, Keitel talked it over with Jodl, and then they, accompanied by Generals Halder, Thomas, and Paulus, and Colonel Kinzel, Chief of the Foreign Armies East section of the General Staff, and other senior officers, flew to Borisov to meet with Field Marshal Bock.

The Borisov conference lasted almost seven hours. The conclusion was unanimous. Bock's plan should be submitted to the Führer for approval. And to ensure that the offensive progressed rapidly, the Fourth Panzer Group, under General Erich Hoepner, should be temporarily detached from Army Group North and attached to Army Group Center.

The New German Plan

Late in the evening of August 11, Keitel and Halder presented the final operations plan to Hitler. Confident that acceptance would assure military victory, both were very persuasive. In response to questions from Hitler and Martin Bormann they argued impressively that nothing could stop Bock. Any Soviet efforts to throw him back would not only fail miserably but also would result in more losses for the Red Army. "The all-out attack on Mos-

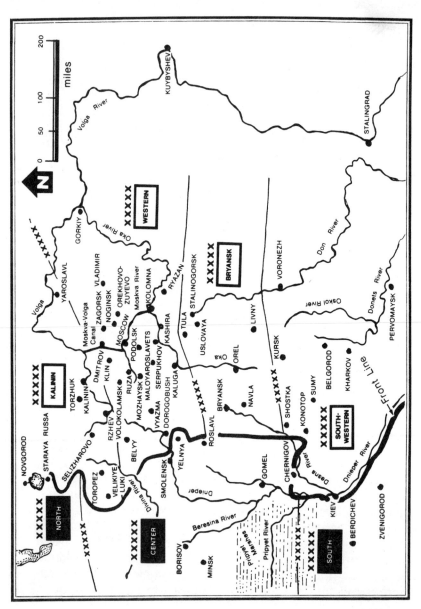

Deployment of Soviet and German Forces Prior to Operation Typhoon, August 27

cow," Keitel said, "should end Soviet resistance, and you, my Führer, will be sitting in the Kremlin, accepting an unconditional Soviet surrender!"

The officers' confidence rubbed off on Hitler. If he still had some reservations, they did not show on his face or in his voice. He summoned General Walter Warlimont, Deputy Chief of Operations, OKW, who was waiting in the next room, and ordered him to annul the old directive and prepare a new one, based on Bock's plan. "We shall call it Operation Typhoon for, like a typhoon, it will destroy everything in its path!"

With Soviet capitulation in sight, Hitler started wondering what to do with Moscow. Should the city be taken and preserved, or should it be totally destroyed, so that no visible sign of it remained. His decision: "No German soldier should enter the capital. Moscow should be destroyed and completely wiped from the earth. The war in the east is one of ideologies, and Germans should show no pity for the *Untermenschen*."

The plan thus approved called for the attack to be launched on August 25, which would give time for redeployment, rehabilitation of equipment, and bringing up of the necessary supplies and reserves. Army Group Center would have 51 infantry divisions, 10 motorized infantry divisions, 14 panzer divisions, and a cavalry division, organized in three field armies (Second, Fourth, and Ninth) and three panzer groups (Second, Third, and Fourth). Together, these forces would number nearly 1,000,000 men and 1,600 tanks. Air support would be provided by some 900 aircraft.

Each army would have a panzer group attached, forming a task force. The Northern Task Force, composed of the Ninth Army and Third Panzer Group, would jump off from southwest of Belyy and northwest of Toropez and, after eliminating the Soviet bulge around Velikye Luki, advance toward Rzhev and Kalinin and spread out around Moscow from the northwest, north, and northeast.

The Central Task Force, consisting of the Fourth Army

and the Fourth Panzer Group, would advance eastward from east of Smolensk toward Vyazma, and then proceed directly on Moscow.

The Southern Task Force, composed of the Second Army and the Second Panzer Group, deployed south of Roslavl and west of Bryansk, was to attack toward Bryansk and Orel, then turn northeast to Kashira and Tula, bypass Moscow from the south, and join with the Northern Task Force around Orekhovo-Zuyevo, and Noginsk, some 50 miles east of Moscow, closing the ring around the Soviet capital. The large Soviet troop concentrations in the Bryansk and Vyazma areas would be encircled and annihilated, leaving Moscow without manpower adequate to organize a meaningful close-in defense.

Protection of the right flank of the advancing force would be the responsibility of General Maximilian von Weichs, commander of the Second Army. He was to organize an operational group composed of five infantry divisions, two panzer divisions, one motorized infantry division, and a cavalry brigade, ready to beat off any possible Soviet counterattack from the area of Gomel and to the east.

No special measures were taken for protection of the left flank, where Soviet forces were known to be incapable of mounting any offensive activities.

As soon as Army Group Center moved out, Army Group South would launch local attacks to pin down Soviet forces in the area, particularly the Soviet Fifth Army, to prevent them from counterattacking the rear of the German troops advancing toward Moscow.

Army Group North was to commence active operations to eliminate the Russian concentration at Staraya Russa and, if possible, complete the encirclement of Leningrad.

Stalin Plans to Defend Moscow

While Hitler was scheming the destruction of Moscow, the Soviet Supreme Command (*Stavka*) received its first confirmation of the forthcoming offensive. On August 12 a message from Switzerland signed by one of the most important Soviet agents, code-named Lucy, revealed that the Germans had decided to launch a decisive offensive against Moscow on or about August 25. The message included a short description of the German operation plan, disposition of forces, and their strength. It tied together bits of information that Soviet intelligence had accumulated during the previous week, and confirmed the prevailing Soviet assumption that the next German onslaught would be aimed at Moscow.

That night the *Stavka* meeting was especially grim. It took place in the Kirov subway station where the offices of the General Staff had been moved shortly after July 22, the night of the first German air raid. Stalin's office was there also, as well as his small makeshift living quarters.

While the possibility of a German breakthrough in the Ukraine—which could result in the destruction of the still mighty Southwestern Army Group—was on everyone's mind, and the fact that German Army Group North was closing in on Leningrad could not be ignored, the meeting was devoted exclusively to the defense of Moscow. No one made an attempt to disguise the situation, make excuses, or blame others for the failures.

Back in the first days of July, when the front was still close to Minsk, the *Stavka* had decided to prepare a continuous line of fortifications some 130 miles long about 30 miles east of the Rzhev-Vyazma line. The fortifications were to be completed early in August. However, although over 150,000 workers had been committed to the project, barely half the work was done. Construction of another defense line was ordered on July 14, when the Germans were approaching Smolensk. It was to be a semicircular line running west of Moscow and east of Mozhaysk, based on fortified areas at key points along railroad lines, highways, and roads leading from the west to Moscow. Even if the construction was expedited, however, it was obvious that these fortifications also would not be ready in time to meet the German attack.

At the front the manpower situation was graver than

ever. Rifle divisions were undermanned. Some had fewer than 1,000 men. Tank divisions were divisions in name only, having only ten to fifteen tanks each. Armies were so reduced that it was doubtful whether they would be capable of putting up serious resistance if the Germans decided to ram through. Reserves were not readily available, and supplies were either short or non-existent.

Still, despite this desperate picture, there was an air of hope at the *Stavka* meeting. Tank production, in spite of the havoc that had been caused by the evacuation of factories to the east, was on the rise, and it was expected that before the end of the year some 4,000 new tanks, including many of the advanced T-34s, would be delivered to the fighting units. A stream of rifles, machine guns, submachine guns, artillery pieces, and ammunition would very soon be coming off the production lines. Mobilization was proceeding fairly well, and nearly 200 new divisions and hundreds of smaller specialized units were being organized and trained. Five well-trained and -equipped armies from Siberia and Central Asia, over 300,000-men strong, were ready to be transferred to the front. They were expected to start arriving late in August. Their departure for the front could be speeded up by a week or so. In the captured territories barbaric German behavior had aroused resentment, and the inhabitants had established numerous partisan groups that could be helpful in opposing the German attackers.

Three Soviet army groups were facing German Army Group Center. The Kalinin Army Group, under General Ivan Konev, was defending the Velikiye Luki-Rzhev-Kalinin axis. The Western Army Group, under the newly-appointed commander, General Grigoriy Zhukov, was defensively deployed in a 200-mile sector directly west of Moscow. And the Bryansk Army Group, commanded by General A. Yeremenko, was protecting the Bryansk-Orel-Tula axis. Among them, the three army groups had nearly 800,000 men, about 500 tanks, most of them light and obsolete, and 500 aircraft, of which only 20% were modern.

There was a consensus among the Soviet leaders that the Germans could not continue their offensive simultaneously along the entire Soviet-German front. Their losses in men and materiel had been very heavy, and replacements were falling far behind. If Hitler decided to make an all-out effort against Moscow, the Soviets reasoned, offensive operations in other sectors would have to be largely curtailed. This would help the Southwestern Army Group and the defenders of Leningrad to strengthen their defenses, and eventually to counterattack. Furthermore, under these circumstances, any eastward advance of German Army Group Center would expose its right flank, creating a grave danger to its lines of communication, which could be cut by a strike from the south. Some of the forces of the Southwestern and Bryansk army groups could be used for such a maneuver, resulting in the encirclement and destruction of the forward German echelon, speeding toward Moscow.

Stalin summed up the discussion, speaking forcefully, with determination. "Well, it seems that the German invaders want a total war of extermination against the Soviet people. So be it. They shall have it, and they will regret it." As a rallying cry he invoked the names of Alexander Nevsky, Alexander Suvorov, Michael Kutuzov, the heroic Russian leaders of the past, and used the earlier invaders—the Tartars, the Teutonic Knights, the Swedes, the Poles, and Napoleon—as examples of Russian ability to rout even the mightiest enemies. "We shall defend every meter of our holy fatherland, just as our great ancestors did! Moscow must be defended at all cost. But we must avoid the mistakes of the past. No more pockets and encirclements. We have already lost too many troops and cannot afford to lose any more. Bialystok and Minsk must not be repeated. The next few weeks will be most decisive. I want Shaposhnikov and Vasilevskiy (Marshal B. Shaposhnikov was Chief of the General Staff and General A. Vasilevskiy was his deputy) to beef up our forces in front of Moscow. We should also start making plans of what to do in case of a German breakthrough.

Serious consideration must be given to a counterattack from the south at the most opportune moment."

The Drive on Moscow

The German offensive on Moscow, the great battle which was supposed to bring the Soviets to their knees, started half an hour before sunrise on August 27, 1941, two days later than originally planned. Time was a crucial factor. The 180-mile drive to Moscow would have to be made before the end of September, or October rains would turn the ground and roads into a sea of mud. Success depended on good weather and the capability of the German Army to reach decisive objectives, including Moscow, before the fall rainy season set in.

At first all went extraordinarily well. Hastily prepared and poorly organized Soviet defenses were no match for the panzer strikes. Few of the hoped-for Soviet replacements had arrived, and those that had were badly trained and inadequately armed. There were very few antitank guns and not many shells. German air superiority was total.

On the extreme right of Army Group Center, the Second Panzer Army (all German panzer groups were renamed "armies" on the eve of the attack) struck toward Navla, south of Bryansk, and, after crossing the Bryansk-Sumy railroad line, turned one of its corps toward Bryansk, while the other continued toward Orel. At the same time, the Second Army easily broke through the Soviet defenses and pressed along the Roslav-Bryansk highway with the intention of enveloping the Bryansk Group of forces from the north and the east, and joining the panzers of Guderian's Second Panzer Army, converging from the south. By September 1 the pocket was closed, entrapping two Soviet armies. Fierce fighting developed as the encircled divisions tried to break loose and flee to the east. Only about 30,000 men escaped, among them the commander of the Bryansk Army Group, General A. Yeremenko, who, severely wounded, was carried out by his men. While sporadic resistance lasted until September 6, only a few divisions were left behind for the mopping up operation. The main force of the army pushed on toward the east.

On September 2 German tanks reached Orel. Their appearance in the city was totally unexpected. Only that morning the Tass communiqué broadcast the news about heavy fighting in the Bryansk area, nearly 70 miles to the west. Street cars and buses in Orel were running as usual, stores and movie theaters were open, and factories working. As the German tanks approached the city, people waved at them, mistaking them for Soviets. The city fell without resistance.

After a two-day delay to reorganize and bring up supplies, Guderian continued toward Gorbachowvo, encountering only minor opposition from *ad hoc*, hastily organized Soviet units composed mainly of stragglers and escapees from encirclement.

On August 28 the Fourth Army, in the center of Army Group Center, supported by the Fourth Panzer Army, launched its attack toward its first objective—the major concentration of Soviet forces in the Vyazma area. By evening it was already evident that the tactical breakthrough had succeeded. To the southwest and northwest of Vyazma, where the Germans were making their main efforts, Soviet fortifications were breached, and the Germans drove eastward without encountering serious resistance. In a deep enveloping maneuver from north and south, spearheaded by panzers and followed by infantry, German troops pivoted and headed toward Temkino, east of Vyazma. In so doing they formed a pocket that sealed the fate of seven Soviet armies. However, extremely determined resistance by the encircled Soviet forces, led by able and experienced generals, including Rokossovsky, Lukin, and Govorov, continued to tie up some 15 German divisions until September 21. This somewhat slowed the German advance toward Moscow, and enabled the

Soviets to bring up those reserves they still had left and to deploy them close to Moscow, along the Volokolamsk-Mozhaysk-Serpukhov defense line.

The Soviet Command had to act very quickly. On September 18 German panzers appeared in front of Mozhaysk and Maloyaroslavets, at the same time others were capturing Kaluga. At some points the Germans were within 65 miles of the Kremlin. The disastrous encirclements at Bryansk and Vyazma had cost the Soviets nearly 600,000 men killed or captured, and nearly 450 tanks and several thousand artillery pieces captured. It was impossible to form any meaningful resistance along the intermittent lines between Vyazma and Mozhaysk. Although some 100,000 troops had either been withdrawn in time or escaped from the encirclement, the men were demoralized and in dire need of equipment, which was very scarce.

On the left wing of Army Group Center, the Ninth Army and the Third Panzer Army also jumped off on August 28. A task force composed of one panzer and five infantry divisions attacked straight north toward Andreapol, in order to cut off and later destroy the Soviet troop concentration in the Velikye Luki salient. The main forces attacked toward Rzhev and Kalinin.

This German attack met surprisingly strong and well organized resistance. The Soviets fought stubbornly and took every opportunity to make vicious counterattacks. The terrain favored the defenders, but after a fierce fight, which included hand-to-hand combat, Rzhev was captured on September 3. The Soviets skillfully withdrew their forces, avoiding encirclement, and continued to resist. The Germans advanced very slowly. By September 20 they had reached a line from Selizharovo to Torzhuk to Turginovo. There they stopped and regrouped for the assault on Kalinin, whose capture was essential for the envelopment of Moscow from the north. It would, moreover, enable the Third Panzer Army and motorized elements of the Ninth Army to pivot southeast to converge with the Second Panzer Army, which was enveloping Moscow from the south and southeast.

When the *Stavka* met at noon on September 20, the overall situation on the Moscow front was grave indeed. There was no longer a continuous front line. The army newspaper, *Red Star*, warned that day, "The very existence of the Soviet state is in danger! Every man of the Red Army must stand firm and fight to the last drop of blood!" Headquarters of the Western Army Group moved to Perkushkovo, a stone's throw from Moscow. Headquarters of the defending armies were no more than 25 to 35 miles from the city. All embassies were evacuated from Moscow to Kuibyshev, and most of the Soviet ministries were sent deep into the Soviet Union, leaving only a skeleton administration in the capital. The most valuable items from the Kremlin and other museums were carefully crated and loaded on special trains for shipment to Siberia and Central Asia. Only essential personnel, the Operational Group, of the General Staff remained in Moscow. The remainder, the so-called Second Echelon, was sent to Gorkiy.

Thousands of Soviet civilians were heading east on foot, in horse carts, and in cars, blocking roads, making troop movements a nightmare. As word spread that the Germans had captured Kaluga and were bypassing Moshaysk, panic broke out. Muscovites started to flee from the danger. Party members, junior and senior officials, and bureaucrats joined the ordinary people crowding the railroad stations, trying to board the scores of trains leaving for the east. Even hospital trains were mobbed, and many wounded were left behind. On the street, unruly crowds ransacked stores, looking for food and other goods. The long-nurtured fear of militia (police) vanished. Militiamen and uniformed NKVD men were attacked and beaten or ran for their lives. It was several hours before special security troops restored order.

A state of siege had been proclaimed in Moscow the day before the *Stavka* meeting. Emergency peoples' courts were established to handle all breaches of law and order. Maintenance of order inside the city limits was entrusted to NKVD troops and the Military Commandant of Moscow, with orders that saboteurs and spies were to be shot on the spot.

Confrontation in the Kirov Station

Stalin opened the *Stavka* meeting on September 20. He emphatically denied rumors that he intended to surrender the city. "Moscow will be defended to the last! Every street shall be turned into a trench, every building into a fortress. Moscow will be a symbol of heroism for the entire nation! Yesterday," said Stalin, "the State Defense Committee ordered two more defense lines built—one along the city border, the other along the ring of boulevards within Moscow itself. The people of Moscow have already started to build them. If there are not enough troops to man them, they will be manned by communist battalions and home guards divisions."

As Stalin paused briefly, Zhukov asked permission to speak. He had just returned from the front, where he had almost been captured by the Germans. Thanks only to the quick wits of his driver, who at the last minute turned off the main road into a forest, did he miss a German panzer patrol. "Despite reverses," said Zhukov, "I am still hopeful that we shall be able to stop the Germans outside Moscow. Bock's communication lines are long, his supplies short, and many of his tanks in urgent need of repair." Zhukov's main concern was the concentrations of German panzers on the flanks of Army Group Center. He referred to the latest intelligence reports that indicated that Bock did not intend to take Moscow by a frontal attack but by a deep encirclement from north and south, closing the ring east of the capital.

Looking Stalin straight in the eye, Zhukov continued. "We should not be concerned with symbols. Our prime responsibility is to preserve manpower. At all costs we must avoid another encirclement. If Guderian and Hoth break through in their respective sectors we shall have to withdraw our forces quickly and form a new defense line east of the ring. We will of course fight fiercely, with all our strength, to prevent the invaders from getting through. But if the worst should happen, we must salvage as much as possible. Thus we shall still have a sufficient force to counterattack when our Southwestern Army Group is ready to strike the Germans in the rear."

Stalin was carefully watching the reaction of the audience. He saw an obvious spirit of defiance. He asked for comments. Several of the generals stood and supported Zhukov's position, and Stalin knew that he had to give in. Thus he eagerly seized on Molotov's suggestion to "let the General Staff prepare a final plan and present it to the *Stavka* tomorrow for approval."

Turning to the issue of reserves, Stalin found that there also his views differed sharply from those of the military leaders. Whereas he wanted all of the reserve armies that were still available to deploy at the Moscow front, Marshal Shaposhnikov and others suggested that the two combat-ready armies that had already disembarked from trains near Moscow, and two recently organized armies that were expected to arrive in a matter of two or three days, would be enough. All home guard divisions and special workers and communist battalions, plus several NKVD regiments also were available to be thrown into the battle immediately.

Shaposhnikov pointed out that there were three full-strength armies from Siberia and Central Asia and one from the Far East on trains west of the Ural Mountains. They should be sent as quickly as possible to the Southwestern Army Group to join a counterattack on Bock's right flank, some 130 miles to the rear of the front line.

Stalin had gnawing doubts about this plan. He argued that General Kirponos (Southwestern Army Group) could spare enough troops to carry out the counterblow either without any reinforcements, or with the help of one reserve army. But General Vasilevskiy's blunt revelation of the difficult situation in the Southwestern Army Group sector, and his vivid description of how a really strong blow from the south, combined with stubborn defense and then counterattack in the Moscow area, would destroy the Germans impressed Stalin. "If most of what you have said is correct," he said, "we shall win. Moscow will become a graveyard for the Nazi barbarians." He ordered the necessary directives prepared.

While the *Stavka* was planning for the defense of Moscow and gloomily contemplating the effects of the fall of the city, the mood in Bock's Army Group Center headquarters was exuberant. Everyone from cook to general mulled over the imminent capture of Moscow and the end of the war. Hitler arrived at army group headquarters in a state of joyful excitement. Shaking Bock's hand he exclaimed several times that the progress of his troops was beyond his wildest expectations. The fate of Moscow was sealed, and the entire campaign might be over in a few weeks. The more forces the Russians threw into defense of their capital, the more would be trapped and annihilated! With Moscow taken, nothing would be in the way of a victorious run to the Volga. "I hope we reach Gorkiy in time to see my soldiers swim in that river before the cold sets in," said Hitler, wringing his hands and licking his lips. "I am happy that I heeded your advice."

Although Hitler was putting on a public show of confidence, in private he revealed considerable concern about the imminent final victory, admitting that it was "not yet in hand." The Soviets still had sizable forces to be reckoned with. Rundstedt was barely holding his front, and in many sectors the Russians had put his troops on the defensive. In the north, Leeb had had difficulties in Estonia. On the Luga River the Red Army had taken the initiative, forcing the Germans to withdraw in several places. In front of Moscow, despite fantastic progress, the Germans had suffered increasingly heavy losses, and one could expect that the battle would intensify, since the Russians would probably defend their capital at all costs.

Hitler closeted himself for almost three hours with Halder, Jodl, Bock, and several senior staff officers and listened in silence to their explanations of the forthcoming final push. When they finished, he agreed to the operation plan they had presented. Once more he ordered that the capitulation of Moscow must not be accepted, and no German troops should enter the city. After the encirclement was accomplished, and the defenders had surrendered unconditionally, Moscow was to be entered by special SS security detachments only. They would take strategic objectives in the city, including telephone exchanges, military barracks, seats of various ministries, prisons, and railroad stations. Any local resistance would be dealt with harshly. For an attempt to kill a German soldier at least 500 Russians living in the neighborhood where it occurred were to be taken and shot or hanged on the spot. No Soviet citizen would be permitted to leave the city without special authorization. Some would be authorized to leave shortly after the takeover. Others would get permission to leave later. And the rest, Hitler shrugged his shoulders, "will not have to wait too long for the final solution." The site of Moscow would be made into a great lake, which would forever cover the former capital of the Russian people.

The Final Assault

On September 27, after a short pause in which the Germans redeployed their forces and built up the two powerful panzer groups on the flanks of Army Group Center, the final assault on Moscow began. In the south the Second Panzer Army moved quickly toward Tula, encountering only sporadic resistance. The Second Army, following the panzers, fanned out toward Voronezh and toward Ryazan. As Guderian's panzers approached Tula, Soviet resistance increased. A mechanized corps counterattacked from Stalinogorsk and Uzlovaya and engaged one panzer corps in heavy fighting. It took two days to beat off the Soviet corps and force it to retreat. But the defenses of Tula held, and Guderian decided to bypass it from the east, leaving the capture of the city to the Second Army. This development slowed the German advance, and it was not until October 5 that elements of the panzer army finally reached the Moskva River at Kolomna. There they were stopped by the newly arrived Sixth Strike Army, which took up defensive positions on the eastern bank of the river.

Again fierce Soviet defense delayed the German time-table. Only after regrouping, and with the support of two infantry divisions of the Second Army that were transferred from the Ryazan axis, did Guderian succeed in establishing a bridgehead on the left bank of the river. On October 8 he pushed on toward Noginsk, some 50 miles away. Soviet resistance weakened, and on October 11 Guderian captured Noginsk.

In the center of Army Group Center, on September 27, the Fourth Army, supported by elements of the Fourth Panzer Army, launched its main effort in the Volokolamsk-Ruza sector and a secondary one west of Novofominsk. As soon as the battle began it was obvious that the Soviets had brought in fresh troops and were determined to bleed the Germans white. The Soviet fortifications proved to be better than anticipated, and thousands of mines had been planted throughout the area. The seesaw battle that developed greatly sapped German strength, and the Fourth Army could advance only 15 miles the first three days. An extremely fierce and vicious battle developed for Istra, Zvenigorod, and Podolsk. All these places changed hands repeatedly. Finally, on October 4, the Soviets suddenly began to withdraw, and the Germans quickly closed on Moscow from the west. At the outskirts of the city they were again halted by a new defense line, this time, however, occupied mostly by Home Guard units, sprinkled with a few seasoned elements. Air reconnaissance reported that the old units were moving rapidly to the east, apparently to be deployed in a new fortified defense line being built between Ryazan, Vladimir, and Yaroslavl. Bock ordered Field Marshal von Kluge's Fourth Field Army not to attack further but to wait until the pocket around Moscow was closed.

On the left (north) flank of Army Group Center, the Third Panzer Army, with an attached panzer corps of the Fourth Panzer Army, jumped off on September 28, broke through the well-prepared Soviet defenses east of Kalinin, and during the following four days captured Klin and Yakhorma, crossed the Moskva-Volga Canal, and reached Dmitrov, where its drive was halted by the Soviet First Army. In the meantime, the Ninth Army encircled and took Kalinin. Then, encountering only limited resistance from retreating Soviet divisions, it followed the Third Panzer Army on a broad front.

The battle for Dmitrov raged for several days. For the Soviets it was very important not to let the Germans through, in order to keep open lines of communication to the east, through Zagorsk and Noginsk. On the other side, Hoth wanted to take those towns quickly and by so doing to encircle Moscow and entrap the Soviet forces still there.

Fighting with determination, German panzers took Dmitrov on October 6 and continued toward Zagorsk, despite desperate Soviet resistance. Zagorsk fell in the evening of October 9, leaving only one major highway through Noginsk still open to the Soviets. Giving his troops no rest, Hoth ordered an immediate drive toward Noginsk, where he expected to join Guderian, approaching from the south. However, Guderian was there first. On October 12 the panzer armies met, about 14 miles north of the town. The mission accomplished, Moscow was encircled. One hour later Bock radioed Hitler.

MOSCOW ENCIRCLED. ALL ROUTES OF ESCAPE CLOSED. WEATHER PERMITTING, MERCILESS BOMBING OF THE CITY WILL CONTINUE UNTIL UNCONDITIONAL SURRENDER. YOUR TRIUMPHANT TROOPS INVITE YOU TO REVIEW THE VICTORY PARADE IN RED SQUARE. HEIL HITLER!

Bock's confidence turned out to be premature. The expected big prize had eluded him.

Elusive Prize

Most of the Soviet troops that had been manning defenses in and around the city had gone before the ring closed, leaving the defense of Moscow proper to local Home Guard and army units left behind especially for this task. Moscow turned out not to be Minsk or Vyazma. The Soviets had learned their lesson. East of the German ring around the city a concentration of Soviet forces stood ready to continue the fight. Even as the champagne flowed at the *Wolfsschanze,* the first local counterattacks had already begun, aimed at assisting units left inside the circle to break out.

In the week that followed there was fierce fighting, as the Germans attempted to retain the operational initiative, while the Soviets tried to seize it. Speed was urged on the German soldiers, but still panzer and mechanized forces had to wait to be relieved by infantry before they could push ahead. While nominally on the offensive, at least temporarily the Germans were unable to launch a serious attack to the east. What they could do, and were doing, was to press closer and closer to Moscow from all sides until, on October 18, there was fighting in all of the Moscow suburbs. Now the question was, would the defenders surrender? Or would they fight to the last, turning Moscow into another Madrid?

The fine weather that had been assisting the German attackers suddenly broke on October 12. Snow began to fall, then turned into incessant, cold rain. It was a severe setback to the Germans. The roads soon turned into quagmires, through which men and vehicles could advance only at a snail's pace. Planes were grounded. Supplies became a pressing problem. Fuel was low. Food was inadequate. Winter clothing for the troops was almost completely lacking. Only 30 per cent of the trucks were in working condition.

There still were ample grounds for Bock's optimism, nevertheless. Moscow was almost in German hands, and with its capture the disintegration of the Soviet regime was expected. However, many intelligence reports reaching Army Group Center were disquieting, to say the least. From a variety of sources came the word that the Red Army was concentrating a considerable force in the Ukraine, between Chernigov and Konotop, along the southern flank of Army Group Center. Some reports indicated that there were at least two full strength armies from Siberia among these troops. Word from the Kiev area indicated that several of the best divisions facing the Germans there were being replaced. One of them was soon identified near Shostka, a town close to the Second Army operational area. On October 16 General K. Rokossovskiy, former commander of the Sixteenth Army defending Moscow, and one of the ablest Soviet military leaders, was seen in Konotop.

At first these and other bits of intelligence were not taken too seriously. Reserves were alerted, but no orders were issued to deploy them close to the area of possible Soviet counterattack. Bock's headquarters was in a state of euphoria. Moscow was on the verge of collapse, and with its fall the collapse of the Soviet regime seemed imminent. It was inconceivable that in such a catastrophe the Soviets, instead of throwing in all their available forces to defend the capital, would open another front. Actually Bock could not do much to sustain another front. Of the five infantry, two panzer, and one motorized infantry divisions originally earmarked for the defense of the southern flanks, all except two infantry divisions were already engaged in other sectors.

During the night of October 18/19 a Soviet deserter, a non-commissioned officer who claimed to be of German origin, crossed over to the Germans. He reported that a Soviet task force of about four armies, including one tank army, would launch an attack from the south toward Roslavl and Vyazma on October 21. Their objective was to cut off all the German forces in the Moscow area.

Soviet Counteroffensive

Bock could no longer disregard the need for defending his dangerously exposed southern flank, which he had so long neglected. But it was too late. At 5 A.M. on October 21 Soviet forces broke through the weak German defenses in a 30-mile sector and, having suffered only minor losses, pushed rapidly toward Roslavl along two main highways. The German situation was further complicated by Soviet paratroop landings at several places in the German rear, some 40 miles behind the front line. This caused havoc to the German logistics system, as depots, truck columns, and communications centers were attacked, bridges and railroads were blown up, and countless small units were either wiped out or forced to surrender.

On October 24, two Soviet cavalry divisions, after a march through seemingly impassable forests, reached Bryansk, where the Germans had a major rear base. The garrison there, not ready for defense, was quickly overrun and almost entirely exterminated. Meanwhile, to the west, Soviet tanks and infantry, advancing almost unopposed, took Zhukovka and headed for Roslavl. The weather, which was initially miserable, got somewhat better, and this improved Soviet performance.

The Soviet counteroffensive marked the beginning of a new phase in the war. For the first time the Red Army had succeeded in mounting a major offensive maneuver, which threatened to envelop and destroy the German forces around Moscow. Bock realized that if the Soviets were not stopped in time, not only would his army group face disaster, but the entire campaign in the east might be doomed. All available reserves must be brought in and thrown against the Russians. OKH shared Bock's concern and had started to move five divisions from Poland and the Ukraine as soon as word of the counterattack came in. But they were not expected to arrive at the front until October 26 or 27. Rundstedt could not help, for he did not have forces to break through the Soviet defenses north of Kiev and attack Rokossovskiy's task force from the rear. Moreover, the Soviet Fifth Army was hanging over his left flank, threatening to strike any day.

With insufficient resources and overextended lines, the

Germans could not stop the Soviets' advance. The attacks continued unabated. On October 25 two airborne battalions were dropped in the vicinity of Roslavl. Panic spread. The Germans withdrew to the north without a fight, leaving all their equipment and heavy weapons behind.

Then, in the morning of October 26 came a new setback. General Zhukov, commander of the Western Army Group, launched a massive counteroffensive from the east toward Moscow, aimed at relieving the city and destroying the German forces in the encircling ring. About 100 Soviet divisions, supported by some 500 tanks and thousands of artillery pieces, attacked on a 100-mile front between Zagorsk and Kolomna, with the main effort from Noginsk toward Podolsk.

The size and strength of the combined infantry-armor attack caught the Germans off guard. To halt the avalanche of Russian troops was next to impossible, despite the desperate stand made by numerous units. The Red Army quickly breached the line southwest of Noginsk and created a threat to Podolsk. Heavy losses were suffered by both sides, but while the Soviet replacements seemed inexhaustible, the hard-pressed German troops could not count on any at all.

Consternation swept the German High Command and the headquarters of Army Group Center. The cold intensified, bringing the troops to the end of their endurance. There was no more talk of taking Moscow. The exuberance of a fortnight earlier disappeared. The question now was how to save the forces at Moscow from annihilation.

The grim truth had a shattering effect on Hitler. His contempt for his generals returned with overflowing bile. His temper grew shorter, and mad outbursts became daily occurrences. Baseless accusations against senior officers, questioning their professional competence, their courage to make hard decisions, and their capability to withstand severe strain, undermined their will to fight.

In a message to Bock, Hitler emphatically rejected his

proposal to withdraw from Moscow to the Smolensk defense line, where he had started the ill-fated offensive nearly two months earlier. Hitler insisted that troops be taken from other sectors of the front and thrown against the Russians advancing on Roslavl, and firmly maintained there were enough German troops around Moscow to halt Zhukov.

The situation continued to deteriorate. General Vasilevskiy, who took over command of the task force when General Rokossovskiy was injured in an automobile accident, took Roslavl, then swirled toward Spas-Demensk and Vyazma in order to cut the Smolensk-Moscow highway, the principal German communication artery.

German forces on the Moscow front could not hold out any longer. Pressure north and south of the city caused them to retreat hastily, without orders from OKH. Confusion became chaos. The threat of encirclement had a profoundly adverse effect on combat performance and morale. Caught between the hammer and the anvil, the Germans' prime preoccupation became survival, with bitter denunciation of the leaders who had caused their misery.

Efforts to halt the advance of Vasilevskiy's task force proved ineffectual. The reserves finally arrived from Poland, but, thrown into the battle piecemeal and without the necessary preparation, they were wiped out, one by one.

The Russians, meanwhile, were enjoying numerical superiority and considerable maneuverability and mobility thanks to the commitment of several cavalry divisions. They had no difficulty in organizing a number of strike forces. Favored by their acquaintance with the terrain, they struck alternately in several directions, with great success.

On November 5 German air reconnaissance reported a concentration of Soviet cavalry only about 40 miles south of the Smolensk-Moscow highway, near Dorogobush. On the same day Zhukov's main forces reached the

Volokolamsk-Mozhaisk-Serpukhov line west of Moscow. To the north the Germans gave up Kalinin, and in the south Tula. The threat of a coordinated Soviet pincer movement was clearly developing.

The Specter of Defeat

Belatedly Hitler came to realize that the Soviets could not be beaten. His illusions and daydreams came abruptly to an end. He cursed himself for listening to Bock, Halder, and "those other stupid generals with whom I had to go to war." If he had only followed his own sound reasoning and attacked in the Ukraine first, he told himself, everything would have been different. Now it was not the Soviets but his own troops who found themselves in a giant *kessel*, with no way out.

Hitler finally decided that he would no longer ignore the pleas from the commander of Army Group Center to withdraw. After all, he was the one who had insisted so bluntly on attacking Moscow. Now let him bear the consequences of his brilliant strategy. On November 7, as Stalin was reviewing the parade in Red Square in honor of the 24th anniversary of the October Revolution, Hitler authorized Bock to issue orders to retreat.

It was high time. The bottleneck through which three field armies and three panzer armies would have to withdraw was less than 80 miles wide. There were only a few roads, and the terrain was inhospitable and very difficult to cross. The Smolensk-Moscow highway was under artillery fire and in imminent danger of being cut.

Having finally obtained the long-awaited permission for a general retreat, OKH did all it could to check the Soviet advance and to withdraw in as orderly a fashion as possible. Roads were mined extensively, all kinds of booby traps were planted, and rear guards were deployed at tactically important points.

Despite these measures, the Red Army retained its momentum, spurred by the realization that the Germans must not be allowed to disengage from the pursuing troops and to organize successive defense lines. Slowly the retreat turned into a flight. Troops were disorganized and lost their fighting capabilities. As rumors spread that the Soviets might close the pocket any day, heavy arms, trucks, and even tanks were left behind, and the soldiers started running for their lives. It was June in reverse. But whereas in June the Soviets were fleeing in nice warm weather, the November weather took its toll on the lightly-clad Germans.

Angered by the disorganized retreat, for which he blamed the weak character of his senior officers, Hitler rescinded his permission to withdraw and ordered Bock to stand fast and continue to fight to the last man. Bock refused. His troops could not hold, he said, and he would not order them to be destroyed. It would be madness to attempt to hold. Unless the Führer changed his mind he could look for another army group commander!

Once again, Hitler yielded to Bock. As the unexpected Soviet victories brought to his mind the fate of Napoleon's armies, which dissolved into nonexistence in the vast expanse of Russia, he was concerned lest any further retreat not only degenerate into total destruction of Army Group Center, which had already lost most of its heavy armament and equipment and nearly 60% of its manpower, but also adversely affect German forces in other sectors of the front, and indeed the whole German nation and his own status. He wanted to dismiss Bock, but he knew that if he did so he would also have to dismiss his army commanders and risk goading the entire army into revolt. The risk was too high. Despondently, he admitted to Goering that "victory cannot be achieved this year. German troops will have to face a bitter winter totally unprepared."

It was the endurance of the German soldiers and the skill of the commanders, not Hitler's leadership, which saved what was left of Army Group Center. As more reserve divisions from France and Germany were thrown into the battle, German resistance stiffened. Combat degenerated into a kind of slugging match in which both advance and retreat became minimal. On November 20 the Soviet offensive, at the end of its resources, and with lines of communication stretching back east of Moscow, came to a halt some 30 miles east of Smolensk.

Thus the major German assault on Moscow failed and turned into the greatest German defeat of World War II. Hitler's hopes of knocking the Soviet Union out of the war in 1941 collapsed totally. The failure sapped the self confidence of officers and men and strained to the limit the relationship between the Führer and his general officers. The German blitzkrieg came to an end; the strategic initiative passed on to the Red Army. The specter of defeat was hanging over the Third Reich.

Afterword

The part of the chapter dealing with the occurrences from the outbreak of the Soviet-German War in June 1941 to the end of July of that year summarizes the true historical events. The rest represents one of the possible "might have beens," if Hitler had acceded to the OKH demands to continue the offensive toward Moscow, instead of turning his efforts to the Ukraine.

Whether or not Hitler's decision not to go after Moscow in August doomed chances of German victory in the East is still heatedly debated by military historians. During years of discussions two opposing points of view have crystalized. One, held by most former World War II senior German military leaders, argues that if Hitler had not interfered with the original plans, and if the offensive toward Moscow had commenced in August, the Soviet capital would have been taken before the arrival of rainy autumn weather, and with the fall of Moscow, the collapse of the Soviet resistance was imminent.

The adherents to the other point of view, among them most, if not all, Soviet military historians, are of the opinion that in August 1941 the German Army Group Center could not carry out a victorious offensive culminating in the capture of Moscow. And, even if Moscow had fallen, it would have been just an episode in the war, a serious setback, but in no way would it have led to the collapse of the Red Army.

In real life, the Germans moved against Moscow at the end of September and in early October, after the encirclement and destruction of the 600,000-man strong Soviet Southwestern Army Group in the Ukraine. In the first days of December they reached the suburbs of Moscow, where they were stopped and forced to retreat by a powerful counteroffensive. However, the German southern flank was not threatened, and the withdrawal, although carried out in most difficult conditions, did not turn into a rout.

Now, assuming that the Southwestern Army Group was not defeated before Army Group Center launched its offensive, this strong Soviet force could have mounted a counteroffensive toward the German flank and rear at the most opportune moment. And this was the case chosen for our command option.

A Soviet counteroffensive from the east, combined with an attack from the flank toward objectives deep in the German rear, was an option that the Soviet Supreme Command could not have overlooked. Such a decision could have had a catastrophic effect on the German forces. Poorly prepared for winter warfare, with their communication lines cut or stretched to the maximum, the retreat of Army Group Center would have been much more costly than it was in December, when it actually happened. It might have even forced Germany to sue for peace.

CHAPTER V

Pearl Harbor

Japanese Preparations

IT IS DIFFICULT to know where to begin the story of what happened at Pearl Harbor. What did happen on Sunday, December 7, 1941, and in the preceding period, was not the result of any short-term decisions on the part of the Japanese Empire but was, rather, the result of a long process that many say had its roots in the Russo-Japanese War settlement, when President Theodore Roosevelt blocked some of the more immediate ambitions of the Japanese.

The basic course of Japanese militarism after the end of the Russo-Japanese War and up to the outbreak of World War II was established in three documents promulgated in 1907: "The National Defense Policy of the Japanese Empire," "The Force of Arms Necessary for National Defense," and "The Principle for Operations of the Imperial Armed Forces." Although revised on several occasions over the years, these three documents stood as the basis of Japanese strategy until 1941, and from these documents came the military operational plans that led to the attack on Pearl Harbor.

This concept of action came into being in February 1941, when Admiral Isoroku Yamamoto, the Commander of the Imperial Combined Fleet, commented to another senior naval officer, Rear Admiral Takajiro Onishi, that the only hope the Japanese had of a successful war against the United States was the destruction of the American fleet at Hawaii.

Onishi, acting under Yamamoto's instructions, ordered a brilliant young naval aviator, Commander Minoru Genda, to study the feasibility of striking a successful, crippling blow against the Americans at Pearl Harbor. Ten days later, Genda reported that, while the risks were great, the mission was indeed possible. Within two months the attack plan was roughed out and a number of senior commanders briefed on the essence of the proposed operation.

While this initial planning was underway, the Japanese government was deeply involved in diplomatic negotiations, the successful conclusion of which might have prevented the need for the Pearl Harbor plan. It was Japan's chief ambition, as exhibited in its relationship with Hitler's Germany, to be accepted as the leader in Asia. To offset this, the United States had mounted a massive diplomatic campaign designed to wean Japan away from the Axis and especially from its ruthless occupation of China. While there appeared to be some official Japanese movement in this direction, it was not without dissent, especially in the early utterances of Foreign Minister Matsuoka, who opted for the Axis alliance as the surest means for obtaining Japanese hegemony in Asia. This issue was further clouded when Germany violently protested Japan's lack of reaction to the Greer Incident in the Atlantic, after which (September 11, 1941) President Franklin D. Roosevelt issued a "shoot on sight" order against German U-Boats. Japan's position was ambivalent at best, and although the Japanese were seemingly ready to reach a rapprochement with the United States, they could not bring themselves to abrogate the pact with Germany. As the American position became more and more intolerant of Japan's desire for the best of both worlds, any idea of a relaxation on the freeze on Japanese assets in America, instituted in July, and the oil embargo placed on Japan by the United States in August, seemed more and more remote. There was little question, in the Japanese view, that by the end of September 1941, President Roosevelt was willing to accept war in the Pacific rather than make any more concessions.

Thus, Yamamoto's planning was seen, by the very few who were privy to it, as a specific means to an end. But the Pearl Harbor attack plan could not be effective by itself, and the DAIHONEI (Imperial Headquarters) spent its time perfecting the various other details associated with the Fiscal 1941 Plan. While all this was going on, the planning effort for the main blow, Pearl Harbor, had been greatly accelerated.

Japan now saw itself isolated from the west. The Americans had made themselves abundantly clear—a negotiated settlement was possible only if Japan quit the Tripartite Alliance and stopped its aggression in China. Without room for further compromise, Japan had only one recourse: prepare for war.

Commander Genda's plan was fleshed out, principally by Rear Admiral Ryunosuke Kusaka, the Chief of Staff to Vice Admiral Chuichi Nagumo, commander of the First Air Fleet. Throughout the summer months, Kasuka had worked on the detailed planning for the mounting of a naval operation of a magnitude never before conceived by the Japanese. Genda, for his part, worked out in the minutest detail the tactical plans for the attack itself. Using Japan's Inland Sea as the test area, Genda experimented with various techniques for attacking large craft in shallow waters. Areas were found that very much approximated the conditions around the major docking areas and mooring sites in Pearl Harbor. After many disappointments, the details for shallow water torpedo attacks were worked out, and Genda was able to report to Yamamoto and Kusaka that his part of the plan was ready. Everything to this point had, of course, been done in complete secrecy.

By the end of August 1941 the diplomatic-political situation had developed to a point where the military felt justified in presenting the plan for war. Yamamoto first briefed the chief of the Naval General Staff, Admiral Osami Nagano and a dozen other key officers, on the plan and then, for the next two weeks, had the plan tested in war games at the Naval War College. The plan did not work as perfectly as had been expected and a number of the senior officers involved, including Nagumo, voiced concern over a strategy that would take the Japanese fleet out of Asian waters to attack the Americans. Would it not be better, some questioned, to continue the conquest of China and to expand the war only by occupying the Dutch East Indies? This might or might not cause the United States to enter the war, but if this occurred, then it was suggested that the place to meet and destroy the American fleet was in the western Pacific. "No," responded Yamamoto. He was convinced, as a result of his years of residence in the United States, that America would enter the war. Thus the place and time to strike the US fleet was by surprise and at Pearl Harbor before the Americans were ready to begin operations. Yamamoto's position prevailed, and the attack planning continued.

On September 13, 1941, seven days after Prince Konoye's government had won cabinet approval to continue negotiations with the United States in a last-ditch effort to avert war, the Imperial Naval Staff issued a combined operations plan for simultaneously attacking Hawaii, Malaya, the Philippines, and the Dutch East Indies. One week later, the chiefs of both the Army and Navy general staffs jointly stated that the government would have to decide on war or peace by October 15 at the latest and, if the decision should be for war, then the operation must begin by mid-November. This stiffening of military opposition to further diplomatic discussion—primarily because of military fear that continued time for talk was dangerously weakening Japan's already depleted oil reserves—led the Konoye government to resign on October 17. With the assumption of the office of prime minister by Army General Hideki Tojo, control of Japan was in military hands. War was now seemingly unavoidable.

Final planning and preparations continued in earnest. About 100 young aviators had already been designated for special training under the leadership of Commander Mitsuo Fuchida, who had been designated as the air group commander for the operation. On October 5 Yamamoto personally swore these pilots to secrecy and gave them the details of the plan. From this point onward torpedo and dive bombing were practiced incessantly; large mock-ups of Pearl Harbor and its environs were studied in great detail, and silhouettes of every American ship known to be in the Pacific Fleet were memorized. Troublesome torpedoes were modified to run straight and true in shallow water, and large-caliber armor-piercing naval shells were converted into bombs to be used in attacking the inside row of battleships riding at double anchor at Pearl Harbor. Enormous amounts of red tape had to be cut also, but this had to be done carefully so as not to tip the secret. Extra tankers had to be sought out and assigned to the task force; both summer and winter gear had to be assembled for the men, who would sail into the cold North Pacific en route to the Hawaiian Islands, lest the issue of winter gear alone serve as an indicator of the Japanese intention to sortie to the north. The list of special tasks seemed almost endless, and many senior officers became more and more worried about the outcome.

While these preparations were in their final stages, the Imperial Navy sent Lieutenant Commanders Suguro Suzuki and Toshihide Maljima for a cruise to Hawaii aboard the *Taiyo Maru*, a cruise ship that must have given the appearance of being lost and sailing all over the North Pacific trying to find the Islands. In fact, the ship's course was very carefully and deliberately chosen and followed the route the attack force would follow to Hawaii. The notes taken by the two officers, both on the high seas and during their stay in Honolulu, became vital parts of the decision for the exact time and date of the attack.

On November 3 the final plan was approved by the chief of the Imperial Naval Staff, and two days later

"Combined Fleet Top Secret Order No. 1" was issued. On November 7 Vice Admiral Nagumo was named to lead the attack force; December 8, 1941 was chosen as the day to carry out the surprise attack.*

By November 15, the ships of the attack fleet began to slip away from their anchorages in Yokohama, Saeki, Kure and elsewhere, leaving behind their radio operators, who continued to fill the airwaves with the typical flow of chitchat and messages that made up the world of marine communications. When the last ship arrived at the secret rendezvous in Hitokappu (Tankan) Bay at Etorofu Shima late on November 21, Admiral Nagumo's fleet numbered over 30 ships, including the carriers *Akagi* (Nagumo's flagship), *Shokaku*, *Kaga*, *Zuikaku*, *Soryu*, and *Hiryu*. Two battleships, the *Hiei* and *Kirishima*, three cruisers, *Tone*, *Chikuma* and *Abukuma*, nine destroyers, and three submarines made up the rest of the combatants. The remainder of the flotilla was fleet tankers and supply ships. This constituted a commitment of almost 20% of the total number of warships available to the Japanese at the beginning of the war and included 75% of the carrier fleet. The Japanese were playing for high stakes.

By November 23 all was in readiness. As one measure of security, those extra supply ships that had surreptitiously brought needed supplies to the fleet were forbidden to depart the bleak harbor at Hitokappu until after December 10. Once given, the security orders were obeyed to the letter, even though the bulk of the personnel involved had no idea of the destination of the task force.

Two days later, on November 25, Yamamoto ordered the fleet to sea; the first step toward war with America was taken. At 8:00 A.M., November 26, 1941 (Tokyo time), the force slipped out of the harbor and in doing so sealed Japan's fate.

---

*According to Japanese reckoning, the attack did, in fact, take place on December 8, as Japanese naval vessels maintained their clocks on Tokyo time and ignored the fact that they had crossed the international date line in mid-Pacific.

America Prepares for War

By the end of 1940, most American political and military leaders realized that war was a distinct possibility; probably with Japan, almost certainly with Germany. The war that had been raging in Europe was going badly for the Allies, and too well for Hitler's Germany. American planners, recognizing that war could come simultaneously in both east and west, had decided that the defeat of Germany would be the first priority. This strategic plan became known as "Rainbow 5". Even before the attack in the Pacific, US forces, especially US naval forces, were engaged in an undeclared naval war in the Atlantic.

Despite this emphasis on the Atlantic and Europe, the Pacific was not altogether ignored. The US Navy had a key role to play in the Pacific. Beginning in 1934, when the Vinson-Trammel Act authorized the construction of a number of new vessels and gave the President authority to build enough ships to bring the Navy up to treaty strength, things looked better for US interests. Then, in 1938, the annual appropriation added more impetus to naval construction. In the next two years additional legislation, not without its powerful critics, authorized an additional 31% increase in naval tonnage. That all the ships were not built or under construction when the war began was due more to shortages in shipyards than shortages in money. When the Japanese attack came, the United States had 17 battleships, 7 carriers, 37 cruisers, 171 destroyers and 111 submarines in commission. Fifteen more battleships, 11 aircraft carriers, and 318 other combatant vessels were under construction. In the active fleet, three carriers, the three-year-old 19,900-ton *Enterprise* (CV-6), the much older 33,000-ton *Lexington* (CV-2), and her sister ship *Saratoga* (CV-3), were in the Pacific. The battleships *Arizona*, *California*, *Maryland*, *Nevada*, *Oklahoma*, *Pennsylvania*, *Tennessee*, and *West Virginia*, along with numerous other craft, were all based in the Hawaiian Islands.

That portion of the Rainbow 5 plan dealing with the

Pacific stipulated that, should war come on two fronts, the Pacific theater was to be contained by naval and air action until the war in Europe could be won. In consonance with this strategy, Army and Navy commanders in the Pacific, especially in the Hawaiian and Philippine Island groups, were required to prepare and submit detailed plans for carrying out defensive campaigns designed to protect US interests in the Pacific, as well as punishing the enemy—obviously Japan—at every opportunity. Although great emphasis was placed on this planning in Washington, it was not until late October 1941 that anything was done to insure that the plans were adequate.

The first indication that everything was not in good order came on November 24, following a war warning message—the second—sent from Washington. This came close to creating chaos in Hawaii, and suggested that neither the Army nor the Navy in the Hawaiian Islands was ready to fight. The war alert order was first of all ignored, and secondly, when it was finally acted upon, the steps taken by both commands in Oahu were found to be unsatisfactory. The Philippines command reacted much more vigorously to the order, and showed a level of efficiency substantially higher than in the Hawaiian group.

Lieutenant General Walter C. Short, commander of the Army's Hawaiian Department, felt that the only threat to his command was from possible sabotage by Japanese sympathizers living among the local populace. His principal action—in fact, his only action—concerned the concentrating of most of his combat strength, especially his aircraft, inside exclusion areas closed to the public. Thus, Hickam and Wheeler Fields, for instance, became crammed with all the Army's 193 fighters and 30-odd bombers, neatly lined up for "easier protection against sabotage."

The Navy did only a little better. Admiral Husband E. Kimmel, the naval commander in the Pacific, after tortuous examination of every possible connotation of the message, finally, in exasperation, told his operations officer, Captain Charles McMorris, to query Washington and ask, "What the hell is going on?" The answer was just as blunt; war with Japan was a possibility, and necessary actions needed to be taken. Kimmel, now furious over the evasiveness of the Chief of Naval Operation's original warning and this later "amplification," personally drafted a message which read:

> TO CNO WASH FR CINCPAC YOUR MSG THIS DATE AT BEST VAGUE X ARE WE TO ASSUME WAR IM-MINENT OR ARE WE TO ASSUME THAT ONLY NECESSARY LOCAL SECURITY INCREASES ARE REQUIRED X LEVEL OF AVAILABLE RESOURCES MAKES UNNECESSARY EXPENDITURE FOR QUOTE POLITICAL POSTURING UNQUOTE EXTREMELY DANGEROUS X CLARIFICATION VITAL X

In response, Kimmel received the following message four days later:

> TO CINCPAC FR CNO WASH YOUR MSG RECEIVED X WAR ALERT MESSAGE WAS EXPLICIT X EXPECT YOUR IMMEDIATE COMPLIANCE X

Now in a towering rage, Admiral Kimmel bowed before necessity and asked for a meeting with General Short. From that meeting on December 3 came the joint decision to act without further concern for Washington's sensibilities. Both Pacific commanders now concluded that Washington was either completely confused, or that something was going on to which they were not privy. As a matter of fact, something was going on of which they were unaware. There was "Magic."

For some time American intelligence had been intercepting and deciphering much of the diplomatic and some of the high-level military radio and teletype traffic passing between Tokyo and several of Japan's embassies and military attaches around the world. While the coverage was spotty and far from complete, it was more information than would normally be available regarding the activities of possibly hostile forces. The manner of collection and the system of decryption were so secret that for a time even the President of the United States was unaware of its existence. Like many others, when first informed of this windfall of information, Roosevelt was skeptical about its true value. However, as more and more information was collected, he realized that a rather complete picture of Japanese intentions was presented. This helped the United States especially in determining the hard line it took in the negotiations with the Imperial government.

Without question, Japan was preparing for war. But how could the information be disseminated to the field without compromising the source? This was the dilemma that faced Washington on December 3, when the two commanders in Hawaii informed their chiefs in Washington that they needed to know what was going on. They added that, unless they received orders to the contrary, they would go on full alert within 48 hours. As a final dig at Washington, the joint message to the Army and the Navy headquarters politely added that if Washington should pick up any additional data that might be of value to the field commanders, it would be very much appreciated if this were forwarded as soon as possible. Both Kimmel and Short congratulated themselves on their telegram—and both were convinced, although they kept their own thoughts, that they were both about to be relieved of command.

Within twelve hours of the transmission of the message, the first of a series of reports was delivered by multiple communication means to multiple addresses in Hawaii. This was because President Roosevelt had been shown the message from Kimmel and Short, and had directed immediate transmission of the gist of all "Magic" information to the appropriate field commands. This was completely contrary to the security restrictions on "Magic," and was protested by Rear Admiral R. Kelly

Turner, Chief of Naval Intelligence. When he persisted in his condemnation of the President's action, he was summarily relieved by Frank Knox, the Secretary of the Navy. In giving his instructions to General Marshall and Admiral Stark the President stated that Japan had laid down its own course, and the United States did not have to stand by idly and wait for an attack. If the Japanese wanted a fight they could have it, but not on their terms alone.

Kimmel and Short now both realized that they were expected to take immediate steps to prepare to defend the Hawaiian Islands, but against what? It was clear from the messages from Washington that no danger to the Hawaiian Islands was perceived in the capital, although an attack in the Philippines was expected.

Short and Kimmel conferred again at Kimmel's headquarters at Pearl Harbor early in the morning of Friday, December 5. Most of Kimmel's senior staff officers were present. Short brought with him only his G-2 intelligence officer, Lieutenant Colonel Kendall Fielder. Short suggested that the principal danger to the Hawaiian Islands was from sabotage of military installations. Fielder said that the large Japanese-American population on the islands could not be trusted. Kimmel agreed that that was a possibility, but pointed out that his own intelligence officers believed that a considerable portion of the main Japanese fleet was at sea, and was not with the convoys which they now knew were approaching Malaya and the Philippines. He stated his belief that, in the light of the damage the Japanese could do by striking a surprise blow at the Pacific Fleet, such a possibility could not be ruled out.

After considerable discussion, by mid-morning the two commanders agreed that they should go on full alert immediately. Short was persuaded of the possible danger when Captain Edwin T. Layton, Kimmel's intelligence officer, reported that his radio intercept stations had lost contact with major elements of the Japanese fleet about

two weeks earlier. At least seven carriers of the Japanese
First and Second Carrier Divisions were among the missing.

It was also agreed that there should be little or no pre-
tense about military activities in the Islands. If there were
Japanese agents in the Islands—there were—there was
not much chance of deceiving them about the presence or
absence of eight battleships in the harbor. At the moment
the battleship task force was at sea, and was returning to
Pearl Harbor for the weekend, as usual. Admiral Kimmel
sent an immediate message to Admiral Pye ordering him
to stay at sea with his battleship task force. Admiral
Halsey aboard the carrier *Lexington* was en route with
Marine aircraft to reinforce Wake Island. He was ordered
to expedite this delivery and then proceed north and east
and rendezvous with the *Nevada* and the *Tennessee* near
the area in the waters north of Hawaii known as Lahaina.
The *Saratoga*, due for return to the West Coast, was put
under sealed orders to proceed away from Hawaii as
planned, that evening. However, she was then to swing
west to join Pye's battleship flotilla to provide air cover.

To all but the most interested observer everything
seemed perfectly normal in and around Pearl Harbor.
Even to the most astute, the only thing unusual was that
Pye had not returned with his battleships to spend the
weekend in Honolulu. At 6 P.M., December 5 (Hawaii
time), Tokyo informed Admiral Nagumo that two battleships (the *Pennsylvania* in dry dock and the old *Utah*,
now a target ship), one Class B cruiser, and four destroyers were in the harbor, and that one aircraft carrier
(*Saratoga*) was preparing to leave within 48–72 hours (in
fact, it left that night).

The Japanese Approach

When Admiral Nagumo on the *Akagi* received this
message he was not surprised. Upset, yes, but not surprised. He had been sure from the beginning that the plan
was doomed. On the second day at sea (November 27)
Nagumo's fears had overwhelmed him, and he had told

his chief of staff, "If only I had been more firm and refused . . ." Nagumo was sure they would be discovered.
Presumably he had prayed that they would be detected
before December 5, the date after which the mission
could no longer be aborted. Seventy-two hours before, the
task force had been ordered to "Climb Mount Niitaka,"
the code message to proceed. Now the abort deadline had
passed. Nagumo, with oriental fatalism, now faced the
task of carrying out a mission he had violently opposed.

The voyage, thus far, had been a near disaster. The
weather was terrible—good for secrecy, but other necessary operations were almost impossible—and men had
been lost overboard during refueling operations because
of the high seas. Now with clearer weather the chance of
being spotted grew proportionately as the Japanese vessels closed the gap between themselves and the Hawaiian
Islands. Nagumo was even more concerned about detection since the last message from Tokyo had also informed
him that it was impossible to tell whether or not Honolulu had put its forces on air alert.

In fact such an alert had been declared. At 8:30 P.M.
December 5 (December 6, Tokyo time), a US PBY naval
flying boat on the last leg of its evening patrol north of
Midway spotted a lone escort destroyer, of the new Japanese *Nashi*-class, making light signals toward the northwest horizon. From that direction came three quick re-
sponses, from different locations! The Catalina
immediately broke away and, apparently escaping detection from the ship below, headed at top speed back to
Midway, the pilot afraid to use his radio for fear he would
be overheard.

Four hours earlier, another PBY patrolling the waters in
the Lahaina area had attacked and, unbeknownst to the
flight crew, had sunk the Japanese submarine I-72. The
submarine, just below the surface, was at battle stations,
watching a US destroyer that had detected its presence
and was stalking it. The first realization of attack came
when the aerial depth bomb hit the I-72's conning tower
and detonated, instantly flooding the boat. The cipher

officer was just completing a message to be sent to inform Nagumo that part of the American fleet was indeed in the Lahaina area. When the I-72 failed to report on schedule, the failure was written off on the *Akagi* as merely some technical difficulty. For Nagumo, however, it only added to his burden of doubt and worry. Commander Genda, on the other hand, bemoaned that only one carrier was in port. He had rightly judged that striking the aircraft carriers was the key to success and would willingly have foregone all the battleships for the chance to sink the three carriers.

American Reactions

As a result of President Roosevelt's edict, complete intelligence information—with interpretation—was being sent to the two major commands in Hawaii. A relatively clear picture of what the Japanese were doing had developed in the Army and Navy headquarters. Even General Short, never considered a mental giant, began to perceive that the threat was indeed real, although, he insisted, sabotage was the only way the Japanese could do serious damage in Hawaii.

Ambassador Grew's messages from Tokyo, the loss of contact with the bulk of the Imperial fleet in home ports, the incident at Lahaina, and the ship-sighting report just received from Midway, all answered two vital questions. Hawaii was indeed threatened, and the attack—if it came—would come from the seas north of the Islands. There was little or no speculation that the Japanese strike would be from the air—although there were still a few die-hard Navy men who refused to believe that airpower alone could sink a fleet—and that it would be soon.

The evening meeting between Kimmel and Short on December 5 (Hawaii time), at Short's headquarters at Fort Shafter, was also attended by Rear Admiral C. C. Bloch, commander of the Fourteenth Naval District. It was decided to transmit the attack estimate to Washington and to the Philippines. Before doing so, however, the three commanders determined to understand more completely the actions which each of them had already taken.

When Short's turn to report came he announced that he interpreted his orders as prohibiting the Army from "firing the first shot." Therefore, most of the actions he and his command had taken had been essentially passive. To this Admiral Bloch replied by asking if, since the Army had the only radars in the Islands—it had five—and since the Army was supposedly training its men in the use of this piece of equipment, it would be too much trouble to man the sites around the clock. Short answered that if the attack came at all it would come between 4 and 7 A.M.; so there was no sense in "wasting manpower" on what might be a "fool's errand." Bloch responded that there were more ways than one to be foolish. Short's face reddened, but before the argument became more acrimonious, Lieutenant Colonel George Bicknell, Short's counterintelligence chief, entered the room without knocking. He reported that the Honolulu office of the FBI had just informed him that the Japanese consulate was obviously burning its files, and that, although the Bureau in Washington had directed that no further action be taken until specific orders were issued, the Federal Bureau of Investigation had gone to its equivalent of full wartime alert.

Bloch turned to Short: "How much more goddamn proof do you need?" Short hesitated and seemed to deflate like a punctured balloon. "All right," he said, "I am in agreement. We are about to be attacked."

Washington was not really prepared for the multiple-address message it received at 5:30 A.M., December 6 EST (12 midnight, Hawaii time). Sent to both the Army and Navy, each through its own channels but addressed to both, the message constituted a break with the traditional separation of the Army and the Navy. Because of the unusual procedure, valuable time was lost at both service departments in getting the message authenticated. Many officers in both headquarters in the nation's capital could not believe such a message had actually been sent.

In general terms the message outlined the results of the analysis of data available in Hawaii, and reported the conclusion that, not only were the Hawaiian Islands about to be attacked, but that the attack would begin within twenty-four hours, and certainly no later than dawn on December 7. Then the message spelled out what each service was doing to minimize the effect of the attack on the Islands. Aircraft were being dispersed, warships deployed, ammunition was being broken out of sealed containers and being put under the direct responsibility of unit commanders. All that was needed, the message concluded, was the authority of the Commander in Chief to carry out an aggressive search for, and engagement of, the "enemy" fleet known to be somewhere north of the Island group.

If the Hawaiian Islands were not attacked, an appended paragraph stated, then the west coast of the United States, or possibly the Panama Canal, might be in imminent danger. This last paragraph struck Admiral Stark, the Chief of Naval Operations, to the extent that he immediately telephoned the White House for a meeting on a subject of the utmost urgency. This was about 9:00 A.M. on Saturday, December 6. Stark suggested that General Marshall attend the White House meeting. He was informed that the Army Chief of Staff had left his quarters at Fort Myer and was horseback riding "somewhere in the south area" of the post. Stark urged that he be informed of the meeting as soon as possible. Marshall was found by an aide and delivered to the White House in his riding attire.

All of this excitement, it seemed to those who attended the brief meeting at the White House, was exactly what Roosevelt had been waiting for. After listening carefully to a recitation of the message from Honolulu, the President said, "All right, it's war." Without asking for opinions, he ordered the military leaders to put the appropriate plans into effect to protect all United States military bases against Japanese attack.

As Marshall and Stark were being escorted out of the President's office, Roosevelt was overheard telling an aide to call the Vice President and the Speaker of the House immediately. Within half an hour war messages were on their way to all commands in the Pacific:

CNO TO CINPAC/COMFOURTEEN 0612262 WAR BE-LIEVED IMMINENT X HAWAII NOW CONSIDERED PRIME TARGET X EXECUTE RAINBOW FIVE TO IN-SURE SECURITY OF NAVAL ASSETS AND TO PRE-VENT ATTACK X DP MARTIAL LAW WILL BE DE-CLARED FOR ISLAND OF OAHU EFF IMMED BY ARMY X SAME MSG BEING TX BY OTHER CHAN-NELS TO OTHER MIL AND CIV AUTH IN HAWAII X YOU ARE DIRECTED TO INSURE ALL REPEAT ALL OTHER COMMANDS AND CIV JURISDICTIONS DASH HAWAII ARE IMMED INFORMED OF CON-TENTS OF THIS MSG X STARK

An almost identical message was simultaneously being sent by the War Department to General Short. No message in American history to the moment caused a greater output of effort than did this one, received almost simultaneously by all commands in the Pacific area. The entire military establishment in the Hawaiian Islands was galvanized into action. All forces went on full alert. The USS *Pennsylvania*, lying in Drydock No. 1, cleared for action. Training her 14-inch rifles on the entrance to Pearl Harbor, she lay like a giant fortress awaiting the attack. Flights of P-39 and P-40 pursuit aircraft (sixty-two of them) from Hickam and Wheeler Fields were deployed to numerous small auxiliary air strips such as Haleiwa, on the north side of Oahu, where their only communication while on the ground was by a field telephone hung on a nail on a support of a small lean-to. The flyable Army bombers and attack planes, B-17s (6), B-18s (17), A-20s (6), however, were still grouped together out in the open in consonance with General Short's sabotage plan at Hickam Field. However, these were guarded by troops and by all of the antiaircraft guns on the island.

The FBI immediately began rounding up known and suspected subversives. In the last of its net was Doctor

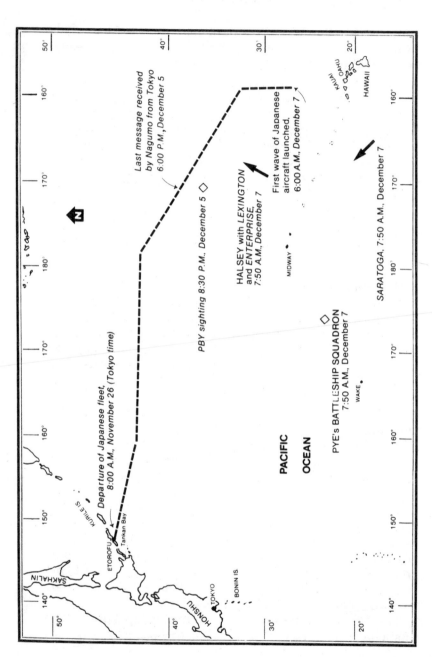

Ship Movements up to 7:50 A.M., December 7

Matakazu Mori, who liked to call friends in Tokyo to talk about flowers. Also taken into custody was one Hana Takahashi, a cleaning woman of indeterminate age, who was, had all the facts been known, the chief supplier of information to the Japanese consular office about ship movements in and out of Pearl Harbor. Without her data, the Japanese were therefore blinded and could not inform Tokyo, and hence, Admiral Nagumo, of the exact disposition of the American fleet.

The Japanese Attack on Pearl Harbor

The opening of the Japanese attack on Pearl Harbor came in a totally unexpected way—by submarine. Known as the Advance Expeditionary Force, and composed of some 28 submarines, eight of which were mother ships for two or more midget submarines, this force had the mission of scouting the entrance to Pearl Harbor, patrolling the waters around the island of Oahu, and, if possible, entering through the antisubmarine net into the inner harbor at Pearl. Once there, the midget subs were to make the best use of each of the two torpedoes they carried. The larger submarines were to take up stations further at sea until time to rendezvous to pick up the midgets off Lanai following the attack. In the meantime they were to engage and sink any American ships that came into their periscopes once the attack had begun. All of these activities were coordinated into the larger plan for the aerial attack on Pearl Harbor, of course, but it was the very presence of these submarines and the detection and sinking of a number of them that most alarmed the US naval command in Hawaii and led to the establishment of full war alert at 5 A.M., December 7, 1941.

At 3:40 A.M., the US minesweeper *Condor*, on patrol outside the net at Pearl Harbor, was making a sweep of the area directly adjacent to the main ship channel when the deck watch spotted what appeared to be the wake of a periscope moving toward the net. *Condor* signalled the destroyer USS *Ward*, "Sighted submerged submarine on westerly course, speed nine knots, require assist." The *Ward*, on outer harbor patrol for the third day, had spotted and reported at least six such sightings in the last three days and each time had received no clear-cut response from shore. This time, however, the response to the *Condor's* message to the Commandant Fourteenth Naval District was swift, and directed to both the *Condor* and the *Ward*: attempt to capture, but definitely stop the sub. Lieutenant William W. Outerbridge, the *Ward's* CO, interpreted the order literally and by 4:15 A.M. had forced the submarine to surface, whereupon its skipper, Ensign Akira Hirowo, attempted to blow it up. But the charge didn't go off.

Outerbridge's message was that he had the sub, the I-20, in tow, that he had found maps and other documents on board, but had no one who could decipher Japanese, and wanted to know what to do with his trophy and his two prisoners. The *Ward* never received an answer to these queries, and some say the *Ward* towed the I-20 until the last day of the war, three months later. Before the answer could be sent, the entire Hawaiian command was put on full alert. And when the Japanese planes appeared over Oahu two hours later, the Americans were ready for them, as ready, that is, as they could be. No one remembered Outerbridge and the *Ward*.

Admiral Nagumo had brought his task force to a point about 225 miles directly north of Oahu by 5:30 A.M., when the observation seaplanes from the cruisers *Tone* and *Chikuma* took off for a final reconnaissance of the area prior to the launch of the main air group for the attack.

No sooner had the two aircraft reached 8,000 feet than their presence was detected by a Kahuku Point radar station. Fighters were ordered aloft to determine their origin and, if Japanese, to attempt to force them down or, if necessary, shoot them down. When the interception was made, the Japanese were able to get off a message saying they were under attack, but that was the last that was heard from them. The two young P-40 pilots would argue for years afterward as to which one of them shot down both of the enemy planes.

Nagumo, in his usual state of distress, was now sure that the whole plan had been tipped but he was irrevocably committed. At 6 A.M., the first wave took off from the carriers—50 dive bombers, 40 torpedo planes, 49 other bombers, and an escort of 45 fighters. One hour and fifteen minutes later, 170 more planes took off in the second wave, while 35 additional fighters circled high above, guarding the fleet. The attack was now on its way.

Within minutes of the takeoff of the first wave, the Kahuku radar station had flashed the message that many aircraft had been sighted north of the island. The Information Center at Fort Shafter began to plot the movement. By 6:45 it had located the aircraft 130 miles north of Oahu on a course aimed directly at the island. To the officer on duty, Lieutenant Kermit Tyler, the whole exercise was just so much hogwash. After all, he was a fighter pilot, and therefore he knew that no gadget could accurately locate planes in the air. More important, it was time for his breakfast, he told his assistant, Sergeant James MacDonald. He left for the mess hall. When the next sighting report came in, placing the aircraft much closer to Oahu and better defining their number—"many, many," the report said—MacDonald took it upon himself to notify Major Kenneth Bergquist, the Officer in Charge. Bergquist could not be reached at home. MacDonald was about to call Tyler at the messhall, when Bergquist entered the command post. MacDonald quickly briefed him, and on ascertaining that the intruder aircraft were almost certainly not a group of American B-17s due in from the States, Bergquist sounded the alarm that sent most of the standby fighters into the air. The Navy's aircraft took somewhat longer to get airborne, and the Japanese planes were just west of Pearl Harbor when the fifteen or so Grumman F4F Wildcats took off. Before that, however, a general alert had gone out as a result of the submarine incident, and there were now many in the two headquarters who thought that the attack would come from the sea and not the air. The radar intercept reports came almost as a relief to those who had maintained an air attack was in the making.

The alert was quickly spread. Aboard every ship in the harbor—there were still a large number which, for one reason or another had not cleared out—the message was the same: "Now hear this! General Quarters—General Quarters. Prepare to repel air attack! Man your battle stations. This is no drill—no drill." The language was different at the Army installations, but the message was the same. Those few minutes of warning helped save numerous lives and helped punish the Japanese when the attack began.

Commander Fuchida's attack group flew above thick clouds that had blanketed the area through which his flight plan took him. Using his homing antenna he had been able to tune in Honolulu's radio station and use it as a beacon. At 7:15 A.M. the station had abruptly and unceremoniously gone off the air. Fuchida was still 80 miles off the coast and could now continue to fly only by dead reckoning along the last bearing he had taken. He did know that the weather over Oahu was partly cloudy, but he also knew that he could miss the island entirely. At 7:49 he crossed the coast just north of Pearl Harbor; he was right on target. But at that very moment, the first of the incoming American pursuit aircraft broke into the tight Japanese formations. The ensuing few minutes cost both sides dearly. The Americans were able to get into the bomber and torpedo plane formations before the Japanese "Zeke" fighters that had been flying high above the attack squadrons could drop down and attempt to drive off the Americans. The Japanese formations were left in some disarray when the Americans were forced to break off because of the heavy and indiscriminate ground fire that came up from below once the planes had crossed over the coast line.

Within this chaotic scene, Fuchida maintained his

composure. His plane had been hit but not damaged, his squadrons battered but not beaten. It was time to signal them whether the torpedo planes would go in first, if surprise had succeeded, or the bombers, if surprise had been lost. The gaps in the flying formations attested to the latter, but the wholly indoctrinated Japanese clung to their plan. Fuchida prepared to fire two "Black Dragon," signal flares. The first one was seen by everyone but the fighter planes. The second one buried itself in a single errant cloud. Although puzzled by the signal for surprise, the torpedo bombers immediately began their runs, skimming across the waters of the inner harbor. When Fuchida saw what was happening, he immediately fired a third flare which the dive bombers rightly mistook for the second, and the torpedo crews missed altogether; so the dive bombers went in on top of the torpedo bombers.

The hail of bullets that both squadrons flew into was awesome. Everything and everyone who could bear on a target was firing. All weapons from personal sidearms to the five-inch guns on the destroyer *Raleigh* were used. Although marksmanship would have been rated as low, volume made up much of the difference. In the first few minutes, at least 26 of the aircraft attacking the naval installations on Ford Island and around the harbor were knocked down.

The aircraft attacking Hickam and Wheeler fields and Schofield Barracks did not fare much better. Those that broke away from the intense, if highly inaccurate, antiaircraft fire were engaged by American fighters. When the second wave of Japanese aircraft flew in at about 9 A.M., their greeting was no less enthusiastic. By the time the attack was over, just before 10 A.M., Fuchida knew that the mission had failed. Only one capital ship was in port, the *Pennsylvania*, and although she had been hit repeatedly with bombs, she was still afloat, as the drydock had prevented the torpedo bombers from attacking her. At least fifteen other ships had been hit, but all were small and of no great consequence. Seven US battleships

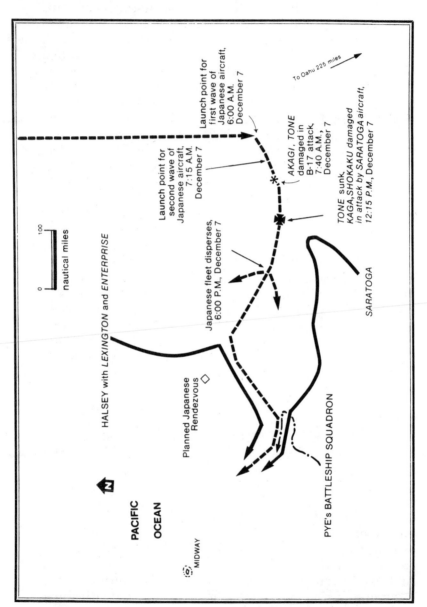

Naval and Air Action, December 7–9

and three aircraft carriers were unaccounted for and had not been attacked. There would be hell to pay when the aircraft returned to the fleet.

But hell was already being paid. Twenty-five minutes after the second wave took off from the carriers, and the carriers had begun their course changes to the rendezvous point where they would meet the returning aircraft, a bomb hit directly amidships on the *Akagi*, killing most of the aircraft recovery personnel on deck, and a number of people in the command group including Ryunosuke Kusaka, Admiral Nagumo's second in command. That bomb and others were dropped by one of the three B-17s flying long range patrol north and northwest of the Hawaiian group. In addition, the cruiser *Tone* was dead in the water, a 500-pound bomb—the only ones available for the B-17s to carry—having surgically removed its stern. Six hours later, the *Tone* went to the bottom, the result of a torpedo run by a Douglas TBD-1 Devastator bomber from the *Saratoga*.

When the B-17s reported in the clear that the attack fleet had been found, the *Saratoga* was about 500 miles away. Steaming at 30 knots, the *Saratoga* was in position to launch her aircraft at 11 A.M. At 12:15 P.M., some 50 of her 86 aircraft attacked the Japanese while they were still refueling and repositioning their returned aircraft. The Japanese had only 24 aircraft in the air at the time, "Zeke" fighters on combat air patrol. American losses were heavy, but, in addition to the *Tone*, the carriers *Kaga* and *Shokaku* were severely damaged and many aircraft were caught on deck and badly damaged.

Now constantly harried by American aircraft from the *Saratoga* and warned that two other aircraft carriers were known to be in the area to the north, Nagumo—in a prearranged move established for just such an emergency—dispersed his fleet. Before they could reach the rendezvous point some 250 miles to the west northwest, the *Kaga*, already badly listing, was sunk and the cruiser *Chikuma* set ablaze, her crew abandoning ship. By this time the *Enterprise* and *Lexington* were closing fast from the northwest.

With three American aircraft carriers in hot pursuit, Nagumo, now in a state of shock, ordered a turn to the southwest to avoid further contact and broke away from the attackers, leaving the slow-moving battleships, *Hiei* and *Kirishima*, behind. At 10 A.M., December 8, Admiral Pye's battleship squadron came upon the fleeing Japanese carrier group and, in short intense battle, sank the carrier *Hiryu*, one cruiser (later identified as the *Abukuma*), and two destroyers. Joined by the *Saratoga*, which was able to overtake the Japanese when they again scattered to avoid the big guns of the American battleships, the battle continued. By 4 P.M. the *Lexington*, damaged in an earlier engagement, and the *Enterprise* had closed into striking range. Before dark, the carrier *Soryu* was set afire— apparently sinking during the night. Next morning the seven surviving battleships found and quickly destroyed the *Hiei* and *Kirishima*.

Later called the Battle of Midway, the action of December 7–9 literally destroyed the Japanese fleet. American losses were 150 aircraft lost, two destroyers sunk, the carrier *Lexington* severely damaged—she sank as she was limping back to Pearl Harbor—and the battleships *Arizona* and *Nevada* sunk with fearful loss of life.

On December 10, the President again went before Congress to announce:

> "Two days ago, I came before this body to ask for a declaration of war against the Empire of Japan. I am here today to inform you that at that very time American air and naval forces had searched out and were in the process of destroying the Japanese fleet that had carried out the premeditated and dastardly attack against the Hawaiian Islands. At 8 A.M., this morning, the United States informed the Japanese government that it intended to prosecute this war thrust upon it by the infamous attack on Pearl Harbor, to the utmost limit of its ability to insure the future peace and tranquility in the Pacific. Although I can-

not report to you any satisfactory answer from the Japanese government, I can inform you that American naval units are now closing on the Japanese home islands to punish the aggressors and to relieve the pressure on our gallant forces in the Philippines and elsewhere in the Pacific. The United States and its Allies are now determined to end once and for all attacks on their sovereignty and will use all of their means to destroy their common enemies."

Afterword

The history of the Japanese attack on Pearl Harbor was, in real life, a severe blow to American naval power in the Pacific. The events portrayed in this account of the opening of World War II are accurate in all respects until the events of December 3. From that point on, the historical facts are altered only to the extent required to reflect the hypothesis that the United States could have responded to the numerous warnings it had received. The incidents following the attack, including the destruction of the Japanese fleet, are, of course, fanciful, but they depict what could have happened if America, especially its military commanders in Hawaii, had been more alert to the true dangers the nation faced on December 7, 1941.

CHAPTER VI

The Japanese Midway Campaign

A New War Plan for Japan

ADMIRAL ISOROKU YAMAMOTO was a thoughtful man. Although he was one of the principal architects of the Japanese war plan that sent a fleet to attack Pearl Harbor in early December 1941, he was pessimistic about the outcome of the war which that attack precipitated. He knew the United States and Americans—particularly the potential industrial might of America—well enough to have doubts about the eventual outcome of the war.

Superficially, he knew, the concept for this new war against the United States was very similar to that which had been brilliantly successful in the Russo-Japanese War of 1904–1905. In both cases the opponent was a superpower with potential resources far greater than those of Japan, but with its center of strength far removed from the Japanese homeland, and from the theater of warfare chosen by Japan. The Japanese military leaders in both cases decided to seize the initiative in a stunning surprise attack before declaring war. Then, while the giant opponent was still reeling from this unexpected blow, the Japanese armed forces would seize key areas in order to establish a defensive perimeter as far from Japan as possible. From these positions they would block enemy offensive blows and make any subsequent enemy offensive so costly, and so time-consuming, that the foe would become war-weary and negotiate peace while Japan still occupied the territories seized at the outset of the war. The success of this plan against Russia had made Japan a great power.

At the outset of World War II the Japanese planned a defensive perimeter on a line south from the northern Kuriles to Wake Island, thence south to the eastern edge of the Japanese-occupied Marshall Islands. From the Marshalls the line went to the so-called Malay Barrier of the Dutch East Indies, and thence north through Malaya and western Burma to eastern China, already occupied by Japan.

During the first four months of World War II, however, Japanese land and naval forces were even more successful in pushing out to the perimeter than they had expected to be. Under these circumstances, Japanese military leaders felt that they should take advantage of their victories to continue their conquests and expand their defensive perimeter. The Doolittle raid on Tokyo on April 18, 1942, made them even more certain that the perimeter should be extended eastward in order to make it more difficult for American carriers to approach Japan. Thus they decided to seize Midway Island, and to establish bases on the Aleutian Islands.

As a first step the Japanese decided to extend their perimeter to the southeast by taking Port Moresby in southeastern New Guinea, and by establishing air and naval bases in the southeastern Solomon Islands. From these bases the Japanese then intended to strike still further southeastward later in the year to capture New Caledonia and the Fiji and Samoan groups. This would cut the Allied air and naval line of communication across the Pacific from the United States to Australia.

In retrospect, all military analysts have praised this Japanese decision to extend their perimeter and their conquests. It was sound strategy for them to take maximum advantage of their successes, and to attempt to keep hammering at the Allies before American industry could rebuild United States military striking strength. But because it was so bold, the critics might not have been so kind if the operations had not turned out so brilliantly.

It was a mid-April evening when Admiral Yamamoto studied the draft of a message his Combined Fleet Staff had prepared for him to send to Admiral Shigeyoshi Inouye, at Rabaul, to inform him of the new strategic decision. Inouye commanded the Fourth Fleet, and he would be responsible for carrying out the first operations of the revised and expanded war plan. But, as he read the message, Yamamoto was troubled by a nagging concern that, at first, he could not even formalize into a coherent thought. There was something wrong about the way the war was going, he thought, despite the victories that so far had crowned the Nipponese efforts. He sat back in his swivel-chair and pondered.

First there had been the report from Ambassador Saburo Kurusu and Admiral Kichisaburo Nomura of their embarrassing meeting with the American Secretary of State, Cordell Hull, on the afternoon of December 8. (It had been December 7 in Washington.)

As Nomura departed, Hull had berated the two envoys for duplicity in continuing negotiations while the Japanese First Air Fleet was actually attacking Pearl Harbor. Hull's fury was understandable, Yamamoto thought. But in his report Admiral Nomura noted that Hull implied an awareness of the prior radio exchanges between Tokyo and the envoys in Washington.

Then there had been indications that the British had been forewarned of the incursion of Admiral Chuichi Nagumo's First Air Fleet into the Indian Ocean in February and March. This was followed by the success of the American air raid on Tokyo on April 18, with the American carriers that launched Doolittle and his pilots approaching Japan in a fashion that would have been overly daring if the Americans had not been aware of the dispositions of the main elements of the Japanese fleet.

Were the Americans reading Japanese secret radio messages? Yamamoto had explored this possibility before the war, and had been assured by the specialists that the new system of one-time codes, with the cipher changed every day, made it impossible for anyone unfamiliar with the codes, and the changing daily cipher, to decode the messages. Yamamato had no reason to doubt the technicians who had given him this assurance, and who had repeated it as recently as late March. But what if they were wrong? What if the most secret Japanese messages were in fact being decoded in Washington as quickly as they were being processed at Rabaul, or Truk, or in Manila?

Yamamoto decided that, until this nagging doubt was resolved, he would act as though the Americans might be reading his messages. The general outlines of the plans would be sent in the presumably secret code, just as though there were no doubt about cryptographic security. But he, Yamamoto, would make some changes in the execution of the plans. In this way he felt he would soon find out the answer. And if the Americans were reading the messages, then he would also have a surprise or two in store for them.

In fact, although Yamamoto never had convincing proof, the Americans *were* decoding Japanese secret radio messages. So they learned all about the new Japanese plan from Yamamoto's messages to Inouye. Although the Americans had only five carriers in the Pacific, in comparison to eleven for the Japanese, and had (as a result of Pearl Harbor) no combat-ready battleships and fewer than half as many cruisers and destroyers as the Japanese, their knowledge of Japanese plans enabled American military leaders to use their forces with optimum efficiency.

The Threat to Port Moresby

The first phase of the Japanese plan was designed to seize the small island of Tulagi in the Solomon Islands, and then later Port Moresby. The amphibious assault forces sent to these objectives were supported by two naval squadrons. The small carrier *Shoho*, with four cruisers and one destroyer, accompanied the assault force to Tulagi on May 3, 1942, and then returned to the Shortland Islands to escort a large invasion force heading toward the Louisiade Archipelago and Port Moresby. To prevent any American interference with this operation, a striking force under Admiral Takeo Takagi consisting of the two larger carriers, *Shokaku* and *Zuikaku*, with four cruisers and six destroyers, hovered east of the Solomons.

While the Japanese were seizing Tulagi, the Americans were concentrating their only two available carriers—the *Yorktown* and the *Lexington*—in the South Pacific. The *Hornet* and the *Enterprise*, returning to Pearl Harbor from the Doolittle raid, were to follow as soon as possible, but they did not arrive in the South Pacific in time to take part in the first important encounter resulting from the new Japanese offensive.

The Japanese landing on Tulagi took place just as the American task force was gathering southwest of the New Hebrides Islands, in the eastern Coral Sea. While the *Lexington* was refueling, the task force commander, Admiral Frank J. Fletcher, dashed north in the *Yorktown* to raid the new Japanese positions at Tulagi on May 4.

The results were disappointing to Fletcher, since his carrier planes were able to sink only one destroyer and three smaller vessels. However, Fletcher had no time to brood about this. On May 5 he was joined by the *Lexington* about 350 miles west of the New Hebrides. The task force at once steamed west to intercept the Japanese invasion and covering forces, which Fletcher knew had just started for Port Moresby from Rabaul and the Shortland Islands.

That same day, May 5, the Japanese striking force, with its two large carriers, sailed around the eastern end of the Solomon Islands and headed into the Coral Sea, about 300 miles northeast of the American task force.

The Battle of the Coral Sea

On May 6 the two carrier task forces headed generally westward on converging courses in the northern Coral Sea. Neither force was aware that the other was near. Scouting was poor on both sides and was hindered by bad weather. Shortly after dark, the two forces actually were within less than 100 miles of each other.

The following morning, May 7, there occurred a confused series of actions between the two forces, marked by serious errors on both sides.

Soon after dawn reconnaissance airplanes from the two carrier forces found each other's ships and pointed the way for attack aircraft to follow. American torpedo planes and dive bombers struck at the *Shoho* and sank her during the morning. Shortly after dark the Japanese attempted an attack on the American carriers that cost them severe losses; only a few of the defending American fighters were lost. However, in an exchange of strikes the next morning—the 8th—the *Lexington* was sunk and the *Yorktown* damaged. The Japanese *Shokaku* suffered considerable damage, but the *Zuikaku* was unscathed despite the loss of a number of planes and pilots. While the Americans also lost a destroyer and an oiler, no other Japanese vessels were sunk.

By this time Admiral Inouye—supervising his forces from Rabaul—became aware of an Australian squadron of three cruisers and several destroyers under Admiral J. G. Grace, which was moving from Australia to intercept the Port Moresby assault force. The Australians survived several air strikes by Japanese land-based planes—and a mistaken attack by American aircraft—without damage and were posing a real threat to the Japanese invasion force. This threat, combined with the loss of the *Shoho*, caused Inouye to call off the invasion plan. The assault force returned to Rabaul.

Meanwhile, in the Coral Sea, Admirals Fletcher and Takagi, both concerned about the heavy losses they had suffered, almost simultaneously decided to withdraw from further action. So ended the Battle of the Coral Sea, the first important sea battle in which no surface ships on either side sighted any of the hostile vessels. It was the beginning of carrier air warfare.

Both sides made a number of mistakes in this battle. Considering only immediate tactical results, the Japanese had slightly the better of it. One of their light carriers was sunk and one heavy carrier was severely damaged. But they had sunk one of the few precious American heavy carriers, had slightly damaged the other, and had sunk a destroyer and a tanker. Though the Japanese had lost more planes in aerial combat, total aircraft losses were about equal because of the number that went down with the *Lexington*. (Actually the Japanese believed that they had also sunk the *Yorktown*, and this error in intelligence was to have a serious effect upon subsequent operations.)

Strategically, however, the Battle of the Coral Sea was an Allied victory. The Americans had prevented the Japanese invasion force from reaching its objectives at Port Moresby and in the Louisiade Islands.

Japanese Preparations for the Midway Expedition

Admiral Yamamoto and his Combined Fleet Staff were completing their plans for the expedition to Midway as the reports from Admirals Inouye, Takagi, and Kara came in from the Coral Sea. Yamamoto knew that the Americans had five aircraft carriers in the Pacific. One of these, the *Saratoga*, was on the west coast of the United States and unavailable. Two—the *Hornet* and the *Enterprise*—had been engaged in the Doolittle raid on Tokyo, and were just returning to Pearl Harbor as the Battle of the Coral Sea was taking place. It seemed to Yamamoto quite a coincidence that the only two remaining American carriers—the *Yorktown* and the *Lexington*—had been waiting so conveniently to oppose the first phase of the new Japanese offensive.

Fortunately, however, according to the reports that reached Tokyo on the 8th of May, both the *Yorktown* and the *Lexington* had been sunk at the Coral Sea. Then, a few days later, Japanese intelligence learned that the *Hornet* and *Enterprise*, after hurried refueling at Pearl Harbor, had rushed to the South Pacific. It looked as though the Americans were still quite unaware of the plans for the Midway expedition. Thus it was most unlikely that there would be any carriers available in the central Pacific to oppose the expedition. Perhaps the Americans were not reading his mail after all thought Yamamoto. He issued his final orders for the Midway expedition with renewed confidence. But there still remained enough doubt (those carriers in the Coral Sea) so that he continued in his determination to confuse the Americans (if they did know about it) by his execution of the plan.

For his expedition Yamamoto assembled most of Japan's Combined Fleet, organized into four major forces. Each of these was divided into two or more smaller groups.

The Northern Area Force, under Vice Admiral Boshiro Hosogaya, consisted of two light carriers, three heavy cruisers, four light cruisers, and twelve destroyers. It was to strike against Dutch Harbor and other Alaskan bases just before the Midway attack to confuse the Americans. Hosogaya was also ordered to establish Japanese outposts on islands of the Aleutians.

The principal striking force was that of Vice Admiral Nagumo, his First Air Fleet, which had carried out the brilliantly executed surprise attack on Pearl Harbor on December 7, 1941, and had just returned from a highly successful raid into the Indian Ocean. Aircraft from Nagumo's four heavy carriers were to soften Midway's defenses and prevent any American naval forces from interfering with the operation. Nagumo also had two battleships, three cruisers, and eleven destroyers.

Behind Nagumo's carriers would be the main body, under the personal direction of Admiral Yamamoto himself. He had seven battleships—including his flagship, the giant *Yamato*, 64,000 tons and nine 18.1-inch guns, the largest warship in commission. In addition he had one light carrier, two seaplane carriers, three cruisers, and twenty destroyers. This great fleet was ready to deal with any American surface forces that slipped past Nagumo's carrier planes.

Approaching Midway from the southwest would be the Midway Occupation Force. This consisted of the Second Fleet of Vice Admiral Nobutake Kondo, with two battleships, one light carrier, two seaplane carriers, nine cruisers, and nineteen destroyers, all protecting twelve troop transports carrying five thousand men. According to the Japanese plan, these troops would occupy Midway the night of June 5–6.

In addition, Yamamoto sent eighteen submarines to the waters between Midway and Pearl Harbor. They were to be in position by June 1 to report any American movements and to attack any American warships that might appear.

This Japanese Combined Fleet was the most powerful naval force that had ever been assembled in the Pacific Ocean. It should have been able to crush any possible American resistance. But Yamamoto did not expect to encounter any American carriers, and his forces were more dispersed than they would have been if serious opposition had been expected at sea. His fleet was spread out in ten separate groups, so far apart that they could not support one another quickly or effectively.

Yamamoto and one trusted staff officer had been studying their charts of the Pacific and doing some calculations. If the Americans had any inkling of the Japanese plans, they *could* have three heavy carriers to oppose the Midway expedition. This was a very small force, even accompanied by all available cruisers and destroyers, with which to oppose the Japanese Combined Fleet with its eight carriers. But if the Americans knew the Japanese plans, and the Japanese were unaware of American plans, three carriers might be able to interfere seriously with the expedition. It would be possible for the *Saratoga* to reach Pearl Harbor from the West Coast in late May, and for the *Hornet* and the *Enterprise* to return from the South Pacific at about the same time. These three ships, and about 20 cruisers and perhaps 30 destroyers, could sail west to defend Midway before the end of the month.

Discovery of American Radio Intercepts

Yamamoto was determined to try to find out once and for all if the Americans were reading his messages. He ordered eighteen submarines to take position between the Hawaiian Islands and Midway by June 1, to report on any American vessels moving westward. But his calculations showed that the American carriers could possibly leave Pearl Harbor for the central Pacific as early as May 25 or 26. A radio message was sent out to Vice Admiral Teruhisa Komaku, the submarine force commander in Kwajalein, addressed to him by his nickname, directing that his command must get on station to carry out their mission four days earlier than originally ordered. (Yamamoto would have been amused if he had known how much head-scratching this message caused at Pearl Harbor and in Washington when it was decoded.) Under forced draft the Japanese submarines reached their stations on the 26th and 27th, and began their patrol.

Then Yamamoto sent a personal message by seaplane to Admiral Hosagaya, commanding the Northern Area Force. He was to make his air attack on Dutch Harbor, as planned—but one day early, June 2 instead of June 3. Then he was to sail south at full speed, to be able to be north and east of Nagumo's First Air Fleet north of Midway by the 5th, and to continue southeast to reach Midway by the 6th, to provide fire support for the planned landing on the island.

As Yamamoto suspected, Americans were in fact intercepting and decoding all Japanese radio messages, and they had very complete information about the Japanese plans. Without this information Admiral Chester Nimitz would have had no possibility of offering effective opposition to Yamamoto. Even with this knowledge of Japanese plans and dispositions, the American situation was truly desperate, for the Japanese fleet was far superior in strength. (See Table 3)

Informed by decoded messages of the Japanese diversion against the Aleutian Islands, Nimitz sent a surface task force of three heavy cruisers, three light cruisers, eleven destroyers, and six submarines to the North Pacific, under Rear Admiral Robert A. Theobald. Under the circumstances, in light of the overwhelming Japanese superiority, this diversion of American forces was a seri-

TABLE 3
Comparison of Forces, Battle of Midway

	Japanese	American
Heavy carriers	4	3
Light carriers	4	—
Battleships	11	—
Cruisers	23	18
Destroyers	65	25
Seaplane carriers	4	—
Submarines	18	25
Carrier aircraft	430	236

ous error. Nimitz should have left the defense of Alaska to the Army Air Force, and concentrated his strength against the main threat. Unfortunately for the Americans, this mistake had serious consequences.

Because of the information about the Japanese plans, all during May the fortifications and garrison of Midway Island were feverishly strengthened. There were 3,600 defenders, with five tanks, 27 guns and mortars, and 32 antiaircraft guns. The island's small airfield was crowded with as many planes as it could hold: 17 modern B-17 bombers and 84 other miscellaneous Army, Navy, and Marine Corps fighters and light bombers. Most of these were old, slow, and inferior to Japanese planes.

Admiral Nimitz assembled all of his available carriers at Pearl Harbor. Admiral William Halsey's *Hornet-Enterprise* task force returned from the South Pacific on May 26. Halsey was ill, and he was replaced by Rear Admiral Raymond A. Spruance. Admiral Fletcher's *Yorktown* also had rushed back to Pearl Harbor, where the damage she had suffered in the Coral Sea—which had been estimated to require three months in drydock—was completely repaired in three days and nights of feverish activity.

Fletcher commanded the three-carrier task force that sailed west from Pearl Harbor in the last days of May. Admiral Nimitz retained overall command, however, directing the battle by radio from his headquarters at Pearl Harbor. In addition to the carriers, 12 cruisers, 14 destroyers, and 19 submarines were available for the defense of Midway. This force was pitifully small in comparison with the tremendous armada approaching from the west. The addition of Theobald's squadron would not have equalized the odds, but it would have reduced them.

The Japanese submarines began to establish their scouting screen west of Pearl Harbor on May 26. By early on the 28th they were all on station. So it was that the *Hornet* and *Enterprise* were sighted on May 29 and 30 by three submarines, and the *Yorktown* was observed by two on the 31st and June 1. Reports of these sightings were received at once by Yamamoto, confirming his worst fears. But of course these radio reports were also being received by Nimitz at Pearl Harbor just as quickly as they came to Yamamoto's desk at sea—confirming the worst American fears. The Japanese knew the Americans were ready, were at least aware of their initial dispositions, and knew that their code probably was broken. So, as the American force waited for the arrival of the Japanese, both sides had quite complete information about the other. Admiral Fletcher's instructions from Nimitz had been: "You will be governed by the principle of calculated risk, which you shall interpret to mean the avoidance of exposure of your force to attack by superior enemy forces without good prospects of inflicting, as a result of such exposure, greater damage on the enemy." Under the circumstances the level of the calculated risk had become very high.

Yamamoto's New Battle Plan

Before departure from Hashirajima, Yamamoto had sent written orders to Hosagaya, Kondo, and Nagumo, regarding a possible redistribution of carriers. Should it be necessary, the redisposition was to be initiated by a radio message—"Execute Plan B." Yamamoto was certain that this cryptic message would not be understood by the Americans, even if they decoded it.

Under Plan B Admiral Hosagaya was to send Admiral Kakuta with one of the two light carriers of his force (the *Junyo*), now called the Second Mobile Force, to join Nagumo's First Air Fleet, now called the First Mobile Force, as rapidly as possible. The other (the *Ryujo*) was to follow Kakuta south as soon as the first diversionary raid on Dutch Harbor was made. When he approached the First Mobile Force, Kakuta was to assume command of a light carrier task group under Nagumo. He and the *Junyo* and accompanying destroyers were expected to join the Mobile Force early on June 2. The *Ryujo* was expected to join shortly after midday on the 4th.

Kakuta was to have additional light carriers in his task group under Plan B. The light carrier *Hosho* was to steam north from Yamamoto's main body to come under Kakuta's command on June 2. The *Zuiho* was to be similarly diverted from Kondo's Second Fleet Occupation Force to become a part of Kakuta's light carrier task force.

When he ordered Plan B into effect on May 27, Yamamoto was taking a risk in reducing the potential air cover of his two largest surface groups. But both of these had seaplane carriers to provide aerial scouting, and he was confident that the antiaircraft defenses of his battleships, cruisers, and destroyers could deal with the most likely aerial threat from Midway itself. In anticipation of this possibility, he had told Nagumo in a letter accompanying the Plan B order that if the Mobile Force scouting planes detected any American carrier strike against the Main Body or the Occupation Force he was to send an intercepting group from the carriers. To facilitate this, the courses of the two surface groups were altered from east to northeast, to converge with that of the Mobile Force, and thus to bring them within supporting range of the carriers.

But Yamamoto did not anticipate such an American diversion of effort. He rightly assumed that the Americans would concentrate their efforts against Nagumo's carriers, and by these changes in dispositions Yamamoto had almost doubled the offensive strength of Nagumo's First Mobile Force. He calculated that by the morning of June 3 Nagumo's strength had been increased by a factor of about 1.11, and by midday on the 4th, after the arrival of the *Ryujo*, this factor would be increased to about 1.60.

Yamamoto discounted the ability of the American land-based planes on Midway to alter this force ratio. As it turned out, he was correct in this assessment. Japanese intelligence had confirmed that the *Saratoga* was still on the West Coast on May 25, and thus could not possibly arrive in time to take part in the battle. Yamamoto was surprised to find that the *Yorktown* (which he had thought was at the bottom of the Coral Sea) was part of the American force. However, following typical, methodical, pre-battle Japanese planning, on May 30 he made a comparison of the opposing carrier aircraft strengths—with the *Yorktown* included—as follows:

	Japanese	American	Ratio
Dawn, June 2	270	225	1.20
Dawn, June 3	300	225	1.33
Noon, June 4	430	225	1.91

Thus, despite the surprise presence of the *Yorktown*, Yamamoto was confident that with a nearly 2-1 numerical superiority in carrier air strength, he should win the battle handily. He was also confident that his combat-experienced pilots and aircraft were at least as good as those of the Americans, and he believed that Japanese armament—bombs and torpedoes—was better. Even though the Americans had an intelligence superiority in their obvious ability to decipher Japanese messages, Yamamoto was confident that his planning had mostly offset this American advantage. He had no doubt of the outcome of the battle. And if this battle was won, he was prepared to change his earlier pessimistic forecast of the outcome of the war.

The Aleutians

As planned by the Japanese, the first action took place near the Aleutian Islands. Eluding a patrol screen of small vessels and submarines, the Japanese carriers made a surprise raid on Dutch Harbor early on June 2. They did a great deal of damage, and lost only two planes to American antiaircraft fire. The Japanese ships then raced out to sea, avoiding the efforts of American Army and Navy land-based planes, and of Admiral Theobald's squadron, to intercept and damage them. The Americans were now alert and ready, but the Japanese were nowhere to be found.

The opening move of the great battle had been clearly won by the Japanese. The Aleutian diversion had been a great success, and it had attracted some American strength from the central Pacific. Admiral Yamamoto now realized, however, that it had failed in its principal strategic purpose since American attention was still focused firmly and grimly on his three great fleets now approaching Midway. But at least he was as aware of that attention as were the waiting Americans. And they did not know that he was aware.

Preliminaries at Midway

During the morning of June 3 American land-based patrol planes sweeping the ocean area west of Midway discovered the Japanese transports and the Second Fleet five hundred miles to the southwest. The B-17's attacked, but scored no hits. In the late afternoon, a Navy torpedo bomber from Midway attacked and damaged a Japanese oil tanker. There was no further action that day. Scouting planes from Nagumo's carriers found no American surface forces northwest of Midway. (Fletcher's carriers were lurking east of the area searched by the Japanese.)

Shortly before dawn on June 4 Nagumo's heavy carriers were 240 miles from Midway. The three light carriers were 20 miles to the north of them. At 4:30 A.M. Nagumo sent 108 planes—about half of his heavy carrier attack force—to strike the island. Leaving only a small defensive air cap, about one hour later the remainder of his planes took off to seek the American carriers northeast of Midway, where they were being covertly shadowed by Japanese submarines, their locations precisely plotted on Nagumo's charts. Kakuta's light carrier group was in reserve and ready to deal with an American strike.

The first Japanese aerial attack force, about 100 miles from Midway, was sighted at dawn, almost simultaneously by American scouting planes and by radar sets on Midway. Twenty-seven Marine Corps fighter planes scrambled up to meet the approaching Japanese strike force and encountered the Japanese 30 miles from the island.

In a brief, fierce struggle the Marine defenders were overwhelmed. Fifteen Marine planes were shot down. Although they succeeded in destroying several attackers, the defending aircraft could not prevent the Japanese from breaking through, and at 6:30 A.M. the Japanese struck the island. Accurate antiaircraft fire shot down a few more attacking planes, but the Japanese damaged most of the installations on the island, and started fires. The attackers avoided the airfield runways, however, since they soon expected to use these themselves. At 7:00 A.M. the 97 surviving Japanese aircraft started back to their carriers.

Meanwhile, just before 6:00 A.M. a Navy patrol plane sighted Nagumo's fleet. Twenty Navy and Marine planes on Midway—alert and awaiting the order—at once took off to attack the Japanese carriers. However, they were unable to penetrate the Japanese screen of defensive fighters. Five of the American planes were shot down, and nine more were so badly damaged as to be useless when they finally limped back to Midway. Only the B-17's, too high to be reached by Japanese fighters, were untouched. But their great height also prevented them from bombing accurately the skillfully maneuvering warships; they scored no hits. The second round had also been clearly won by the Japanese.

The Carrier Battle

But the American carriers had not yet entered the fight. Spruance's *Enterprise-Hornet* group was closer to the Japanese than Fletcher's *Yorktown* when the bombing of Midway began. Spruance—cautious but aggressive—decided to steam closer to the enemy to be sure that his planes would have enough fuel so that they could take their time in attacking. Also, he figured that the Japanese planes that were attacking Midway would be refueling and rearming by the time the American planes arrived. But Spruance was unaware of two critical factors. The scouting planes had made a mistake in reporting the location of Nagumo's fleet; the Japanese carriers were forty miles further away than their reported location. Worse, the Japanese knew precisely where Spruance was, and their strike planes were already approaching his carriers.

At about 6:30 A.M., the *Enterprise* and *Hornet*—widely separated to avoid giving the enemy a good target—began to fly off their attack planes. It took an hour for all the planes to get off and to assemble in four separate groups: torpedo planes and dive bombers from each carrier. When the air groups were assembled, they headed for the Japanese Fleet.

For Admiral Nagumo the battle was going according to plan. Between 7:00 and 8:30 his Mobile Force was under attack by land-based planes from Midway, and his vessels were taking evasive action as the defense fighters of the two task groups shot down or drove off the American attackers. Then, while this activity was going on, an American submarine thrust up its periscope in the middle of the heavy carrier group and fired two torpedoes (both of which missed) before attacking Japanese destroyers forced the submarine to dive deep below the surface. This was the USS *Nautilus*, largest submarine then afloat, which had headed toward the carriers after hearing the initial radio reports of the American scouting planes.

By 8:30, with the American land-based planes and the submarine driven off, Nagumo and Kakuta could give their attention to the coordination of two very difficult efforts. First, the heavy carriers had to take on the planes returning from their successful attack on Midway. At the same time, the light carriers had to be ready to deal with the anticipated American carrier strike forces. By 9:00 all of the planes from Midway had been taken aboard the heavy carriers, and Nagumo turned these carriers north to close with Kakuta's group, while the planes rearmed and refueled. He suspected—though in the fog he could not be sure—that more than 100 American carrier planes were a few miles away. The planes and vessels of both carrier task groups were alert.

The sky was cloudy, and because of the incorrect report of the position of the Japanese carriers, the *Hornet* and *Enterprise* planes had a hard time finding their target. The torpedo planes, flying under the clouds, however, finally discovered Nagumo's carriers and turned in to attack at about 9:00, just after Nagumo had changed course.

First came the *Hornet's* 15 torpedo planes. But, as they were approaching the carriers, they were struck from above by alert Japanese defensive fighters. All 15 of the American planes were shot down before they could launch a single torpedo. The 14 torpedo planes of the *Enterprise* suffered almost as severely. Ten were shot down, and none of the four survivors scored a hit.

Above the clouds, the *Hornet* dive bombers completely missed the Japanese and had to return to their ships on their last drops of gasoline. The *Enterprise* dive bombers almost missed too, but their leader, Lieutenant Commander Clarence McClusky, Jr., discovered the Japanese heavy carriers just before his planes would have been forced to turn back.

At this time the Japanese defensive planes and aircraft gunners had just repelled the torpedo bomber attack, and thought they had repelled all of the Americans. They

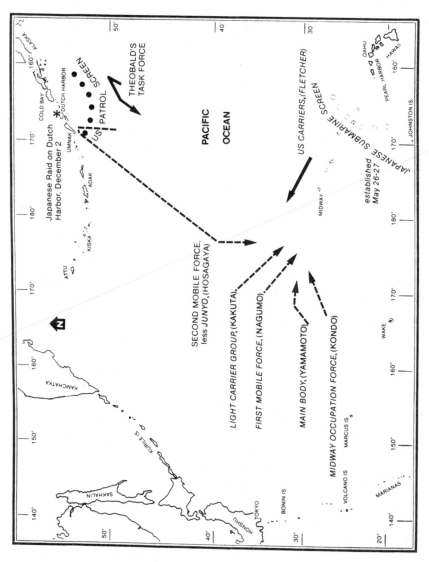

Positions of Major Japanese and US Naval Forces. Dawn, June 4

were caught completely by surprise as the *Enterprise* dive bombers screamed down at them. As Spruance had hoped, the decks of the Japanese carriers were crowded with the planes that had just returned from the Midway strike and were being refueled. The American bombers got several hits on both the *Akagi* and the *Kaga*. The planes on deck burst into flames, and uncontrolled fires soon enveloped both carriers, putting them completely out of action.

Just as the *Enterprise* dive bombers were scoring so heavily, the *Yorktown* torpedo planes and dive bombers arrived to launch a combined surprise attack against the carrier *Soryu*. She was also set afire and left in a seriously damaged condition. When the American attack was over, at 10:25 A.M., three-fourths of Nagumo's heavy carriers had been knocked out of action. But the Americans paid a heavy price. Pounced on by Kakuta's fighters, only 43 of the 135 strike planes returned to their carriers.

Nagumo, on board the stricken *Akagi*, was reluctantly persuaded by his staff to transfer from the carrier to one of his cruisers. Despite being considerably shocked by this sudden turn of the battle, he immediately made plans to redress the balance. He knew that he still had substantial numerical superiority both in the air and on the surface.

Japanese search planes had discovered the *Yorktown*, but missed both the *Enterprise* and the *Hornet*. Nagumo, on his new flagship, ordered Kakuta immediately to send out his remaining attack groups to strike the three American carriers, since he knew from submarine reports that the *Hornet* and *Enterprise* would not be far from the *Yorktown*. Joining in this strike was the attack group from the *Ryujo*, which had just joined Kakuta's task group.

Just after noon, as the three American carriers were beginning to take their planes back on board, the Japanese approached. On the *Yorktown* the handful of landing planes were waved off, and the vessel took evasive action. However, a few of the attackers got past the *Yorktown*'s defensive fighter planes and antiaircraft fire from the carrier and her escorts, and hit her with three bombs. The

Yorktown's speed was reduced, but the deck damage was soon under control, and she began to take on her planes again.

The situation was far worse, however, for the Americans a few miles to the west. The *Hornet* and *Enterprise* had just taken aboard the pitiful remnants of their strike groups when the Japanese attacked. Although Spruance's defensive fighters met the attackers aggressively, they were badly outnumbered, and soon all were shot down, even though they took a heavy toll of the Japanese. The remaining Japanese bombers and torpedo planes, executing the coordinated attacks they had so assiduously practiced in training, scored several serious torpedo and bomb hits on both American carriers. Within moments both were in flames. Those Japanese planes that had not expended all of their armament now turned against the cruiser and destroyer escorts. Although a few were shot down, three cruisers and two destroyers were hit, and one of the cruisers was clearly in sinking condition as the Japanese planes returned to their carriers.

Meanwhile Nagumo had refueled and rearmed the *Hiryu* planes that had made the earlier attack on Midway. At 2:30 P.M. these planes appeared over the *Yorktown,* most of them armed with torpedoes. Despite her fighter plane screen and very heavy antiaircraft fire, several attackers got through to hit the limping *Yorktown* with two torpedoes. The ship began to list heavily and slowed to a stop. At 3:00 P.M. Admiral Fletcher ordered her to be abandoned. The crew was taken off by nearby destroyers, and one destroyer stayed with the stricken vessel in hopes that she might be salvaged and towed back to Pearl Harbor. Soon after this Fletcher attempted to turn the direction of the battle over to Spruance by radio. It was then that he discovered that the *Hornet* and *Enterprise* were also both out of action, and that Spruance had shifted his flag to a cruiser.

The carrier air battle—and with it the sea battle, for all intents and purposes—was over. The Japanese had clearly won an overwhelming victory. Two American carriers had been destroyed and were sinking; the third was barely afloat. The Japanese had also lost three heavy carriers, but they had one undamaged heavy carrier and four light carriers left. And since these vessels had taken on the remaining planes of the stricken *Kaga*, *Akagi*, and *Soryu*, Nagumo still had more than two-thirds of his original air strength. All of the American carrier planes had been lost.

Closing Actions

Nagumo now shifted his flag to the *Hiryu* and prepared for the final phase of the battle, to provide support to the surface forces attacking Midway.

Yamamoto, informed of the results of the carrier battle, his plans triumphant, now ordered Kondo to move against the island. The Main Body and Nagumo's battered but still battleworthy Mobile Force also closed in on the tiny island. At sea there were a few *entre acte* performances as the main scene was being shifted.

During the afternoon the American submarine *Nautilus*, still tracking the Japanese carriers, discovered the burning, sinking carrier *Kaga* and attacked her. But two of the American torpedoes missed, and the third failed to explode when it struck the carrier's side. The stricken vessel sank a few hours later; at about the same time the *Soryu* blew up. During the night the survivors on the *Akagi* and *Kaga* struggled to save their vessels, but in vain. Shortly after dawn on June 5, Japanese destroyers took off the survivors, then sank the two burning hulks with torpedoes.

During the evening of June 4 Yamamoto ordered Admiral Kondo, who was nearest to the Americans, to engage the remaining American surface force with his four battleships, nine cruisers, and nineteen destroyers. Meanwhile a submarine and cruiser division began to shell Midway as the Main Body and the transports closed in on the island.

But Fletcher and Spruance had expected that the Japanese would attempt just such an attack on their remaining vessels. To avoid the vastly superior Japanese surface forces they steamed east during the night. Sometime after midnight Yamamoto realized that he would be unable to catch the retiring American task force. He ordered Kondo to move in to provide gunship support to the amphibious attack against Midway.

As they were turning back to the northwest just about midnight on June 5, two Japanese heavy cruisers, the *Mogami* and *Mikuma*—part of Kondo's striking group— collided while trying to avoid the American submarine *Tambor*. Early the following morning these two cruisers, limping westward at reduced speed, were discovered and attacked by American submarines. Both were hit, but the *Mogami* suffered little damage. However, the *Mikuma* was stopped in the water. Japanese destroyers drove off the American submarines, and one of them began to tow the *Mikuma* westward. However, the American submarines returned to the attack, and another torpedo hit the crippled cruiser. This was the end for the *Mikuma*, sunk with a loss of one thousand lives. The battered *Mogami* finally reached Truk, where she was under repair for two years.

The Midway Assault

Following the Japanese victory at sea, the outcome of the land battle on Midway was never in doubt. After two days of pulverizing bombardment from the air and from the great Japanese armada of surface vessels, Japanese troops stormed ashore on June 9. More than half the defending Americans had been killed or wounded in the pre-assault bombardment. The survivors fought tenaciously and gallantly, but the Japanese, despite severe casualties, could not be denied. By evening of June 9 the small group of survivors surrendered. Midway was in Japanese hands and destined to remain under occupation for the next eighteen months.

Aftermath

Meanwhile, far to the east, American destroyers had been towing the helpless *Yorktown* back to Pearl Harbor. Late on June 6, the Japanese submarine *I-168* discovered the ships and attacked. One of her torpedoes immediately sank the destroyer USS *Hammann*, while two more crashed into the *Yorktown*. That probably would have been enough to sink the carrier. However, a strike force from the *Hiryu* attacked the stricken *Yorktown* about an hour later and hit her with ten bombs. That was the end for the sole surviving American carrier.

Losses in the Battle of Midway were heavy on both sides. The Japanese lost three carriers and a heavy cruiser, with several other vessels damaged. They lost nearly 200 carrier planes and about 100 pilots. They also lost a total of 3,500 men killed at sea, and a horrendous total of 1,700 killed and 3,300 wounded in the land assault.

American losses, of course, were much heavier. More than 5,000 sailors, Marines, and airmen were killed at sea, including nearly 200 highly-trained pilots; six ships—three carriers, one cruiser, and two destroyers—were sunk; more than 200 carrier planes were lost (shot down or sunk with their carriers), and 76 land-based planes were destroyed either in the air or on the Midway runway. The heaviest cost, of course, was the nearly 4,000 Marines and soldiers killed, wounded, or captured during the bitter struggle on Midway Island.

A minor but interesting sidelight to the battle was the successful transfer of command by three of the senior admirals, from a sinking flagship to another vessel: Nagumo from the *Akagi*, Fletcher from the *Yorktown*, and Spruance from the *Hornet*.

Midway was one of the great sea battles of history. However, it did not decisively affect the outcome of the war, although it undoubtedly prolonged it for more than a year. For a time at least Japanese control was assured in the great reaches of the Southern Resources Area and contiguous regions Japanese forces had so handily won at the outset of the war.

Tactically, both sides had performed almost faultlessly, but the odds in favor of the Japanese were such that the Americans were unable to gain any advantage. Yamamoto and Nagumo, aware of their superiority, never gave the Americans a chance. On both sides planning and execution were marked by skill, gallantry, and determination.

One basic factor led to the result: Yamamoto's realization that American knowledge of the Japanese secret codes was presenting Nimitz with an accurate picture of Japanese intentions and dispositions. Because of this he was able to make plans to offset this initial American advantage.

Before the Battle of Midway Japanese carrier strength in the Pacific had been approximately double that of the United States; following the battle the Japanese retained three large and four light carriers; the Americans had now only one large one in action. But the Americans had thirteen carriers in shipyards approaching completion, while the Japanese had only six. Thus, by the end of 1942 the United States would have a slight preponderance in carriers and carrier aircraft, and a little better than parity in surface vessels of all major types. As long as the war continued, this American preponderance was bound to grow, since—as Yamamoto had warned at the outset of the war—Japan could never hope to match American industrial war production capability.

It seems likely that, if Admiral Yamamoto had not suspected the American ability to decipher the Japanese codes, the Americans would have been able to surprise and ambush the widely scattered groups of the Japanese Midway expedition, with a resulting defeat to Japan. In that case, the war probably would have ended with an American victory in 1944 or 1945—depending on how the United States related its Pacific war against Japan to its Atlantic-African-European struggle against Germany.

As it was, we know that the war dragged on until early 1946, when the destruction of the Japanese fleet in the climactic Battle of Luzon, combined with three long-range B-29 atomic bomb attacks from Chengtu in China, forced Japan to sue for peace.

Afterword

Save for one slight fact—and its logical conse-quences—this narrative of the Battle of Midway is completely faithful to history. That one altered fact was Admiral Yamamoto's suspicion that the Ameri-cans had broken the Japanese codes. Even that fact may not be as altered as it seems to be, since it seems most unlikely that Yamamoto would not have speculated about this possibility. But, whether he did or not, neither at Midway nor during the remain-ing ten months of his life did Yamamoto take any apparent action based upon such a suspicion.

Even if Yamamoto had not suspected the Ameri-can eavesdropping on Japanese secret messages, the changes in his plans and dispositions which are sug-gested in the preceding pages would have been quite logical had not he—and most other Japanese military men—been so carried away by six months of unbro-ken successes that they took some risks that were unnecessary. Even with the Japanese as completely surprised by the presence of three American carriers as they were in fact on June 4, 1942, if Yamamoto had had the Second Mobile Force available to sup-port Nagumo's First Mobile Force, the course of the battle almost certainly would have been similar to that which is imagined in this chapter. The result: an overwhelming Japanese victory.

This should demonstrate, if there are any doubts, that Midway, like Waterloo, was "a close-run thing."

CHAPTER VII

The Stalingrad Campaign

The Stage is Set

THE WINTER OF 1941–1942 brought the first sharp setbacks of World War II for the Wehrmacht, which hitherto had been accustomed to easy victories. After stopping the Germans at Moscow, the Russians had seized the initiative and thrown the Germans back all along the front. However, when the sun shone warm again in the late spring of 1942, and dried the endless plains of southern Russia, the Wehrmacht again had stabilized the front. Both the German Armed Forces High Command (*Oberkommando der Wehrmacht*, OKW) in Berlin, and the German Army High Command (*Oberkommando des Heeres*, OKH) in Russia, were assessing the situation and preparing plans.

Time was clearly working against the Axis powers. Soon the Allies would activate their almost world-wide resources. Hitler knew this, although he was counting on the Japanese to keep the Americans busy. At a minimum, another major victory over Soviet Russia was essential, and soon.

There was reason to expect such a victory. The German armies had repeatedly demonstrated that they were tremendously superior in mobile warfare to the ponderous, poorly-led Russian armies that had three times lost the flower of their officer corps: in the Revolution and Civil

174

War, 1917–1919; in the great purges, 1937–1938; and in the catastrophic defeats of 1941, in which the Wehrmacht had captured more than four million prisoners, in addition to inflicting horrible casualties and heavy materiel losses on the Red Army.

But German military power had also waned. Germany's tank inventory had declined from 3,660 to 3,300. By June 1942 the army alone had suffered 1.3 million men killed, wounded and missing, 40% of the total that had been mobilized. German manpower shortages made it impossible to replace losses fully. Thus infantry units were down to 30% of authorized strengths in Army Groups North and Center, and down to 50% in Army Group South. Overall, German military capability had so declined that it would be possible for only one army group to undertake an offensive in 1942. For this, Army Group South was selected, largely for reasons of economic strategy in which Caucasus oil was preeminent. On April 5 Hitler signed Directive 41. This called for the initial offensive in three successive coordinated steps:

- First, a drive eastward from south of Orel toward Voronezh, thence, southeastward, west of the Don River, toward Stalingrad;
- Next another offensive from Kharkov due east to the Don River to meet the mechanized forces of Step One, which would be attacking southward from Voronezh;
- Thereafter, a third offensive from Taganrog toward Stalingrad, there to meet with the combined force of Steps One and Two, attacking with its left shoulder along the Don river.

After this operation had been completed, the second phase of the offensive would begin: expansion into the oil-rich Caucasus area. As regards Stalingrad, it was contemplated that the attacking force would merely "bring the city under fire from heavy weapons so that the enemy can no longer use it as a center of armament industry and communications." The German General Staff did not intend to do the enemy the favor of committing infantry or

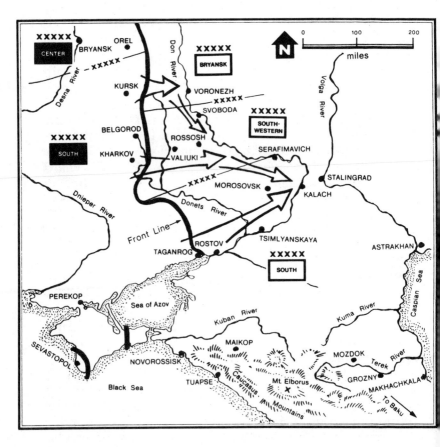

German Operational Concept for Directive No. 41

armored divisions in an urban battle of attrition in houses, cellars, and factories, should the enemy defend the city.

The directive was prudently restrained. It concentrated forces on one objective at a time; forces and objectives were in harmony. Nevertheless, it contained one serious error: "The enemy has suffered extremely heavy losses of men and materiel," it stated. This statement was true; but it was followed by a false conclusion: "During this winter, he has expended most of the reserves earmarked for later operations." When these words were written, Stalin was in the process of raising ten new infantry armies of six divisions each, two new tank armies, three new tank corps, two new infantry corps, one new cavalry corps, seventeen new independent infantry brigades, nine new independent tank brigades, and numerous smaller formations. Thus, the foundations of the forthcoming German summer offensive were shaky, since they were built on a faulty appreciation of enemy capabilities.

The Curtain is Raised

On June 28, Army Group South launched the first phase of the offensive. The total forces participating in the offensive were 68 German divisions, and 29 divisions of Germany's allies and satellites (Hungarian, Italian, Romanian, and Slovak divisions, Walloon and Croat contingents, and volunteers from almost all European countries). Fourteen additional allied divisions were soon committed, 111 divisions in all.

Everything went well with the first step—at least so it seemed. The Second and Fourth Panzer armies reached Voronezh in four days; German commanders avoided the temptation to allow themselves to be dragged into a prolonged battle for the city, which was contained by a small screen of light forces. Thus this force, which advanced down the west bank of the Don River in early July, had little trouble in driving several disorganized Soviet units ahead of it. A few of the Russians were able to escape across the river, but most were overrun, captured, or dispersed.

Meanwhile, in the second step, the Sixth Army began its drive eastward from Kharkov. Spearheads of the Fourth Panzer Army and the Sixth Army met near the Don, midway between Svoboda and Serafimavich. Many Soviet units escaped across the Don, but more than 100,000 Russians were captured in the Valiuki-Rossosh pocket. The Sixth Army reached the eastern tip of the Don River Bend on July 14, less than eighty kilometers from Stalingrad.

On July 7 the Seventeenth Army and the First Panzer Army jumped off in the third step, driving due east. Rostov fell to the First Panzer Army on July 10. Again many Russian units, having learned well the lessons of twelve months of bitter defeat, were able to withdraw across the Don. But by July 20 more than 300,000 had been bagged by the Germans. Of the escaped Soviet units, many were disorganized; most others were very low in morale. The Soviet Southwest Army Group had not been destroyed, but it was only barely a viable fighting force.

On July 7 a new German Army Group A had been established under the command of Field Marshal Wilhelm List, to take over the direction of operations in the Stalingrad-Caucasus area. Under List's command were the First and Fourth Panzer Armies, and the Sixth and Seventeenth Armies. At the same time General Maximilian von Weichs replaced Bock as the Commander of Army Group South.

Moltke was fond of saying that no battle plan lasts longer than the first clash of opposing armies. Nevertheless, one of the marks of a military genius is to prepare a plan so carefully, and then fight in accordance with the plan's concept so flexibly, that the operation is able to go "according to plan." The first phase of the operation envisaged in Directive No. 41 had been one such operation. The second phase began on July 12, two days after Rostov was seized.

While the Sixth Army was establishing itself on the west bank of the Don near Kalach, the Seventeenth Army and the First Panzer Armies struck south across the lower Don between Rostov and Tsimlyanskaya into the Kuban Steppes. The Romanian Third Army and the Italian Eighth Army were committed north of the German Sixth Army to consolidate a strong defensive position along the Don and to protect the left flank of the Sixth Army. The Fourth Panzer Army was shifted south of the Sixth Army, and on July 16 the two German armies began their part in setting the stage for the second phase of the offensive by a drive due east from Kalach toward Stalingrad.

List was concerned about the growing gap between the diverging spearheads of his two offensives. He established a system of motorized patrols linking the advancing troops as best they could across the Kalmyk Steppe. But the patrols saw little action, at least during the last two weeks of July, save for exhausting motor trips.

The harried staffs of the Soviet Southwestern and Southern Army Groups were too busy attempting to extricate their battered units from new disasters to be thinking about any counteroffensive maneuvers—even if they had had the resources for such activities, which they did not. Reinforcements were arriving for both Soviet army groups, but these had to be committed to replace the forces recently captured by the Germans, and in front of the onrushing drives of the Sixth and Fourth Panzer Armies eastward toward Stalingrad, and of the First Panzer and Seventeenth Armies southeast into the Caucasus.

During the last week of July the Russians received a welcome respite, as all four of the German armies were stalled by shortages of gasoline. The Sixth Army was also perilously short of ammunition. However, by August 5 the Germans' logistical difficulties had been overcome, and the advance was renewed. On August 8 General Friedrich Paulus, commanding the Sixth Army, reported by telephone to Field Marshal List that his patrols were probing stiffening Soviet resistance in the suburbs of

Stalingrad, and that his artillery was firing on Soviet concentrations east of the Volga more than 10 kilometers north and south of the city. He asked if he should attempt to seize the city.

List reminded Paulus that Directive No. 41 specifically warned against a commitment of troops to an urban battle in Stalingrad. "If it falls into your hands like a ripe melon, naturally you should take it," List added. "Your mission now is to consolidate, forming a powerful northern bastion to protect the offensive into the Caucasus." He then briefly summarized for Paulus the provisions of a new Directive No. 45 from OKH, which had emerged from discussions in late July between OKH and the staffs of Army Group A and Army Group South.

There were two principal problems that had needed to be thrashed out in this staff conference. First, despite the terrible losses inflicted upon the Soviets, they still had viable fighting forces east of the Don in the Voronezh, Southwestern, and newly established Stalingrad Army Groups. The long, overextended German line from Voronezh south to Stalingrad was obviously vulnerable if the Soviets were able to mass sufficient troops to attempt a counteroffensive to drive behind the advancing spearheads of Army Group A. Furthermore, the southern drive of Army Group A was creating another extended flank, a possible invitation to a Soviet thrust westward across the Kalmyk Steppe toward the lower Don.

The second problem was how to maintain the speed and power necessary for a successful drive through the Caucasus to Baku and the Iranian border without more troops, when there were no more troops. The line along the Don could be thinned out, but this would make the danger to the northern flank and rear of Army Group A even worse than it already was. The Fourth Romanian Army, now arriving in the area of Weichs' Army Group South, could be shifted south to support the First Panzer and Seventeenth Armies, but List was strongly opposed to that. He suggested that the Romanians, under Weichs' command, could relieve the Sixth and Seventeenth Armies in the Stalingrad area, and that these two armies then should be given to him to reinforce the drive into the Caucasus.

General Franz Halder, Chief of Staff of OKH, refused to consider this suggestion. He pointed out that this would leave a stretch of nearly 600 kilometers, from Voronezh to Stalingrad, defended by four allied armies—Second Hungarian, Eighth Italian, and Third and Fourth Romanian. He reminded List that the Soviets still had some bridgeheads west of the Don. He also reminded the army group commander that this vulnerable line must be securely held to prevent any possible threat to the rear of Army Group A.

Halder then gave the OKH decision. The Fourth Romanian Army would be assigned to List, who would retain responsibility for both the Stalingrad and Caucasus regions. He could shift the Fourth Panzer Army to join the southeasterly thrust into the Caucasus, rather than putting the Romanians there, but he must leave the German Sixth Army to hold the northern shoulder in the Stalingrad area. This, added Halder, would assure that there was some good, solid German *wurst* in the sandwich, between slices of possibly more porous allied bread.

This was the essential decision of Directive No. 45. List was to secure the line of the Caucasus Mountains, the Caspian shore from Astrakhan to Baku, and the line of the Volga from Stalingrad to Astrakhan. A decision as to whether to continue the advance southward to the Turkish and Iranian frontiers would be postponed, and would be made on the basis of the situation existing after List reached his assigned objectives.

By August 15 the German Sixth Army had securely anchored itself on the Volga, north and south of Stalingrad, easily beating off several weak Soviet counterattacks. Stalingrad itself remained in Soviet hands and was kept under intermittent German artillery fire. The right wing of the Sixth Army was extended slowly down the west bank of the lower Volga, while the Fourth Romanian Army, against scant opposition, was advancing even more slowly across the Kalmyk Steppe toward Astrakhan. The Seventeenth Army was consolidating control of the northern ridge of the Caucasus Mountains, and the German flag was flying on top of Mount Elborus, highest of the snow-covered Caucasus peaks.

German alpine troops, Romanians, and Walloons descended into the lush subtropical valleys beyond the passes. North of the mountain range, at Mozdok, one oil field was already in German and Slovak hands. The First Panzer Army had seized Grozny, south of the Terek River. Germans and new allies—Russian, Turkoman, and Kalmyk volunteers—came within reach of the Caspian Sea and knocked at the gates of Astrakhan. By the end of the month the Fourth Panzer Army was advancing between the Kuma and Terek rivers, approaching the Caspian Sea. German and Croatian soldiers stood at Stalingrad and looked beyond the Volga into the vast Kazakh Steppes. Indeed, as Hitler had required in April, Stalingrad had been "reached" and had been "brought under fire from heavy weapons so that the enemy could no longer use it as a center of armament industry and communications."

The German victory had been tremendous, and would be even greater before the offensive came to an end. But it had been achieved at great cost, and, for all their magnitude, the accomplishments had been less than had been hoped for. Shortages of manpower, fuel, and ammunition were critical. The front of List's army group now stretched over 1,500 kilometers; on the average each of his 50 divisions was responsible for a front of 30 kilometers. This was bad enough for the Sixth and Fourth Romanian Armies—where the division fronts actually exceeded 40 kilometers on the average—but it forced the advancing divisions of the First and Fourth Panzer Armies to operate virtually independently of each other, with open flanks and large numbers of effective Soviet fighting units behind them. Enough of these bypassed Russian groups were sufficiently active to interfere seriously with the already strained logistical system attempting to provide the panzers with fuel and ammunition.

Furthermore, new Soviet units were continually appearing along the front, both north and south of Stalingrad, and in the Caucasus. Among these new units were the Sixty-sixth, Twenty-fourth, Sixty-third, Sixth, Sixtieth, Sixty-second, First Guards, and Fifth Tank Armies, plus several independent tank corps, infantry corps, and many other formations. And other new units had been committed further north. Admittedly, the Germans were still far superior in quality and leadership, and were inflicting disproportionate losses of killed and wounded upon the Russians, but the German divisions were the same ones that had launched the offensive many weeks before. Losses accumulated and replacements were few. Altogether, the German Army in Russia was by now more than one million men below authorized manning levels. Strengths of combat units were especially low. The divisions were exhausted and short of supplies, and now realized that they were opposed by an enemy that—despite disastrous defeats—was dedicated, numerous, and reinforced.

As August turned to September, the German advance continued, but at a much slower pace. By September 15 Romanian guns were firing on Astrakhan, and a strangely-mixed force of Germans, Romanians, Russians, and Cossacks held most of the west bank of the lower Volga, and most of the northwestern shore of the Caspian Sea, from the Volga delta to Makhachkala. It was now obvious to List that his resources were inadequate to reach Baku. He ordered all units to halt in place, dig in, and wait further orders.

Thus, for the second time in the war, the initiative passed to the Russians again. What should the Germans do? Hitler himself had stated the solution late in March, when he planned the offensive: "When the offensive comes to a halt, forces must be withdrawn to reserve. Not regiments. Divisions." Right though he was, this meant shortening overextended fronts, releasing territory, losing prestige. Ultimately it meant that the offensive had failed—and had failed in a situation where time was working in favor of Germany's enemies.

Clearly, a most difficult and painful German decision was required. A prerequisite to the decision was a convincing estimate of the enemy's capabilities. But German intelligence was groping in the dark, trying in the age-old manner to produce an overall picture from tiny pieces of information, many of which were of doubtful credibility themselves.

On August 3 it was reported to Hitler that the Russians' tank losses allowed them either to replace current losses in existing units or to raise new units, but not both. This was good news. But twelve days later OKH intelligence had an alarming update: although the Soviets had committed most of their infantry divisions, they still had at least 73 in reserve, plus 86 tank brigades and 20 cavalry brigades, in all more than half of the striking power already committed. However, there was no intelligence concerning the combat readiness of these reserves, their officers, their NCOs, their training, their weaponry, their equipment. These were valid questions, and nobody could reliably answer them. However, early in October Halder felt confident in saying that "at present, the Russians are not in a position to launch a major offensive with far-reaching objectives."

But, even though a Russian attack was considered unlikely, a good general staff could not ignore the possibility. Yet in such unlikely event, where and when could the enemy strike?

On August 29 OKH intelligence produced a paper called "Considerations on Future Development of the Enemy Situation." This concluded that "during the forthcoming winter the enemy will again be able to commit a large number of new formations." But this important conclusion was watered down by the very next sentence: "Generally speaking, at present there is no indication that the overall German/Russian force ratio will change decisively in favor of the Russians in the foreseeable future."

Considering the enemy's likely course of action, many options across the entire Russian front were listed, and it meant little that one of these was a possible Russian offensive across the Don River, north of Stalingrad.

As time progressed, OKH intelligence more and more believed that the likely target of a Russian winter offensive would be Army Group Center. This culminated in a November 6 assessment: "More and more clearly the main effort *(Schwerpunkt)* of future Russian operations . . . can be recognized in the sector of Army Group Center. It is yet uncertain if the Russians still intend to launch a large operation across the Don. . . . However, as can be recognized, their preparations for an attack in the south have not yet progressed so far that we need to reckon with a larger operation carried out simultaneously with the expected offensive against Army Group Center."

In retrospect it is difficult to understand why Halder—who had in July so clearly recognized the dangerous potential of a Soviet offensive across the middle Don between Voronezh and Stalingrad—did not give this possibility more attention in October. There were evidently two principal reasons. In the first place, Soviet losses had been so great during the summer of 1942, and the quality of Soviet forces had so clearly declined, that Halder was convinced that low morale and poor troop quality were not offset by the increase in number of Soviet troops, even though German strength had been declining at the same time. The quality differential was such that German commanders were using a rule-of-thumb that a successful German attack could be made if the Soviets did not have more than a two-to-one numerical superiority, and that they could defend successfully against odds of six-to-one or more.

The second reason for Halder's failure to give adequate consideration to a possible offensive across the Don was that the quality of his own staff had substantially declined during the past year and a half. Even with frantic efforts to train good young officers for the General Staff, there were not enough such young officers, and there was not time to give them sufficient training. So, all of the higher-level general staffs—including OKH—had been forced to send good officers to newly-formed divisions, corps, and armies, and to replace the numerous casualties that had occurred—particularly at division level—in the General Staff Corps. With smaller staffs, and fewer people of first-rate quality, staff capabilities declined. Both opportunities and threats were missed.

The Crisis Develops

Thus, with Fall approaching, the right wing of Army Group South and the left wing of Army Group A were in a potentially dangerous situation the moment the Russians regained the initiative. The Sixth Army—which still was outside Stalingrad—was particularly vulnerable, and its flanks were so weakly protected that they almost invited an enemy attack. South of the city, in the Kalmyk Steppe, and northwest of Stalingrad, along the Don, Romanians were deployed. Beyond these to the north were an Italian army, and then a Hungarian army. Many of the Romanian divisions and the Italian alpine divisions would later fight courageously. But none of the allied divisions was in any way prepared for a winter campaign in Russia and against Russians. Clothing was insufficient, equipment and weaponry were poor, training was not up to German standards, and hardly any of the allied divisions had officers and NCOs of the caliber required to lead men in battle against Russians.

What should the Germans have done? Reserves, strong reserves were needed, to enable commanders to react to whatever the Russians would do. Lack of defensive depth meant disaster the moment the Russians achieved a breakthrough. Hitler was among the few who saw and understood the writing on the wall. Again and again his strange but logical mind was close to the solution. Even as the Sixth Army approached Stalingrad, as early as August 16, he expressed his deep concern about the vulnerability of the flank on the Don, and he repeated this several times later. On November 4, out of the blue, he ordered the 6th Panzer Division and two infantry divisions to be moved from France to Russia. Even more strange, he ordered these divisions to Army Group South, not to Army Group Center, which had been tumbling from crisis to crisis throughout the year, and which was expected by German intelligence to be the target of an enemy major offensive to commence soon. The availability of these three divisions was to have a significant effect on the coming battle.

In addition, the allied armies on the Don received stiffening by the assignment of a few German divisions. Also, some artillery, antiaircraft, and antitank units were put under their command. And the XLVIII Panzer Corps was created and placed behind the Romanian army. But its Romanian tank division was judged by its German corps commander as unfit for action. The Romanians were barely trained, and 87 of their tanks were of pre-war Czech make and vintage, with only 20 German tanks (Mark III) with a limited capability against the Russian T-34. The German 22d Panzer Division, also part of the XLVIII Panzer Corps, was down to 33 tanks, less than a battalion. The corps was little more than a pennant on the situation map. There was not even enough strength to try to eliminate Soviet bridgeheads along the Middle Don.

Crisis and Catastrophe

On November 11 German signal intelligence produced an analysis of Russian radio traffic that partially raised the curtain that had so long concealed Russian reserves, capabilities, and intentions. Carefully, the report listed and located a very large number of newly-deployed major Russian formations. From this the analysts concluded that large enemy ground and air forces were about to launch a two-pronged major offensive across the Don River north of Stalingrad, and across the Volga south of the city. "Deployment has progressed far," the report said flatly.

In passing on this report, OKH intelligence analysts did not take seriously the threat of a Russian offensive south of Stalingrad. In spite of apparent deployment for two attacks, the imminent Russian operation was evaluated as only one significant offensive. In a report to the Army Chief of Staff, OKH intelligence evaluated Soviet intentions as follows: "They will attempt to cut the railway to Stalingrad. . . . Available forces are too weak for more far-reaching objectives."

When Halder read this intelligence report, on the morning of November 12, he immediately thought of the staff conference with List and Weichs and their staffs, in late July. He demanded a copy of the signal intelligence report which had been so cavalierly discounted. When he read this, he at once came to the conclusion that the OKH intelligence assessment was wrong, the signal intelligence warning was almost certainly correct.

Having reached this conclusion, Halder had two options. One was to report his assessment to Hitler, who was —after all—Commander in Chief of the Army, and await instructions from the Fuhrer. The other was to take the action he thought was necessary and then, in due course, to report this to Hitler. He did not hesitate. He took the second option.

Halder sent an urgent message for Field Marshal Erich von Manstein, recently appointed commander of Army Group North, to come to OKH headquarters at Vinnitsa, and he called for an immediate conference of the chiefs of the staff divisions of OKH.

The conference did not last long. It began, and ended, with a Halder monologue.

"Gentlemen: Our latest signal intelligence estimate suggests that the Russians have a capability of undertaking a major offensive across the Don River between Voronezh and Stalingrad, with a subsequent attempt at a double envelopment of the Sixth Army by a thrust across the Volga south of Stalingrad. OKH intelligence discounts this possibility, but reports it as one of several enemy capabilities.

"I have reviewed the signal intelligence report which was partially a basis of the OKH intelligence report. The signal intelligence report indicates that such a Soviet counteroffensive north, and also south, of Stalingrad is very likely. At this moment I am not prepared to evaluate either of these conflicting intelligence assessments. If OKH intelligence is right, we have little to be concerned about. If the signal intelligence report is right, Army Group A in general and the Sixth Army in particular, are in serious danger. If we prepare ourselves to meet the threat implied by signal intelligence, we could impair our ability to meet a threat to Army Group Center. If we do not prepare ourselves for the threat to the Stalingrad area, Army Group A could be faced with disaster.

"Accordingly, we have decided to create a new Army Group Don, to be responsible for the area south of Voronezh and north of Astrakhan-Rostov. This army group will be commanded by Field Marshal von Manstein, who is now en route to this headquarters. His command will include the following armies: German Sixth, Hungarian Second, Italian Eighth, Romanian Third, and Romanian Fourth. It will also include all reserves that can be assembled in the Kharkov and Rostov areas in the next two weeks. I estimate these to be about twelve divisions, to be organized and allocated as the new army group commander directs.

"Within twenty-four hours I expect from this staff the following:

"1. A revised estimate of the situation, considering the possibilities of both an enemy single envelopment and a double envelopment of the Stalingrad salient, and

"2. The concept of a counteroffensive plan designed to intercept, then encircle and destroy enemy forces attempting such a single or double envelopment."

The following afternoon General Halder, accompanied by Field Marshal von Manstein, received the staff briefing Halder had requested. When it was over, Halder turned to Manstein:

"My dear Field Marshal, we do not know that the

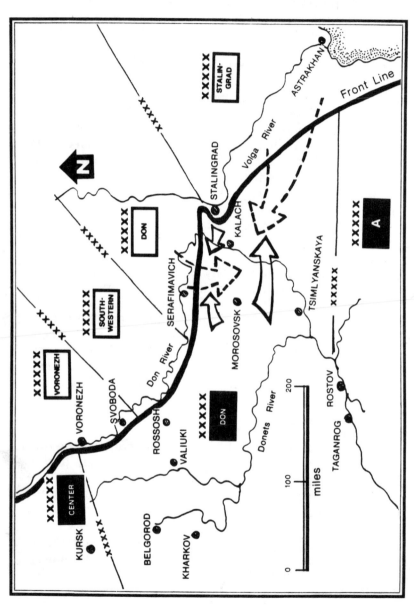

Soviet Counteroffensive, November 19, and Subsequent German Counterattacks

Soviets have the capability of performing, or even attempting, what has been suggested here. But it is a possibility. And if they could do anything like this the consequences to Germany could be disastrous.

"Our response to such a Soviet move, which has been suggested here by the OKH staff, is based upon a realistic assessment of the forces which will be available to you and to Army Group Don. We have perhaps ten days in which to prepare ourselves for this operation. This is not much time, but I believe it is enough. I will be closely in touch with you during the next ten days. Please feel free to call upon me, or any segment of the OKH staff, for whatever assistance you may need.

"Obviously there must be complete secrecy in the concentration and administration of your force, in the preparation for the operation, and in the pre-battle deployment. Use of radios must be kept to an absolute minimum; land lines and messengers must be used for routing communications. But of course, *Herr Feldmarschall*, I need not tell you about such things, other than—as now—to remind you to include security instructions in your very first conference with your staff and commanders."

Manstein's thin-lipped smile showed that he both understood, and did not resent, such elementary instructions from the Chief of Staff of OKH, who in 1939 had been his directly superior officer in the old OKH, and who now, though junior in rank, was nevertheless his operational superior. These two austere, brilliant, but otherwise very different men, knew each other well. Manstein was a Prussian aristocrat, Halder of middle-class Bavarian origin. But in 1942 they were perhaps the two most able and skillful members of that unique military monastic order, the German General Staff.

On November 19, two powerful Russian armies of the Don Army Group struck the two corps of the Third Romanian Army from bridgeheads they had retained west of the Don. The following day, two Soviet armies of the Stalingrad Army Group struck the Fourth Romanian Army south of Stalingrad.

In the northern pincer, the two attacking Russian armies had about 600 tanks. Opposing this Soviet armor was the Romanian division commanded by the former police chief of Bucharest, with its 21 German tanks and 87 obsolete Czech tanks. In reserve were two German armored divisions with 74 tanks. The southern spearhead was launched by two armies with about 400 tanks. They attacked two Romanian divisions which had no tanks, and later encountered a German motorized infantry division with 52 tanks.

Between these two large pincers, the German Sixth Army at Stalingrad had 180 tanks and assault guns. It was directly opposed by the Russian Sixty-fifth Army (48 tanks), Twenty-fourth Army, (about 150 tanks), and three additional armies, and by army group reserves that had among them seven tank brigades and two tank regiments, perhaps 200 tanks.

Finally, the Russians had in overall reserve the First Guards Mechanized Corps, with unknown tank strength, probably fewer than 100.

In summary, along the Stalingrad front, 300 kilometers south from Serafimovich through Stalingrad, the Germans had 314 tanks and assault guns (including the useless Romanian tank division). Overall Russian tank strength approached 1,500.

Finally, mention must be made of quality. By 1942, half of the tanks produced by Russia were T-34s. On the other hand, fewer than 100 of the German tanks were Mark IVs, the only ones able to do battle on even terms, or better, against the famous Russian T-34.

The Soviet *Stavka* and Soviet commanders were well aware of this force differential, and were quite confident that, despite the overall qualitative superiority of the Germans, they had assembled sufficient superiority in manpower and weapons to overcome the qualitative difference. Furthermore, the commanders of the two offensive thrusts—Konstantin Rokossovskiy, commanding the Don Army Group, and Andrei Yeremenko, of the Stalingrad

Army Group—were leaders who, in the process of survival of the fittest in the bitter crucible of defeat, had competence matching their German counterparts.

But there was one thing of which the Soviets were not aware. Concentrated in the Don River Bend, around the railroad center of Morozovsk, was the Task Force Kempf, consisting of the XLVIII Panzer Corps, the II SS Panzer Corps, each with four divisions, and the partially assembled XL Corps, with two recently-arrived infantry divisions, and one infantry and one panzergrenadier division en route by train. The XLVIII and II SS Panzer Corps each had three panzer divisions and an infantry division, and each corps had about 300 tanks. When assembled, the XL Corps would have about 60 tanks. Of the 660 tanks, more than half were Mark IVs.

The Soviet Don Army Group accomplished its initial breakthrough of the Romanian Third Army more rapidly and more easily than the *Stavka* had expected. On the morning of November 21, just as the assault south of Stalingrad began, T-34 tanks of the Don Army group advancing southward on both sides of the Don River were approaching Kalach. Unexpectedly, in mid-morning, the Soviets found themselves struck vigorously from the east and the west. The attackers from the east were units of the German Sixth Army, waiting in reserve for this eventuality. Those from the west were from the 13th Panzer Division of the XLVIII Corps. As the Soviet advance shuddered to a halt, panzer columns of the XLVIII Corps struck further to the rear, just south of the northern stretch of the Don River Bend. Behind the German panzers were Italian and Romanian infantry, quickly re-establishing their old positions along the Don. By nightfall the bulk of two Soviet armies, including more than 400 tanks, had been virtually isolated in the Don River Bend. One other army was reeling back northward from Kalach, east of the Don. By the morning of November 23 the German and Romanian positions along the Don, and between the Don and the Volga north of Stalingrad, had been re-established, and the XLVIII Panzer Corps was systematically whittling away at a pocket of 100,000 Russians and 400 tanks.

The Soviet thrust south of Stalingrad was defeated almost as quickly but not so dramatically. As the Soviets advanced west from their bridgeheads on the right bank of the Volga, they were met late on the 21st by the II SS Panzer Corps. There was a confused melee of intermingled tanks and infantry through the night, and in the morning of the 22d the first great tank battle of the war was fought between the Soviet Fifth Tank Army and the II SS Panzer Corps. The Soviets had a slight numerical superiority—about 400 tanks against about 300—and had an additional qualitative advantage of about 200 T-34s against 100 Mark IVs. But German tactical and technical skill more than made up for the numerical odds, and by nightfall the Soviets had lost 250 tanks and were in full retreat back to their bridgeheads.

On November 23 Hitler announced to the German people and to the world the great German victory at Stalingrad. He assured his countrymen that the war in the East had now been won. It would, perhaps, take until July of 1943 to consolidate the victory. But the fall of Stalin and Communism, he promised them, were now inevitable.

However, in July 1943 there was another great battle between Kursk and Kharkov. The XLVIII Panzer Corps and the II SS Panzer Corps, which had been primarily responsible for the victory at Stalingrad, again proved their superiority over their Russian foes. They almost broke through at Kursk. But they did not; there were too many Russians. Kursk-Kharkov was the turning point of the war, which ended in May 1945, with Soviet troops occupying Berlin.

Afterword

The above account diverges from the historical facts in only a few instances. The most important of these are the following.

The initial offensive of Army Group South was in fact watered down from the plan of Directive No. 41. The second step of the offensive was launched too far north—in other words, too close—to the first step, and as a result many Soviet units were in fact pushed back in retreat, rather than being encircled and destroyed. And the third step from Taganrog was never pursued with the vigor that was essential to complete the destruction of the Soviet forces west of the Don. Thus probably as many as 300,000 Soviet troops that should have been encircled were permitted to withdraw across the Don, and were available for subsequent operations.

In the account presented here, the Germans adhered faithfully to the strategic concept of Directive No. 41, in which the offensive toward Stalingrad was to provide a secure base for subsequent operations in the Caucasus, and no effort was to be made to occupy Stalingrad itself. In fact, however, in the middle of the offensive, Hitler issued Directive No. 45, which provided for simultaneous, diverging offensives to seize Stalingrad and to occupy the Caucasus. It was a dispute with Hitler over this dangerous strategy that led to the relief of General Franz Halder as Chief of Staff of OKH, and his replacement by General Kurt Zeitzler. In this account, since there was no basis for strategic dispute, it is assumed that Halder would have remained as chief of the German Army General Staff.

But what is clear from the analysis on which this revised version of history is based is that the Germans were already in a situation in which a victory over the USSR had become virtually impossible. This suggests that Stalingrad—as it actually occurred—was a less decisive battle than either Moscow or Kursk, even though it was the *symbolic* turning point of the war. At Moscow the Germans were stopped, and thus probably lost their one and only chance for victory in the East. At Kursk the Soviets were finally able to seize the initiative from the Germans, never to release it until the end of the war.

Had the Stalingrad-Caucasus Campaign actually been fought as planned, and thus as suggested in the above account, the second decisive battle would probably not have been fought at Kursk, and it might have taken place in 1944 instead of 1943. But, as a result of the Soviet victory at Moscow in 1941, it was inevitable that a battle like Kursk would take place in 1943 or 1944. Thus it seems reasonable to assume in this excursion from history, that hypothetical history and actual history could have converged on the decisive battlefield of Kursk.

CHAPTER VIII

The Rome Campaign

THE ITALIAN CAMPAIGN is often viewed as one of World
War II's "sideshows"—a grinding slugfest not at all romantic in the sense that the North African campaign was
romantic, a backwater front dwarfed by the immense
military efforts in Northwest Europe and along the Eastern Front. But Italy, for all its lack of the glamor and dash
associated with the war against Rommel in the Western
Desert or the gargantuan dimensions of the struggle in
Northwest and Eastern Europe, was something more than
a sideshow, for it was in Italy that, by hard fighting in the
most adverse terrain and weather conditions, the Western
Allies first breached the defenses of Hitler's *Festung
Europa* and inflicted a painful—perhaps irreparable—
defeat on the German army.

Allied victory in North Africa, sealed by the German
defeat in the Battle of Tunisia (May 3–13, 1943), was a
prerequisite to the amphibious invasion of Sicily (July–
August 1943), itself a springboard to the Italian mainland.
The capture of Sicily, completed on August 17, 1943,
opened the Mediterranean as an Allied sea route and provided the Allies with airfields in easy flying distance of
Calabria, Naples, and the entire South Italy operational
area. The Allied air forces were now in a fair position to
contest the Luftwaffe for control of the airspace over
southern Italy. Field Marshal Albert Kesselring, the Ger-

man commander in southern Italy, correctly anticipated an early invasion of the Italian mainland.

Meantime, in July, Benito Mussolini, the rotund, almost comic embodiment of Italian fascism, had been driven from power by a war-weary Italian nation. His successor, Marshal Pietro Badoglio, began secretly to negotiate an armistice with the Allies. The armistice was signed on September 3, the parties agreeing that its terms would become effective on September 8, when it would be published.

The Salerno Campaign

Simultaneously with the Italian defection, British troops landed in Calabria, at the toe of the Italian boot (September 3), and began to advance northwest; their objective was Naples. Kesselring, expecting the main Allied attack in the Naples-Salerno area, held back his main forces and carried out a delaying action in the south. Again, he anticipated correctly. The main Allied attack, made by Lieutenant General Mark Clark's US Fifth Army, was an assault landing at the Gulf of Salerno on September 9. On the same day a British division was landed at Taranto on the heel of the Italian boot.

The fighting at the Salerno beachhead lasted eight days. The landing itself was virtually unopposed, but Clark's men quickly encountered stiff resistance from German defenders deployed in mobile defense. Four shallow beachheads had been established by September 12, when the Germans launched a massive counterattack that penetrated the beachhead perimeter in the Allied center. The Allied toehold was seriously imperilled, but continuous naval gunfire and the beginnings of effective Allied close air support, combined with stubborn resistance by the American and British ground units, frustrated the German plans on September 15.

Kesselring now recognized that the Fifth Army beachhead at Salerno was firmly established, and that further attempts to drive the Allies into the sea would be impracticable. With the British Eighth Army moving up from the south and posing a threat to the rear of the German forces ringing the beachhead, he ordered a withdrawal northward beginning on September 16. The Germans withdrew slowly, launching sharp local attacks to deceive the Allies and, later, fighting effective delaying actions in the hills beyond the beachhead. The withdrawal yielded the port of Naples to the Fifth Army on October 6 but the Allied advance was halted along the line of the Volturno River. There the Germans constructed a strong defensive line, capitalizing on the twin advantages of terrain and the worsening October weather (heavy rains left the river in flood condition). Nevertheless, on October 12, all six divisions of the Fifth Army attacked and breached the line of the lower Volturno; on October 14 yet another German withdrawal began.

The next objective for the Fifth Army was a deep German defensive zone south and east of Cassino, covering the approaches to the Liri and Sacco river valleys, the historical routes to Rome from southern Italy. The German Barbara Line, which the Allies first encountered, improved the already formidable combination of rugged hills, deep ravines, canals, and mountains between the Volturno and Garigliano Rivers. This covering zone was planned by the Germans as a series of delaying positions, to be held successively while the even stronger Bernhardt Line was completed. This defensive zone was based on a series of rugged peaks east of the deep, canyon-like Garigliano Valley.

The Volturno Campaign

On October 15 the Fifth Army moved against the Barbara Line, beginning the long, hard process of battering its way through the succession of German lines below Rome. Kesselring hoped that winter weather, rugged terrain, strong fortifications, and German skill and determination could stall the Allies indefinitely.

The advance from the Volturno bridgeheads was painfully slow; Kesselring's expectations seemed justified. The Germans defending the Barbara Line withdrew in a series of classic delaying actions, relying on demolitions, roadblocks, mines, self-propelled guns, artillery, and rear-guard elements to slow the Allied advance.

By late October, however, the Barbara Line had been overrun, and the Fifth Army prepared to assault the stronger Bernhardt Line defenses. A few minor successes were achieved in early November, but the offensive soon bogged down before the key German defensive positions on Monte Camino, Monte Maggiore, and Monte de la Defensa. To add to the travail of the troops, the weather worsened; the winter cold was now accompanied by constant torrential rains. On November 15 General Clark concluded that the advance could not be continued. His men were exhausted, and unit strengths and combat effectiveness were sapped by casualties. The Fifth Army at this point needed rest and replacements. A brief period of static warfare ensued, the armies content to patrol and exchange artillery fire. The delay before the Bernhardt Line defenses, however, allowed Kesselring time to put the finishing touches on yet another deep defensive zone—the Gustav Line.

In early December the revitalized Fifth Army renewed the assault, overrunning the mountain strongholds of the Bernhardt Line. The 15th Panzer Grenadier Division, the mainstay of the Bernhardt Line defense, was forced to withdraw, since its communications with Cassino and the Garigliano area were threatened by the Allied advance. The Germans evacuated the Bernhardt Line and occupied prepared positions in the Gustav Line.

The fighting from the Salerno beachheads to the Gustav Line had been bitter. The Germans gave ground only grudgingly and extracted a blood toll for every meter advanced; the bad weather and difficult mountainous terrain had added to the severity of the battle. But this campaign had merely been prelude to the battle for the Gustav Line. The Barbara and Bernhardt Lines had been only covering positions—the glacis of the main Gustav Line position which Kesselring meant to hold at all costs.

In Kesselring's scheme of defending the Italian peninsula south of Rome from successive lines of strategic fortified barriers, the Gustav Line was the key. It extended completely across the peninsula from Minturno to Ortona and was solidly based on the rugged terrain of the Apennine Mountains. On the Fifth Army front the broad, swampy Garigliano River and the swift-flowing Rapido formed a moat for the German defenses echeloned in depth on the mountains behind. Here the Allies had but two routes of advance to Rome and beyond: the old west coast road (Highway No. 7, the Roman Appian Way), which followed the narrow coastal plain through Minturno, Gaeta, and Terracina before debouching onto the Pontine Marshes and continuing across the Alban Hills to Rome, and the equally ancient Highway No. 6 (the Romans' Latin Way), which cut through the Apennine massif beginning at Cassino and followed the Liri-Sacco River Valley to Valmontone and Rome. From time immemorial these roads had been the only practicable military approaches to Rome from the south, and numerous battles had been fought for their possession.

Kesselring's engineers improved on these terrain advantages by constructing a powerful, continuous fortified zone several miles deep. Its chief features were pillboxes, bunkers, minefields, and wire obstacles. In addition, work was begun (albeit in a leisurely fashion) on yet two more lines—the Hitler Line, running inland from Terracina, which was meant to reinforce the Gustav Line, and the "C" Line (often erroneously called the Caesar Line by the Allies and Western historians), which covered the Alban Hills south of Rome.

The Anzio Campaign

Faced with this formidable combination of rugged terrain, restricted axes of advance, and deeply-echeloned fortifications, and mindful of the slow and arduous course of the Volturno-Winter Line campaign just ended, the chief Allied military leaders devised a strategy to outflank the German defenses. The new plan centered on a daring amphibious landing about 160 kilometers behind the Gustav Line defenses at the small, twin resort towns of Anzio and Nettuno, just 50 kilometers south of Rome. The Fifth Army's VI Corps, which consisted of the British 1st and US 3d and 45th Infantry Divisions plus two-thirds of the US 1st Armored Division, and other units, was selected for the mission. The objective of this force was to land at Anzio-Nettuno and move rapidly inland to the Alban Hills to block the enemy's lines of communications along Highways 7 and 6. It was hoped that such a move would threaten the rear of the German troops holding the Gustav Line and force them to withdraw up the Liri Valley.

The initial Anzio-Nettuno landing was made on January 22, 1944, by the British 1st and US 3d Divisions. The landing achieved surprise and consequently was virtually unopposed by the scattered German units in the beachhead area. However, rather than driving inland to the commanding mass of the Alban Hills while German resistance was weak, Major General John P. Lucas, commanding the VI Corps, elected to consolidate the beachhead and await reinforcements. Given time to recover, the Germans rushed their own reinforcements to the beachhead area and prepared to resist seriously any further Allied advances.

The German Fourteenth Army commander, General Eberhard von Mackensen, responsible for defending the Anzio area, rapidly built up a strong force from units of his own and the Tenth Army. On the Allied side, elements of the 1st Armored and 45th Divisions were landed beginning on January 25, and General Lucas began finally to advance the beachhead line. However, in heavy fighting during January 25–February 2, the VI Corps was unable to break through the German defenses. On February 2, the beachhead was just 30 kilometers wide at its base and about 15 kilometers deep. The Germans still held all the commanding ground in the vicinity of the beachhead—ground that provided magnificent observation of the entire beachhead area for their artillery.

At this juncture Mackensen launched limited objective attacks to weaken the VI Corps and pave the way for a massive future offensive planned to annihilate the beachhead. These limited objective attacks began on February 3 and continued without let-up until February 12. Allied counterattacks achieved little, and, by the end of this phase, many Allied units were depleted and exhausted.

Mackensen had achieved the preconditions necessary for the planned offensive to eliminate the beachhead. His force now consisted of nine divisions and two independent infantry brigades; opposing this was an Allied force of four reinforced divisions. His plan was to split the beachhead and capture the port of Anzio. The main effort would be along the Anzio-Albano road, or the "Bowling Alley," held by the US 45th Infantry Division. An attacking force of almost 50,000 men and 452 guns was massed along a narrow front for this purpose.

The "Bowling Alley" offensive was launched at 6:30 A.M. on February 16, 1944, following a short, intensive artillery preparation. The Germans achieved tactical surprise and by 10:40 had driven a wedge almost two-and-one-half kilometers deep into the center of the 45th Division. However, the Americans were soon provided with massive close air support and heavy naval gunfire support, which slowed, but did not stop, the German assault.

During the next three days of intense fighting the Germans inched ahead, but by evening of February 19 they had been completely halted at the 45th Division's final defensive line. Having advanced about six kilometers since the beginning of the engagement, the German Fourteenth Army ceased its attack.

The "Bowling Alley" offensive had come within an ace of success, but German skill and aggressiveness had been more than met by Allied stubbornness and firepower. Still seeking a decision, the Germans shifted their effort against the 45th Division's right neighbor, the 3d Division. Fresh German units assaulted this sector of the beachhead perimeter from February 29 to March 3 but sustained heavy casualties and were unable to budge the Americans. Following this failure the Germans went over to the defensive.

Stalemate

From March 3 to May 23 the beachhead area was relatively quiet. The great offensives of February were succeeded by static warfare. The Germans were incapable of denting the complex fortified defenses of the beachhead perimeter, and the Allies, for their part, lacked the men and materiel to push the Germans out of their trenches ringing the beachhead.

Meantime, on the Gustav Line front, the Allies achieved some minor successes. The Fifth Army, from January to March, battered against the German defenses along the Garigliano River, and at the south end of the Liri Valley ("the gateway to Rome"). The British X Corps crossed the Garigliano and established a bridgehead along the slopes of the mountains overlooking Minturno (January 17–20). However, further inland, near the junction of the Garigliano, Liri, and Rapido Rivers, the British 46th Division failed in its attempt to gain Sant' Ambrogio and the high ground beyond, and the US 36th Division, attempting an assault crossing of the Rapido below Monte Cassino, was repelled with nearly 2,000 casualties (January 20–22). Other attacks made in the Monte Cassino area by the US II Corps pushed up to the northern edge of the Cassino massif but stalled a few kilometers short of Highway 6 in the Liri Valley (February 1–14).

The failure of the Cassino assaults effectively ended the Fifth Army's winter offensive. The Garigliano front quieted, and the Fifth Army's boundary with the British Eighth Army was shifted southwestward toward the coast as the Eighth Army assumed responsibility for undertaking a new offensive in the Cassino sector. The Fifth Army, in the meantime, began the build-up for renewed offensive operations in the spring, when improved weather conditions would facilitate mobility.

The "Diadem" Plan

The planned Allied spring offensive, code-named "Diadem," had three main objectives: to breach the Gustav Line in the Aurunci Mountains beyond the Garigliano and at Cassino (where the Eighth Army had failed to make appreciable progress); to overrun the Hitler Line, then being constructed behind the Gustav Line in the Liri Valley; and to break out of the Anzio beachhead and link up to cut off the German Tenth Army.

On the main Fifth Army front along the lower Garigliano the fresh US II Corps (85th and 88th Divisions) was near the Tyrrhenian Sea, while the French Expeditionary Corps (FEC) was on its right, linking with the Eighth Army near the southern approaches to the Liri Valley. The VI Corps at Anzio had been heavily reinforced and was poised for the breakout attempt.

The initial Fifth Army attack plan was for the US II Corps and the FEC on May 12 to thrust through the Aurunci Mountains that dominated the Garigliano bridgehead. The II Corps was to drive through the hills south of Minturno, while the FEC seized Monte Majo and the Ausonia Defile. Aided by elements of II Corps at Monte La Civita and Spigno, the FEC was then to advance across the Ausonia Valley into the Petrella Massif. Then both corps would advance northwest to meet elements of the VI Corps, which, eleven days after the II Corps attack, would be starting its breakout from the Anzio beachhead.

The Anzio breakout scheme, code-named "Buffalo," contemplated much more than an irruption from the beachhead and link-up between the Fifth Army's separated corps. It aimed besides to destroy the right wing of the German Tenth Army by cutting its line of retreat from the Cassino front at Valmontone, a mountainside town just under 20 miles from the VI Corps' beachhead perimeter that sat astride Route 6, the ancient Rome-Cassino highway and main supply line for the Germans in the Garigliano-Cassino sector. As General Sir Harold Alexander, Supreme Allied Commander in the Mediterranean, envisioned the operation, this move would be the key to the decisive defeat of the German armies in the battle for Rome. While the II Corps, the FEC, and the Eighth Army battered the Germans in the south and drove them headlong over the mountains, the VI Corps, having thrust aside the weaker Fourteenth Army, would complete the victory by blocking Route 6 and creating the conditions for the annihilation of the Tenth Army's right wing. If everything went according to plan, the Germans would have great difficulty in recovering from the blow in order to establish themselves on a new defense line further north, as they had done so many times in the past. Alexander's "one-two punch," as he described it, would eliminate the bulk of organized German resistance below Rome and, if properly followed up, could even lead to total German collapse in Italy. And, since the operation would nearly coincide with "Overlord," the great Allied invasion of northwestern France slated for early June, its ramifications would be doubly profound.

General Clark and Valmontone

A major actor in the forthcoming drama would be Mark Clark, the mercurial Fifth Army commander. Clark was suspicious of British intentions, having been embarrassed once already when the Anzio beachhead operation failed to deliver Rome and instead degenerated into a bloody stalemate, and he doubted now that Alexander's plan would achieve the lofty goals predicted for it. He was especially concerned by the role assigned his VI Corps at Anzio. To gain Valmontone the corps would first have to make a breakout to the east, through the formidable fortifications of the German Fourteenth Army, and would then have to continue to the east, leaving most of the

Fourteenth Army in its Alban Hill entrenchments, over-looking the flank of the VI Corps.

As Clark and Major General Alfred M. Gruenther, Chief of Staff of the Fifth Army, looked at the map in the operations room, Clark remarked that this would, in effect, be a flank march in front of an entrenched enemy. A young lieutenant colonel standing behind the two generals, who had recently been an instructor in military history at West Point, remarked:

"Napoleon said, 'Never make a flank march before an army in position, above all when it occupies the heights at the foot of which you must defile.' "

Clark turned quickly to look at the younger officer.

"Exactly, that's what bothers me about this move. As I recall, Frederick the Great had an army shattered at Kolin when he attempted such a maneuver against the Austrians. We could be giving the Germans an opportunity to strike the flank and rear of the VI Corps, cutting it off from its base of supply. The risks are substantial." He turned to his Chief of Staff. "What do you think about that, Alfie?"

Gruenther had a reputation for having the keenest bridge-playing and staff-analysis mind in the Army. With a typical tight-lipped smile, he responded: "General Clark, I don't recall verbatim the maxims of Napoleon, like our young friend here. But I remember that he also said: 'One can only maneuver around a fixed point.' The VI Corps would not be making a flank march in front of an entrenched enemy. It would be exploiting a break-through, in order to envelop the flank of the Fourteenth Army. The enemy entrenchments overlook our own en-trenchments, which have been strong enough to repulse every past effort he has made to push us off the beach-head. The left flank units of the VI Corps will be carrying out secondary attacks all along that front, to pin the Four-teenth Army in its positions. I see no danger to flank and rear. On the contrary, we will have created the kind of opportunity for a strategic envelopment that Napoleon would have jumped at."

Gruenther walked up to the map.

"The VI Corps, built up to a strength of two British and five-and-one-half US divisions, should have no trouble in fulfilling the role outlined for it. Moreover, the 85th and 88th divisions of the II Corps, advancing across the Pontine Marshes toward the beachhead from the south, will provide a further measure of security for the beachhead by filling the place of divisions drawn off for the stroke at Valmontone."

Clark thought for a moment. There might be a more direct route to Rome—the prize Clark yearned for, and which he considered the Fifth Army had earned. But the proper object of Diadem, as Alexander had pointed out, was the destruction of German divisions. It was obvious that Gruenther was right. The maneuver should smash the Fourteenth Army. Furthermore, it was obvious that Rome would fall into his hands ultimately when the German line of retreat along Route 6 was blocked. So, despite his misgivings, he said:

"Alfie, you are right. We shall follow the Army Group directive to the letter. The VI Corps breakout will be pointed toward Valmontone."

Initiation of "Diadem"

On May 11, at precisely 11:00 P.M., 1,660 guns on the Fifth and Eighth Armies' front opened fire on the Gustav Line defenses, heralding Diadem's opening phase. A short while later, on the main Fifth Army front, the II Corps and FEC attacked. As this attack progressed, the Eighth Army offensive got underway, with British and Indian troops thrusting across the Rapido, and Polish infantry struggling to overcome the defense of German paratroopers at Cassino. At Anzio the VI Corps artillery joined in the bombardment, but no attacks were launched from the beachhead line.

The II Corps and FEC attacks met with success, as both American divisions and the French troops broke through the German defenses and pushed on, the battered German

XIV Panzer Corps withdrawing before them. On the French right the Eighth Army made steady, if unspectacular progress into the Liri Valley. The Germans, alarmed by the prospect of a collapse along the Gustav Line, began to milk the Fourteenth Army at the quiescent beachhead for troops to stem the Allied tide in the south.

D-Day for the planned breakout from the beachhead was set for May 23. The main effort was to be made by the US 3d Infantry and 1st Armored Divisions. The 3d Infantry Division was to strike northeastward toward Cisterna into the zone of the LXXVI Panzer Corps. The 1st Armored Division was to make a breakthrough in coordination with the 3d and exploit the breakthrough by thrusting north toward Velletri and the Alban Hills, then continuing on toward Valmontone and Route 6. Partly to deceive the Germans as to Allied intentions, and partly to tie down the I Parachute Corps and prevent shifting of German units to assist the LXXVI Corps, the two British divisions on the left of the beachhead front were to undertake a simultaneous holding attack.

Breakout from Anzio

At 6:30 A.M. on May 23, after an unusually heavy artillery bombardment, the Allied units began to attack. Against bitter German opposition the 3d Division advanced approximately half way to Cisterna on the first day. The German defense, by elements of the 362d Infantry Division, which garrisoned the town, and part of the 1028th Panzer Grenadier Regiment, continued strong during the 24th. However, as Allied pressure continued in the Cisterna area, German resistance collapsed. On the 25th, the 3d Division seized Cisterna and Cori, some five miles beyond. On the left of the 3d Division, the 1st Armored Division advanced with two combat commands abreast. Combat Command A (CCA) on the left made good progress. By dusk on May 23 CCA had advanced about 500 yards beyond the embankment of the Rome-Naples railway that for so long had delimited the German for-

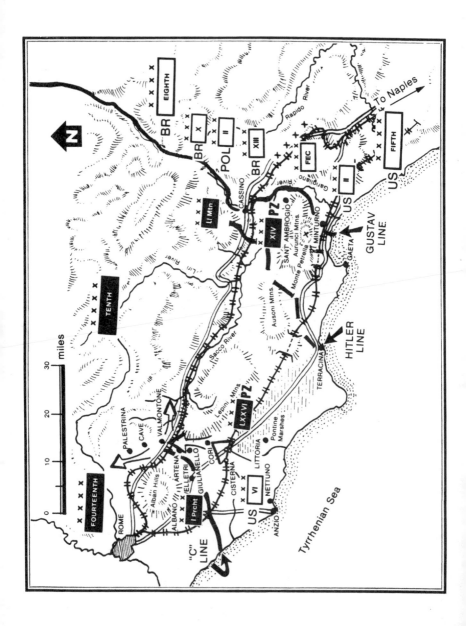

ward line of resistance at Anzio. Combat Command B (CCB) on the right had considerable difficulty at first. Its attack bogged down in unmarked American mine fields laid down earlier as part of the Anzio defenses, and its units then suffered severely from direct antitank gunfire from the German defenders. The 1st Armored renewed its attack on the 24th. By the end of the day its units, ranging ahead of the 3d Division infantry, had cut off Cisterna from the rear and forced the evacuation of Cori. By the end of May 25 the division had reached the edge of the enemy's main defenses at Velletri.

On May 26 the VI Corps continued to drive north and northeast in exploitation of the breakthrough achieved in the attack from the beachhead. The 1st Armored Division's CCA and the US 34th Infantry Division (which had been in corps reserve at the beachhead) combined to mask the remnants of the LXXVI Panzer Corps that had retreated to the fortified "C" Line in the Alban Hills after the Cisterna debacle. On the CCA's left, the US 45th and British 1st and 5th Infantry divisions demonstrated briskly against the German I Parachute Corps, effectively preventing its intervention in the coming decisive battle. In the meantime, the Valmontone strike force, consisting of the 1st Armored Division's CCB, the 3d Division, and the Canadian-American 1st Special Service Force (1st SSF—elite motorized infantry), concentrated for its attack in the rolling terrain between Cori and Giulianello. The VI Corps artillery began to displace forward to support the forthcoming attack, and Allied fighters and fighter-bombers ranged the skies overhead, attacking disorganized German formations with impunity.

Viewed from the German side, the situation could hardly have been worse. The breakout offensive had wrecked the 362d Infantry Division and severely battered other LXXI Corps units. To form a local reserve and buttress the C line defense, the I Parachute Corps had had to release mobile and ad hoc combat units to its sister corps. Since the Fourteenth Army itself had no reserve (in fact, it had been milked of combat formations to oppose the Allied drive in the south), Kesselring's Army Group C headquarters on the 23d ordered the Hermann Goering Panzer Parachute Division (then stationed at Pisa preparatory to a move to France) to rush south to reinforce the LXXVI Corps at Valmontone by the morning of May 26.

The Battle for Valmontone

In fact the German projection that the Hermann Goering Division would arrive at Valmontone on the morning of May 26 was too optimistic. The first and only unit of the division to arrive that day was the highly mobile but lightly equipped Panzer Reconnaissance Battalion. The rest of the division, harried continually by Allied fighter-bombers and plagued by mechanical difficulties, was strung out for dozens of miles along the northern approaches to the Tiber bridges. Of the division's 60 Pz. Kpfw. IV tanks, not more than 11 actually passed the Tiber on their way to the front; the rest were disabled. One-third of its 75mm self-propelled antitank guns and 20% of its heavy weapons also were lost, although personnel losses were light.

On the southern front, meanwhile, the II Corps and FEC offensive continued, the leading elements of the II Corps making contact with the beachhead forces in the Pontine Marshes below Anzio on May 25. The badly damaged German divisions opposing the II Corps advance fell back across the Lepini Mountains toward Route 6 and Valmontone. The 85th and 88th divisions and the US 36th Infantry Division, which had been transported to the beachhead by sea, were now available to add their weight to the Fifth Army forces ranged against the German fortifications in the Alban Hills. If Clark had any lingering doubts about the security of the beachhead and his left flank and rear, they were now allayed by the tremendous beachhead build-up made possible by the II Corps breakthroughs at the Gustav and Hitler Lines.

Everything was now set for the important advance on

the Valmontone Gap. Major General Lucian K. Truscott, Jr., the VI Corps commander, took personal charge of the formations concentrating for the advance near Artena, some three miles south of Valmontone. At 6:00 A.M. on May 27 the advance began, with the 1st Armored Division on the left, the 3d Division in the center, and the 1st SSF on the right. Initially, German opposition was light, being confined to long range artillery and *Nebelwerfer* (artillery rocket) fire from the flanking Alban Hills. The VI Corps artillery and Allied fighter-bombers soon suppressed this fire, however.

Truscott did not know the strength or disposition of the enemy in the Artena-Valmontone sector, but 1st Armored and 3d Division patrols had clashed with Germans in scout cars and half-tracks at Artena on the 26th and chased them a mile north of the town to Artena Railway Station, where the Germans organized a defensive line along a railway embankment. Truscott knew from prisoner-of-war reports that these Germans (who had shown more fight than the disorganized remnants of the beachhead defenders) were from the Panzer Recon Battalion of the Hermann Goering Panzer Parachute Division, a formation not previously reported in his sector but known to be moving toward the Valmontone Gap; so he judged that this division would constitute his primary opposition. Other German units—including a hodge-podge of GHQ flak and antitank units, plus the shattered remnants of the 715th Infantry Division from the German left flank of the beachhead, and a few "Alarm" (Field Replacement) battalions—might be expected to join in the resistance. "Not a very impressive collection," observed General Truscott, who prepared to oversee the operation from a command post near Artena. "The Hermann Goerings will undoubtedly fight hard, but the rest—well, they're already broken. We must not allow them to rally on the Hermann Goerings."

Speed was of the essence, but the VI Corps force had some three miles of difficult terrain to traverse before it punched through the Valmontone Gap. From Artena, following the axis of the Artena-Valmontone road almost due north, the first obstacle was the railway embankment at Artena station. Beyond the embankment, which skirted the Alban Hills on the left and thereby enveloped the left flank of the advance, the road crossed rolling countryside, the ground rising continuously toward Valmontone. On the left of the road, nearest the Alban Hills, the terrain was rutted by numerous gullies and valleys; on the right of the road the terrain was relatively flat and open. Much of this tract was cultivated, and there were numerous vineyards and farms. Nearing Valmontone, there was a large, solidly-constructed villa and beyond this, another tall railway embankment.

This terrain offered many advantages for the defender, not least of which were the two railway embankments—considerable obstacles as the Germans at Anzio had proved when they based their defense on the embankment connecting Campoleone and Cisterna. On the other hand, the wide expanse of flat, featureless terrain on the American right offered a natural avenue of approach for armor and mechanized infantry.

A reinforced division, defending this ground from fortifications, might have delayed the VI Corps long enough to permit the escape of the Tenth Army's right wing, but, on May 27, the Germans did not have the resources to man the Gap. Furthermore, the C line—which ought to have been extended eastward to cover the approaches to the Gap—ran instead only as far as Labico, some two miles northwest of Valmontone. The Gap itself was covered only by "emergency fortifications," mines, wire obstacles, and a few firing trenches. The Germans' position was nearly hopeless, but if they could buy time by bluff and fierce resistance, the next day might bring the rest of the Hermann Goering Division and, possibly, other units to their support. As yet, the I Parachute Corps had not been seriously pressed; solidly based on the C Line, it might be able to provide units to sustain the Valmontone flank.

But this was the most optimistic case, and the course of

events proved rapidly that it was not to be. Truscott had over 300 tanks advancing up the Valmontone Corridor. Against this force the Germans mustered just four Tiger (Pz. Kpfw. VI) tanks of the 508th Panzer Battalion, five "Elefant" (heavily armored tank destroyers) of the 653d Antitank Battalion, and 23 Italian assault guns of the Parachute Assault Gun Battalion, XI Flak Corps. The American force numbered well over 30,000 men; the Germans by tremendous exertion had scraped together about 4,000 defenders, many of whom were demoralized. They fought in small combat teams under junior officers. Coordination of the defense was impossible because of the length of the front (about four miles) and because Allied air and artillery attacks knocked out wire communications almost immediately when the attack began.

From about 7:00 A.M. to 9:00 A.M. German resistance was strong and tenacious. The German armor, roaming behind the Artena railway embankment from fire position to fire position was particularly troublesome. It slowed but did not stop the advance. Penetrations of the German line at the embankment were made beginning about 9:00 A.M., and from that point German resistance began to wane. One by one the German combat teams were "pocketed" and compelled to surrender. By 10:00 A.M. strongpoints at Artena Station and the villa below Valmontone had been reduced, and penetration became breakthrough. The German infantry that remained attempted to escape the trap on foot, but they were rapidly overtaken by American armor and mechanized infantry. Hundreds surrendered, but many of the elite Hermann Goering paratroopers chose death instead. Colonel Hamilton Howze, leading a 1st Armored Division task force at Valmontone, marveled at their bravery but concluded sadly that what followed was literally a massacre. It was the third time in the course of the war that the Hermann Goering Division had been "destroyed."*

*The BBC announced the division's destruction "with particular satisfaction" on its evening broadcasts of the 27th.

End of the Rome Campaign

By 12:00 American armor was mopping up in the Valmontone-Palestrina area, and the battle for Route 6 had ended. Truscott now pivoted the bulk of his force on his right flank and assumed a broad blocking position across Route 6. Like hunters in a blind, the VI Corps Valmontone force was now positioned to intercept the retreat of the Tenth Army's right wing, then being driven up the Liri Valley by British and FEC "beaters." The 34th and 36th US Divisions passed across the rear of Truscott's force, penetrating the mountains in the direction of Palestrina and Cave to cut off German groups attempting to retreat on the trails and paths that crisscrossed the high ground beyond. Following these forces on the 28th, dog-tired soldiers of the 85th and 88th Divisions began the systematic envelopment of German forces remaining in the C Line defenses west of Lariano.

The "one-two punch" envisioned by Alexander's brilliant plan began to bear fruit beginning on the afternoon of the 27th, as tired and dazed remnants of the German XIV Panzer Corps, which had opposed the advance of the II Corps and FEC on the southern front and had attempted to escape without transport across the Lepini Mountains, began to come in. Truscott's men collected masses of prisoners, men identified as belonging to four divisions: the 29th Panzer Grenadier, the 94th Infantry, the 15th Panzer Grenadier, and the 26th Panzer. Not normally one to show emotion, Truscott beamed when his staff announced that the day's haul of Germans exceeded 18,000. The Fifth Army's POW cages were swollen further in the days following, when prisoners identified as belonging to the Tenth Army's LI Mountain Corps were brought in.

There was very little fight left in the Germans below Rome now. The Fourteenth Army's I Parachute Corps, which had been largely a spectator to the debacle that had befallen its sister corps, conceded Rome on the 28th (the city was declared an open city to prevent its destruction) and retreated posthaste north of the Tiber. Skillfully extricating itself from the Allied pursuit, it joined with the remains of the Hermann Goering Division and fell back across the Campagna to Viterbo, then Siena and Florence. On its way it abandoned much of its armor and heavy equipment. In Berlin, meanwhile, Hitler, in violent rage, ordered German forces in Italy to "stand fast and oppose the enemy wherever he may show himself." Strategic reserves, which the Germans could ill afford to divert to Italy, were dispatched to Kesselring from France and the Balkans. Almost as an afterthought, but not unexpected in the circumstances, on June 2, 1944 Kesselring was sacked and ordered to report to Berlin. On June 6 Allied forces began landing in Normandy; the German house of cards began to totter.

In the last analysis, the Allied victory in the Rome campaign decidedly shortened the war. One German army was destroyed and another rendered virtually impotent. The Germans subsequently found it impossible to stand anywhere south of the Alps. German casualties exceeded 90,000, of whom at least 60,000 were prisoners. Their material losses included 500 artillery pieces and 200 tanks. The cost of the operation to the Allied 15th Army Group was about 25,000 men.

The End in Italy

Importantly too, Rome had shown just how effective air and ground forces' superiority, combined with bold tactics, could be. The long winter's stalemate had given way to a spring and summer of mobile warfare in which superior Allied resources could be utilized to their fullest to capitalize on the victory. Alexander and Clark—two unlikely candidates—emerged as "masters of mobile warfare." The British and American press, so long at loggerheads, were agreed on this at least.

Kesselring's successor in Italy was Generaloberst Heinrich Gottfried von Vietinghoff, formerly the commander of the Tenth Army. The remnants of the two German armies were integrated with the strategic reserves Hitler had released and a mixed German-Italian formation called the Ligurian Army commanded by Italian Marshal Rudolfo Graziani. In early August, when the Allied pursuit from Rome reached the foothills of the Alps, the Germans prepared a last-ditch defense of the mountain passes leading to southeastern France, southwestern Austria, and Yugoslavia. There had been scant time to construct fortifications, but in the east at least, along the Adriatic front, the Germans were able to occupy the still formidable trace of Austrian fortifications left over from World War I. From east to west Vietinghoff had the Tenth Army in the Udine and the eastern slopes of the Dolomites, the Fourteenth Army in the Lake Garda region, and the Ligurian Army in the Milanese.

The new German defensive alignment presented Allied planners with several problems, for, although the front was definitely widened, it could also be held by fewer troops, since routes through the Alps were few and narrow and tortuous. The Allied solution was to maintain the relentless pressure they had been applying since May, but also to envelop the German defenses in the west from France. In Operation "Dragoon," launched on August 15, Fifth Army divisions invaded France via the Riviera and, pressing inland, entered Italy through the back door of the Haute-Savoie passes. The hybrid Ligurian Army was trapped between two powerful forces and compelled to surrender. By mid-September the British Eighth Army in the east had forced the Ljubljana Gap in Yugoslavia and was poised to break out of the mountains into the mid-Danube region of eastern Europe. And British and US troops made amphibious landings at Trieste and along the Istrian coast in landing craft made available by "Dragoon's" success. The Fifth Army, which had been less successful in the Lake Garda region, shifted its axis of advance to follow the British on the end around through the Ljubljana Gap, then burst into open country from the Loibl Pass. Moving west behind a screen provided by the British, Fifth Army units successfully enveloped the Germans remaining in the Alpine redoubts north of Lake Garda.

Having completed the destruction of German forces in Italy, the Allied 15th Army Group next moved to occupy Yugoslavia and parts of Austria. Operating freely in the rear of German armies facing the Russians, the Allied forces were able to move swiftly. German resistance was negligible, since from September on the Germans were more concerned with moving north and west away from the Russians and the 15th Army Group. On September 25 British and Russian soldiers met at Gyor on the Danube; that day Mark Clark's Fifth Army entered Vienna in triumph.

Afterword

Clark's concept of the Fifth Army's role in the Rome campaign differed materially from that of Alexander. Whereas Alexander emphasized the primacy of the Eighth Army's drive up Highway 6 in the Liri Valley and sketched a secondary role for the Fifth army, Clark saw greater possibilities for his divisions, chief among them the capture of Rome. This chapter has outlined the course the Italian campaign might have taken had Clark followed Alexander's army group directive for Diadem to the letter. In fact, Clark decided to pay lip service to Alexander's plan, and, instead of directing his main thrust from the beachhead against Valmontone, chose instead to attack northward against the C Line defenses in the Alban Hills with the mass of the VI Corps. The bulk of five divisions, the 1st and 5th British, and the 45th, 1st Armored, and 34th US, butted their way slowly through the C Line defenses from May 25 through June 3, 1944; only one division, the US 3d Infantry Division, reinforced by the 1st SSF and an armored task force from the 1st Armored Division, was assigned the task of cutting Route 6 at Valmontone.

The operation to cut Route 6 was mounted on June 1—not May 27 as it might have been. And since five days had been lost to the VI Corps in fruitless attacks against the C Line positions, the full Hermann Goering Division was in position to dispute the Valmontone corridor of June 1. It took two days of hard fighting to drive the Hermann Goering Division beyond Valmontone; meanwhile the imperiled left wing of the German Fourteenth Army and right wing of the German Tenth Army escaped the destruction that probably awaited them had Alexander's plan been fully implemented. Kesselring was able to use the battered but still largely intact XIV Panzer Corps to anchor his army group's right flank south of Florence, and the Italian campaign again became an affair of Allied head-butting against skillfully defended German fortifications. The war in Italy lasted ten more months instead of merely two, and east-central Europe was lost to Soviet domination.

CHAPTER IX

Normandy: The Great Allied Failure

Hitler Seeks a Man for the West

IN EARLY 1942 the German swastika flew over most of Europe, the various nation states of the continent having fallen to the Wehrmacht one after another, beginning with the *Anschluss* in Austria and ending with the seizure of France that culminated in the catastrophic British evacuation at Dunkirk. All that remained to be done to secure the West was to take England, and that appeared to be only a matter of time.

The considered opinion among the German leadership, especially the strutting Hitler, was that the Allies could not possibly invade western Europe in the foreseeable future. After Nazi Germany completed the defeat of the Soviet Union—and, despite recent December setbacks, that appeared also only a matter of time—the bulk of the German armed forces could be freed for use against the British Isles. Having taken personal command of the army in December 1941, Hitler was confident that matters would soon be going better.

But, as is so often the case, situations change and change rapidly, not only by design but also by happenstance. Within less than a year three major events collectively caused an almost total reversal of the German estimate regarding the chance of an invasion of the continent.

The three events were: Hitler's decision not to invade England, because he "knew" the British were about to sue for peace; the fact that American aid and some forces were in the process of being deployed to the European area; and last, and possibly most unexpected of all, the Soviet Union's defense of the homeland stiffened to the point that by the end of January 1943 a German Army, commanded by a field marshal, was about to surrender to a Soviet commander at Stalingrad.

A change in German strategy was therefore essential. Even though Hitler fumed and raged, he accepted the fact that the coast of France, along with the remainder of the periphery of western Europe, was now a vulnerable feature in Germany's security system. Hitler and his chief advisors also seem to have understood that now there was no going back, the chance to invade England had passed. Furthermore, the island nation was the most obvious springboard for any planned assault on Fortress Europe. To take prompt action to deal with this growing danger it was necessary, first of all, to find the right man to deal with the problems, and then to provide him with the wherewithal to accomplish the job.

One of these problems was partially solved in March 1943, when Field Marshal Erwin Rommel was ordered out of Africa. Rommel was one of the most acclaimed, if not universally popular, officers in the German Army and, as such, was in Hitler's good graces. Leaving his command in Africa, Rommel was ordered to report to Rastenberg, Hitler's headquarters in East Prussia, where, upon his arrival, he was immediately ushered into the Führer's presence.

Rommel at Rastenberg

After Hitler had lavished high praise on the Field Marshal, the two were left alone to talk. Although the conversation was quite wide-ranging, it seemed to Rommel that Hitler kept coming back to one central theme—the defense of the West. In response to a comment, Rommel told the Führer that he was extremely worried about the situation in the West and that he feared that OKW (*Oberkommando der Wehrmacht*) had underestimated Allied airpower. He also conveyed these fears to Lieutenant General Fritz Bayerlein, an old friend whom he met soon after he had arrived at the Führer's headquarters. He confided to Bayerlein that he was not sure he had gotten his point across to Hitler, but that he had tried to suggest that the stiffening of Soviet resistance required new thinking about the East, possibly even a withdrawal, so as to shorten interior lines, and permit a new buildup of strength. (Rommel did not know that others had given Hitler similar assessments.) Hitler had given Rommel the opening for his comments when the Führer boasted that, by January 1944, German aircraft production would be 7,000 planes a month and that tanks would be rolling off the assembly lines at a rate of 2,000 a month. Rommel had congratulated Hitler, he confided to Bayerlein, but he thought that the German leader was having a flight of fancy.

Nevertheless, the timing seemed right for telling Hitler what he thought—Rommel was never known for his circumspection—and he proceeded to do so. If the Allies were able to open a second front in the west, Rommel pointed out, especially by seizing the French coast opposite England, Germany's situation would become critical. Rommel estimated that the Allies would have to be held in check for at least two years to allow for a rebuilding of German strength. (Rommel did not tell Hitler, but confided to others, that the idea of a reinvigorated German military capacity should have as its main and immediate goal the seeking of an honorable peace settlement.) When Hitler objected to Rommel's proposal about delaying the war effort, the field marshal stated that his appraisal was really only an extension of the Führer's own thoughts on the expected production ability of German industry by 1944. Thus, Rommel's original proposal suddenly became Hitler's own, personal view of the future.

When Hitler pressed Rommel for details on his views, the field marshal saw that what had started out as a suggestion was rapidly, almost too rapidly, being considered as a new military objective. Even though he was apprehensive about Hitler's irrational haste, Rommel determined to press on. He suggested that Germany's success depended on repulsing an Allied invasion in the west before any appreciable lodgement could be made. To accomplish this would require the destruction of the invasion forces at sea or while they were on the beaches. To Rommel's surprise, Hitler agreed and added that in time the Allies could achieve air superiority in the West and that this would make it very difficult to stop an invasion before it began. Having made this point, Hitler closed the meeting, much to Rommel's relief. On his departure, the field marshal made the mental note that this was probably the last he would hear about the affair until the news of the Allied landings was announced. To his surprise, he was proven wrong.

Shortly after departing Rastenberg, Rommel took command of German forces in northern Italy and was there through the summer of 1943. By August he had all but forgotten the meeting with Hitler. He therefore was surprised when he was again ordered to report to the Führer to review a report just received from Field Marshal Gerd von Rundstedt, the German commander in western Europe. Rommel felt uneasy about this as Rundstedt, while surely no friend of his, was his senior, and Rommel knew that he would have to be careful in what he said.

Upon his arrival at Rastenberg, Rommel was shown Rundstedt's report. It was what Rommel expected, a listing of one deficiency after another, with particular emphasis on the poor quality of manpower available in the West and the extremely low morale among the numerous non-German troops, particularly the Russians, that were part of his command. With these problems and the chronic deficiencies he outlined, Rundstedt concluded that his resources were inadequate to stop a possible invasion from across the English Channel. In order to have sufficient strength in all likely landing areas, so as to have a reasonable chance of pinning the Allies into a beachhead, he would not have enough reserves to strike a counterblow.

When Hitler asked Rommel's opinion, the field marshal was able to reply that he was in complete agreement with Rundstedt's report, as it stated the facts. He added, however, that he would have wished to see some more concrete proposals for dealing with possible contingencies. Rommel acknowledged that, without a very detailed examination of the situation, he was in no position to comment on what more could be done. He did indicate, however, that it was not clear from the report whether OB West (*Oberbefehlshaber* West), Rundstedt's headquarters, had completely evaluated the alternatives. Hitler was silent for a few moments. He shifted the subject to the situation in southern Italy, where the Allies had recently landed south of Naples. Hitler criticized the handling of the situation by Field Marshal Albert Kesselring, commander of Army Group C. Rommel did not comment. Hitler then thanked Rommel and concluded the conversation. Rommel returned to Italy that night convinced he had done himself more harm than good by his rather evasive answers to the Führer.

This may well have been the case, but only Hitler knew for sure. The purpose of the meeting, according to Hitler's aides, had been to review the final details of Rommel's assumption of command of OB Süd (*Oberbefehlshaber* South), the German forces headquarters in Italy. But when it was announced that all forces in Italy would be consolidated under Kesselring, as OB Südwest, Rommel was out of a job, as were all of his staff in Army Group B. All of the assets of Rommel's headquarters were transferred to Kesselring's headquarters, except for the staff. Rommel assumed that he had been summarily relieved, probably because of the unsatisfactory meeting with Hitler.

Rommel to the West

Three days later, on November 21, 1943, Rommel was ordered to proceed to Munich, where he was to establish a new command called Army Group for Special Employment, directly subordinate to *Oberkommando der Wehrmacht* (OKW). Rommel was directed to survey the entire coast area from Denmark to Brittany and was to prepare operational plans for each sector, including a special study of the availability of forces in unthreatened areas. In effect, to his amazement, Rommel was being given planning authority over all of the forces in France, Belgium, the Netherlands, and Denmark, completely bypassing the theater command of Field Marshal Rundstedt. Although Rundstedt still retained operational authority, obviously this too could readily be transferred to Rommel's new headquarters any time Hitler so desired.

By this move the Führer had gained effective personal control over the Western Theater, much the same as that he already held over the Eastern Front.

It was obvious to Rommel that he would have to consult Rundstedt's headquarters about the current status of planning. When Rommel arrived at St. Germain-en-Laye, OB West headquarters outside Paris, he was greeted by the 68-year-old aristocrat, who, without preamble, accused him of engineering the plan, with "the Bohemian corporal, Hitler," and of totally undercutting the authority of OB West. Although Rommel protested his own ignorance of Hitler's plan until he had received his orders, Rundstedt would not be mollified. He promised Rommel (to whom he referred privately as "Marshal Bubi") that despite the anomaly of the situation, he would cooperate with Rommel, but that neither he nor his staff would participate in the new planning process.

Without misconception as to his relationship with Rundstedt, Rommel ordered his staff to begin a detailed analysis of the various sectors of the coastline that constituted the primary avenues through which the Allies might contemplate the invasion of Europe. It soon became obvious that this was indeed a monumental task. From the outset, Rommel refused to believe that no more could be done than Rundstedt had already contemplated. As a start, in the area immediately facing England, the most likely point from which to launch an invasion, every inch of the coast was surveyed from Antwerp in the north to La Rochelle in the south. From this analysis, the coastal area was divided into four zones: the Antwerp to Boulogne-sur-Mer area, including the Pas-de-Calais; the Boulogne-sur-Mer to Deauville area; the Deauville to Brest area; and the Brest-La Rochelle area. The first two areas were controlled by the Fifteenth German Army; the latter two were the responsibility of the Seventh Army. Together, the Seventh and Fifteenth armies constituted Army Group B. Responsibility for the southern coast of France on the Atlantic, and for the Mediterranean coastline as well, was assigned to Army Group G, with its First and Nineteenth Armies.

Although the Mediterranean coast could never entirely be scratched off the list as a possible landing area, its priority was considerably lower than the area around Calais, considered by Rommel—as by Rundstedt—as the prime likely landing area for an Allied invasion. The second most important zone was considered to be the area between Deauville and Brest in the Normandy-Brittany region. Next in priority was the Mediterranean region; the area south of Brest on the Atlantic coast of France was never seriously considered in any of the German planning, since it was too far from Allied supply bases for a significant invasion.

An initial, if somewhat innocuous effort at the fortification of the French coast—the so-called Atlantic Wall—had been started in 1942 in conformity with Führer Directive No. 40. Little had been accomplished by the time Rommel arrived on the scene in late 1943, due primarily to the uncooperative relations between the service elements of the German Wehrmacht and OB West, and to the shortage of material necessary to construct the type of fortifications described in the directive. Since

Rundstedt would not deign to deal directly with Hitler—even though the Führer held him in high regard—he had been ineffective in getting anything out of Keitel and Jodl, Hitler's senior military assistants in OKW.

Rommel, on the other hand, by virtue of his new position, and having Hitler's ear, was able to demand and get more effort into the construction of fortifications as a part of his scheme for the defense of the French coast. On the basis of his area priority list, Rommel was able to influence the building of more fortifications along the coast in the Pas-de-Calais sector. The Normandy coast, considered less likely as a landing site, was to have second priority, while the Mediterranean area was to be relatively ignored for the present. With Hitler's approval, *Organization Todt,* which had been building U-boat pens along the coast at Brest, St. Nazaire, and Lorient, was directed to step up work on coastal defense emplacements. Reichsminister Albert Speer promised to supervise the effort personally.

Rommel and Rundstedt were in full agreement in believing that the Pas-de-Calais area was the most likely area for Allied attack. This area was the closest point to England on the European coast, and it contained both Calais and Antwerp, two of the most strategically important ports in northern Europe, ports of the type the Allies would need following any initial landing on the continent. Most of the German defense efforts were, therefore, concentrated in this area, but some effort was also put into the Normandy sector.

The Me 262

About this time there came an unexpected contribution to improving the German defenses of western Europe. Hermann Goering, by his very presence and his constant optimism, had done much to weaken the German war effort. Now, suddenly, he became a strong advocate of Rommel and his proposals for the defense of the West, even though the evidence suggests he personally disliked

Rommel. Goering's motive in this move was that he saw in what Rommel was doing a means of making the Luftwaffe the first military air service in the world to possess operational jet fighters.

Since 1940, when the first jet aircraft was flown in Germany, the Messerschmitt plant had been turning out Model 262, twin-jet fighters and fighter-bombers. There were fewer than 100 of these in late 1943, but these were more than enough to cause the Allies some serious problems if introduced into the war. Hitler had not allowed any of them to be used, however, claiming they were being held for a plan so secret that even Goering could not be informed of its details. Indeed, the plan was secret, for it was known to Hitler alone and went with him to his grave. Thus, the jets had never been used, although the best pilots in the Luftwaffe had been assigned to fly them in the Special Air Group known as KG 200 (*Kampfgeschwader* 200), which maintained a number of secret air bases throughout Germany and in several locations in occupied Europe.

All the work of constructing these aircraft was performed underground in a labyrinth of huge tunnels that honeycombed the mountains behind the picturesque Bavarian village of Oberammergau, the site of the Passion Play. After the aircraft were built they were transported to Landsberg about 30 miles away, on special trucks, which trundled through the quiet Bavarian countryside in the dead of night. At Landsberg, the outer wing sections were assembled onto the planes, and they were given a few flight tests, usually by KG 200's chief test pilot, Hanna Reitsch, the most famous woman pilot in Germany. These flights always took place at night. Special underground hangars hid the planes during the day.

As the number of these jet aircraft increased they severely taxed the hangar storage capacity at Landsberg. Luftwaffe officials urged that they be deployed to other bases and actively employed, especially on the Russian front, but Hitler would not be budged.

When Rommel was appointed to command the Army

Group for Special Employment and charged with planning the defense of the West, Goering saw an opportunity for using his new weapon. In his capacity as Commander in Chief of the Luftwaffe, Goering himself briefed Rommel on the Me 262s, stressing their effectiveness against bombers, their almost irresistible capabilities in support of ground activities, and in particular the "absolute ability of the Me 262 to overcome any known opposition." Although Goering was exaggerating to some extent, it was a fact that the Me 262A1 fighter model of this aircraft could literally fly circles around all Allied bombers then in active service over the continent. They were much faster and more than a match for most Allied fighters, armed as they were with four 30-millimeter automatic cannon. Thus, when Rommel was able to convince Hitler to release this potent weapon to the arsenal in the west, a significant step was taken toward overcoming growing Allied air superiority over northern France and Belgium.

By June 6, 1944, when the Allied invasion of Europe began, nearly 150 Me 262 fighters and fighter-bombers, plus 12 reconnaissance models, were available. The reconnaissance models, which could outfly anything in the air at the moment, were put into active service first on June 1, 1944, and served thereafter as the eyes of the Germans. They were able to penetrate English airspace at will, photographing the invasion buildup and escaping before Allied interceptors could be vectored on them by the radar network of the British Isles. One reconnaissance Me 262 was shot down by Allied antiaircraft fire on June 3, but since it exploded in mid-air—violently, according to observers—and the wreckage scattered over a broad expanse of the English Channel off Slapton, little real technical data was retrieved by the Allied Command. Thus there was little hint of the devastation these aircraft would cause to the invasion force a few days later.

The question of the employment of these aircraft was only one of Rommel's problems of planning for the defense of the West. First among these problems was the basic issue of allocation of still substantial German resources between the Eastern and Western Theaters that pervaded every aspect of planning at the German High Command. At Rommel's insistence, a meeting was set up with Hitler where the field marshal proposed that the German army break contact with the Soviets and withdraw to a much shortened defensive line, where the military strength of the Wehrmacht could be rebuilt. Hitler would not hear of this, even though all of the senior military officers present, including Goering, supported the proposition. Instead, Hitler promised to limit operations on the Eastern Front to allow for a faster build-up in the West. Rommel, although not satisfied, accepted this decision as the best that might be hoped for. Hitler, on the other hand, had noted all those present who had openly sided with Rommel and secretly vowed to deal with them when victory was at hand. Right now he needed them, or they all would have suffered the fate of a number of other "doomsayers" who had argued against the Führer's specific desires.

German Defensive Buildup

The slowdown in German military operations along the Eastern Front allowed for some shifting of resources to the West, but the key element was the release of effective forces for the Atlantic Wall. Rommel had hoped for unit reinforcements from Russia, but instead OB West got individual replacements of men, and train loads of equipment, much of which had been earmarked for Russia. These were still not enough to fill Rundstedt's shortages, but more than either field marshal had expected. In the end, the shifting of manpower and supply emphasis to the West weakened the Eastern Front and, when the Soviets started their own offensive timed to coordinate with the landings in western Europe, these shortages played heavily in the outcome of the war.

Of more immediate importance however, was the fact that most replacements were being sent west instead of east, to fill the seriously understrength German divisions in the Seventh and Fifteenth armies in France. By the time the Allied invasion began, in June 1944, the German army along the Atlantic Wall was near full strength, with rested, battle-hardened troops in all units. Serious deficiencies still existed in some critical skills, but the luxury of numbers made it easier to accommodate these shortages.

While these steps were to prove significant in the forthcoming events, of even greater importance was the reorganization of numerous resources already available.

Much to Rommel's relief, early in 1944 his relationship with Rundstedt had been clarified by the redesignation of his Army Group for Special Employment as Army Group B controlling the Seventh and Fifteenth armies. Rommel's headquarters was incorporated with that of existing Army Group B, and was nominally under Rundstedt's OB West. However, as Rundstedt had somewhat wryly remarked to him after Rommel had established his Army Group B headquarters at La Roche-Guyon, the OB West headquarters had in effect become a line of communications agency, with Rommel virtually the field commander of all operational forces in the West, except for two groups controlled directly from Berlin. The first of these was the OKW reserve, which consisted of the I SS Panzer Corps, with its 1st SS, 12th SS, and 17th SS Panzer Grenadier divisions, and the independent Panzer Lehr Division. The second group was the German Third Air Force, the air support element in the West that had, up to this time, been assigned directly to Goering's headquarters, *Oberkommando der Luftwaffe* (OKL). This air army included, in addition to the aviation units, all antiaircraft and parachute troop units, organized into the III Flak Corps. By a direct approach to Hitler, in which he spelled out his plans for pushing the Allies back into the sea, Rommel in February was able to get these two major units put under his direct control. Rommel also tried to get Hitler to order the 319th Infantry Division withdrawn from the Channel Islands back to France, but when Hitler flushed and began to lecture him on the fact that by holding the islands Germany held a piece of England, Rommel quickly backed off. He was able to convince the Führer, however, that all military government functions in France, Belgium, and Holland should be taken out from under high command control and given to OB West.

When Rommel returned to La Roche-Guyon from Berlin, he immediately ordered that the I SS Panzer Corps and the Panzer Lehr Division be incorporated into Panzer Group West under the command of General Leo Freiherr Geyr von Schweppenberg, who was charged with the coordination of all German armored forces in the theater. Rommel also ordered Field Marshal Hugo Sperrle, commander of the Third Air Force, to send an air force planning group to his headquarters to help coordinate the air-ground battle that would eventually have to be fought.

There were two problems still to be settled. The first was whether the German economy could continue to supply the materials, especially the steel and concrete, necessary to construct the type of fortification system envisioned by Rommel as the best means of holding the Allied invasion to the shoreline. The second, and no less important problem was a constant updating of intelligence data and its correct evaluation to insure that the right coastline was defended.

At the beginning of his tenure in the West, Rommel had been convinced that the Pas-de-Calais area was the most likely point for the main effort in any cross-Channel attack. But, by the end of 1943, he was no longer quite so positive in his assessment and began dividing his attention between the Pas-de-Calais and Normandy, which was beginning to look like a good possibility. In doing so, of course, he increased his reliance on the war economy to supply what fundamentally became twice the original estimated requirement for building supplies. This, he soon found, was an impossible task.

The German economy had shown signs of gradual improvement since the drain of East Front requirements had lessened because of the slowdown of operations in that theater, but it was nowhere near its peak output. Nor could it be as long as the Allied bombing continued. Despite the efficient efforts of Albert Speer, the bombing and the long-term drain on the system caused by the requirements of the Eastern Front had weakened the nation's ability to supply the now critical needs of the Western Defense. Steel was literally being ripped from bombed-out buildings in Germany, and non-essential railroad tracks in occupied countries were being taken up for use in the construction of the most vital strongpoints along the coast. But still the bombing continued and grew in intensity and little could be done to weaken the Allies' ability to inflict this damage.

Preparing to Meet "Overlord"

German intelligence (*Abwehr Ausland*) under Admiral Wilhelm Canaris had penetrated the security cloak thrown over the plan the Allies called "Overlord," the invasion of the continent. Canaris could not with absolute certainty, however, identify the area for the main phase of the attack or the timing involved. For months German radio intercept stations had been monitoring the BBC, seeking from among the daily barrage of cryptic messages that were sent to the French underground certain key phrases which were known to be critical to the invasion. Besides words, passages from musical scores were being transmitted by the BBC on a regular basis, all part of an immense cryptic communications system maintained between England and the resistance forces on the continent. German intelligence operatives, some of them disgruntled Frenchmen, had penetrated this network, and the meaning of some of the transmissions was in the hands of German intelligence. Besides this, a German agent code named Cicero, who worked as a valet in the British Embassy in Ankara, had supplied almost all the details of Overlord to the *Abwehr*, except the two critical items of time and place. Other bits of information were collected wherever they might be found: from the comments of an American general at the bar in Claridge's in London, or from the boasting remarks of a British battalion commander, who unknowingly, specifically identified locations in the Normandy area by his remarks about the objectives of his force.

Although these and other indiscretions on the part of individuals caused great concern when they were reported to the German High Command, there was still no absolute proof that Normandy was to be more than a large scale demonstration timed to conceal the real main attack area in the Pas-de-Calais. It was still up to the Germans to decide which way to lean. That decision was made early in 1944 as a result of an in-depth analysis of all information gathered by intelligence, and by relating this to the outcome of wargames conducted in the field by the OKW staff. From this analysis it was possible to identify Normandy as the main target area, and the beginning of June 1944 as the prime time for the Allied invasion.

With this information, Rommel then had two immediate internal tasks to accomplish. The first was to shift emphasis in fortification construction to the Normandy area, with all that entailed, and the second was to reposition his forces to be ready for the presumed primary threat.

The bulk of the German forces in western Europe were in the Fifteenth Army zone in northern France and the Low Countries. Because more troops would be needed in the Seventh Army area—that included the Normandy peninsula—necessary plans had to be made and executed to move critical units south. But these moves had to be accomplished with the utmost secrecy, as any untoward movement might have forced the Allies to reconsider their options and change their primary landing areas back to the Pas-de-Calais. As would be proved later, Rommel gave his wholehearted support to the Normandy build-up but could never completely overcome the nagging doubt about the Calais area being the prime objective. Because of this the shifts that were made in the locations of German units were not wholesale in nature, nor were they conspicuous.

As for the issue of redirecting the major share of the coast defense construction to what was now the main priority area, Rommel and his planners were baffled. Since a number of fortifications were already under construction around Calais, Rommel decided to continue work on them, while making a number of changes in the scheme for defending the Normandy area. These modifications were approved by the OKW and by Hitler, but only after a long, acrimonious session in which the Führer raged over the defeatist attitude of his generals in refusing to believe in the fundamental strength of the German economy.

Back at his headquarters, Rommel began a new review of the possible landing areas along the Normandy coast to determine the most suitable areas for large scale landings. This study showed that the likely area for the landing was a thirty-mile stretch of coast between Grandcamp-les-Bains and Ouistreham. To accomplish the defense of this area, especially those stretches of beach that favored landings by large numbers of troops, Rommel ordered the construction of strongpoints composed of heavy field fortifications. These positions were to receive first priority, while smaller beaches more suitable to surprise operations and demonstrations were to be defended by smaller strongpoints tied together with support artillery fire from batteries located well to the rear of the beaches, outside the field of observation and, if possible, the range of naval gunfire. All haste was to be put into the flexibility of German reserve forces to respond to calls for help from the units regularly stationed along the coast. Although every attempt was made to reinforce these units, the bulk of replacements and equipment that became available after this point in time went to the reserves so as to insure their maximum level of readiness. Thus, although the Germans failed to achieve Hitler's long-held dream of an impregnable Atlantic Wall, they did accomplish the monumental feat of bringing the German army in one portion of France to a state of readiness that at least approximated its condition in 1940.

Most of these preparations were known to the Allies as soon as they occurred, but the real nature of what was going on was obscured by the methods with which the Germans appeared to operate. The Allies noted the construction in the Normandy area, but they also witnessed the continued construction of the fortifications in the Calais region. German troops on the move were observed and reported by the French resistance, but these moves were seemingly not extensive, and observed along the entire northern coast. All in all, the Allies thought, the Germans were simply tidying up. Time was growing short, and if an assault was to be launched against the continent during the summer of 1944, planning either had to continue for Operation Overlord, or it would have to be cancelled for 1944. General Dwight D. Eisenhower, the Supreme Allied Commander, made the decision to continue as planned, even though the German defensive picture had become somewhat more clouded than it had been. Part of the Allied decision to proceed was based on the realization that any delay would force a delay of months for the favorable conditions necessary to the invasion. Furthermore, it was also obvious that any delay would only aid the Germans as they strengthened their defenses.

Thus, the plans for Overlord continued apace, and this, in turn, limited Germany's time for preparation. Under Rommel's leadership much was being accomplished. Yet there was no way of diminishing the effects of the continuous Allied bombing that was extracting an extremely heavy toll, especially from German industry. To offset this, many vital plants were being put underground in caves similar to the one at Oberammergau where the Me 262s were built. Also, everything possible was done to improve the effectiveness of air defense against the Allied bombing formations. For one thing, the Germans decided that the British were reading the encoded Luftwaffe radio traffic; to stop this all mission traffic was ordered sent by landline—telephone and teletype circuits. Entire new encryption systems also were developed and changed frequently, to impede the ability of the Allies to read those messages that had to be sent by radio.

The special air group KG200 was ordered to step up its operations. This included not only preparations and training for use of the reconnaisance version of the Me 262 as a means of observing Allied preparations for the invasion, but also readiness to employ the combat models of the jet when the attack began.

Because of the secrecy surrounding the Me 262, special precautions were undertaken to reduce the possibility that the Allies might identify and bomb their airfields. In addition, after careful analysis, locations close to the coast were designated and readied as auxiliary airfields. In some instances straight stretches of road were earmarked as standby runways, where the jets could be refueled and rearmed. This was no easy task, since the Allied air interdiction of northern France was increasing steadily in intensity.

By the end of May 1944 all that the Germans could do to strengthen the Atlantic Wall had seemingly been done. The defense against invasion now depended on those fortifications that had been completed and upon the flexibility of the German armed forces themselves to respond to major threats. Efforts to improve the defenses were not interrupted, but Rommel personally could relax briefly. He planned a brief vacation.

The Warnings

At about 9 P.M. on the night of June 1, 1944, German radio intercept stations that habitually monitored the usual innocuous stream of BBC announcements beamed at Europe picked up an unusual message: "*Les sanglots longs des violens de l'automne.*" Admiral Canaris had warned that this was the first part of an announcement to the French underground that the invasion was about to begin. This particular message, Canaris had warned, would designate a two-week period for the attack, while the second part would indicate that the landings would begin within the following 48 hours.

An alert was immediately sent to all commands of Army Group B, and predetermined actions were taken to prepare for the defense. Among the procedures that had been laid down in anticipation of this message was the alerting of every unit within France and the other coastal countries, and the cancellation of all leaves, schools, and other activities that took troops away from their units. Because of this, Erwin Rommel cancelled his own planned leave and remained at his headquarters. Troops were put on fifty percent alert, and any and all unusual incidents, no matter how insignificant, were reported to higher headquarters for evaluation. The forces guarding the Mediterranean coast were also put on alert as a precautionary measure. Because of the stringent procedures, there was little chance that someone would not "get the word."

Nothing happened for four days, until Sunday, June 4, when an Associated Press teletype operator inadvertently flashed a message around the world that the invasion had begun. Although a retraction was sent out immediately, German intelligence correctly assumed that the time was getting close when the real attack would be made. Rommel's headquarters at La Roche-Guyon was a beehive of activity, as staff officers scrutinized the numerous reports, many of them contradictory, that flowed into the command post in a steady stream. Conflicting as the information may have been, the sum total of data convinced Rommel that the invasion was only hours away. At noon on June 5, he ordered a full alert, sending all German forces to their primary battle positions. This alert was to last for 24 hours, unless extended. Even if the invasion did not come during that period, Rommel told his staff, it would be an excellent test of all the training and preparations that had gone before. All of this was done even though Rommel could not see how the Allies could undertake the landing given the terrible weather conditions that hung over the Channel and over the coast of France.

The rest of June 5 passed without incident until 10:15 P.M., when the German intercept stations picked up the second half of the message that was the alert for French resistance to prepare for the invasion within 48 hours. Just as Canaris had said it would, it came over the radio amid a flurry of other messages: "*Blessant mon coeur d'une langueur monotone.*" The invasion was about to begin. By midnight all German commands had been notified, and the full alert order was extended indefinitely.

The Assault Begins

At 15 minutes past midnight the first parachute troops of the US 82d and 101st Airborne Divisions began to land in designated areas on the Cotentin Peninsula. Although these specially-trained Pathfinders approached the French coast in low-flying aircraft, their approach was detected, and their aircraft were taken under fire as soon as they crossed the French coast. Still, most of the para-troopers managed to get to their objectives and began marking the landing zones to be used when the main force arrived. At the same time, British paratroopers and glider troops began landing further east in the vicinity of the French village of Ranville, where they had the mis-sion of destroying the bridges over the Caen Canal and the Orne River. Most of this force was destroyed even before the gliders were free of the transports that towed them. Those that were not hit in the air were smothered in the hail of fire that met them as they reached the ground.

Soon the German Seventh Army headquarters at Le Mans was besieged with reports of parachutists landing everywhere, of strange flares being sighted, and of two stationary green lights about ten feet above the water, one near Ouistreham and the other just east of Arromanches-les-Bains. As it turned out, the lights were affixed to the masts of two British midget submarines that were to serve as the boundary markers for the landings of the British

Second Army on Gold, Juno, and Sword beaches. Without them the British forces would have had to rely on
navigation alone to insure they were in the right place.
When they did land, the entire force went ashore exactly
where they were supposed to, but the fact that the Germans were alerted made the landings that much more
difficult.

Troops of the 3d British Division found themselves
pinned down on Sword Beach and were in the process of
sorting out their situation when the first wave of German
aircraft, including several Me 262s, attacked the sandy
stretch, choked with men. Although the air attacks
caused considerable confusion, they were but the precur-
sor of the ground action that followed when German panzer units arrived. The tanks crossed the bridges over the
Orne that were supposed to have been taken out by the
failed Allied airborne landings east of the river. The German counterattack struck the left flank of the British force
and, before it could be slowed, had badly mauled the
troops ashore and had forced a delay in any attempts to
land more troops on that beach.

The American landings at Omaha and Utah beaches
faced equally grave problems. At Utah Beach, for example, the Germans had flooded the low, marshy area directly behind the beach, thus restricting movement from
the beach inland to five causeways. The German 709th
Infantry Division, deployed in this area, had prepared the
causeways for demolition. Soon after the first wave of the
4th US Infantry Division began moving toward the shore,
these causeways were blown up.

As the Americans struggled ashore, intense German fire
upon their landing craft, and attacks by German jets upon
the landing armada itself, took a heavy toll when the assault wave touched the beach at la Grande Dune. This
was 1,000 meters southeast of les Dunes de Varreville where
the landing had been planned. This was sheer luck, since
the Germans had completed work on the defenses at la
Grande Dune but had hardly begun final preparations at
les Dunes de Varreville. This error, in effect, sealed the

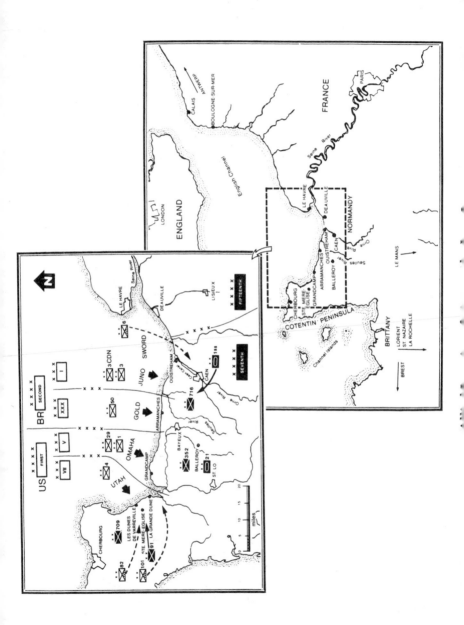

fate of the VII US Corps landings. By 9:45 A.M., June 6, H-hour plus 3:30, the lead elements of the 4th Division were in serious trouble.

Although some elements of the two American airborne divisions had been able to rally and move to their assigned objectives after they began landing at about 1 A.M., for the most part the units were so scattered all over the Cotentin Peninsula that there was no hope of gathering sufficient force to help relieve the pressure on the beach. The 82d and 101st Airborne divisions had, in effect, ceased to exist as effective units. The 6,600 paratroopers of the 101st Airborne, loaded on some 430 C-47 transports, had reached the French coast with no real trouble, but such heavy clouds hung over their approach that the aircraft became very badly scattered. German records showed later that at least 1,500 paratroopers were killed or captured in the first hours after the landing. Most of the division's equipment was airdropped into swamps and marshes where it rested undisturbed until recovered by the victors in following weeks.

At first light, troops of the German 91st Infantry Division were out in force, mopping up small groups of paratroopers all over the countryside. Major General Maxwell D. Taylor, who jumped with his men, could not be located, and Brigadier General Don F. Pratt, the division's assistant commander, in charge of the follow-on glider force that was to reinforce the parachute troops, was killed in the landing when his glider was wrecked. Those who were not killed in the night glider assault landing (the first ever attempted) were killed or captured on the ground, as the glider landing areas had not been secured by the paratroops. The only unit of the division that was not mauled in this manner was the 327th Glider Infantry Regiment that could not be airloaded and was, therefore, coming in to join the division by ship on June 7.

The jump of the 82d Airborne Division was, if anything, even more of a catastrophe. Landing to the west of the 101st's area, the 82d Airborne Division's several drop zones formed a rough circle around the town of Ste. Mère

Église. The division was to seal off the southern approaches to the corps area, but its dispersal over a 35-mile wide area made this impossible. Although individual small units were able to gather up their men and fought bravely, they were simply overwhelmed by the numerically superior and alerted German forces. Daylight brought on what amounted to a pheasant hunt, with German patrols flushing out American paratroopers all over the area.

Allied Disasters

With the airborne landings in a total shambles and the 4th Division on the wrong beach and cut off from immediate movement inland, the VII Corps was in serious trouble. The corps commander, Major General J. Lawton Collins, was in the process of informing the First Army commander, Lieutenant General Omar Bradley, of this fact when a new element was injected. German aircraft, mostly jets, began attacking the beaches and, on several occasions, the landing armada itself. Three Me 262s, barely skimming the water, came upon Collins' flagship, the U.S.S. *Bayfield,* and hit it with three bombs that effectively knocked out much of its communications. The jets had come in so fast that there was simply no time to react. They were gone before the smoke from the explosions from their bombs had settled. To regain communications, Collins and a few of his senior staff officers had to transfer to a destroyer.

On the beach, Colonel James Van Fleet, commander of the 8th Infantry Regiment, had watched in dismay when the German aircraft attacked the beach choked with his men. He saw the jets come in, chased by a swarm of P-51s, but soon saw that the speedy American pursuit craft were incapable of catching the even faster jets. The first strafing did the most damage, but the second and the third waves of German fighters also took heavy tolls. By 3 P.M., the elements of the 4th Division on the beach had not moved more than a few hundred yards and had sustained extremely heavy casualties. Any idea of reinforcing the beach by pushing another wave of troops ashore seemed impossible for the moment. Communications were still not fully reestablished after the *Bayfield* incident, and Bradley, aboard the U.S.S. *Augusta,* had his hands full with the situation on Omaha Beach, where the situation was even worse.

Omaha Beach was the responsibility of the U.S. V Corps, commanded by Major General Leonard T. Gerow. The shoreline that the assault would have to cross was less than five miles in width, and any deviation in landing at exactly the right place would have confronted the troops with reefs, tidal shallows, and 100-foot high cliffs just a few feet from the water's edge. Although the Germans had strengthened the entire area with a maze of pillboxes, emplacements, and barbed-wire obstacles, they had concentrated the bulk of their effort into that five-mile stretch of beach and had zeroed the massed artillery of the 352d and 716th Infantry Divisions, all placed well back from the beach, on that sandy expanse. As a final move, the 21st Panzer Division was placed in the wooded area west of Balleroy, where a good road system allowed for rapid movement either east or west toward the coast.

Following an extremely heavy naval bombardment of the landing area, two regiments of the US 1st Division began the assault. After sustaining heavy casualties getting to the beach, the lead elements were only just beginning the task of consolidating their positions when the first counterattack began. The fire over the beach was murderous, but the Americans held on until the second wave got ashore. The beach area was now clogged with troops and equipment, but movement out of the beach area was delayed by the confusion of minefields, tank obstacles, and barbed wire entanglements that had to be cleared by sappers from the Engineer Special Brigade, which had accompanied the leading infantry units ashore. Major General Clarence R. Huebner, commanding the 1st Division, joined his men ashore with the second wave and, after appraising the situation, notified Gerow that the beach area could accommodate no more troops until movement inland had begun.

But despite the outstanding leadership of the officers of this battle-hardened division, the units simply could not break through the defenses. Only at a few places, where local defenses were overwhelmed, or covered by dense smoke, could any advance at all be made. These areas were so small and scattered, however, that they could not be effectively exploited. The assault ground to a halt, in part due to the utter exhaustion of the troops, most of whom had been seasick because of the arduous Channel crossing.

Almost as if they sensed the situation, at this moment the Germans committed their jets in strength. About 15 Me 262s swept the length of Omaha Beach, raking the exposed troops with automatic cannon fire. Other jets engaged the Allied fighter cover. Behind them came several waves of medium bombers and Stukas, which attacked the landing ships as they lay off the beach. German aircraft losses were tremendous. Even the numbers of jets began to thin out noticeably as Allied airmen learned how to "gang up" on them to knock them down, and antiaircraft gunners aboard the ships offshore began to compensate for the speed of these unique aircraft. But the attacks continued, making it impossible to reinforce the beach with more troops.

Rommel had kept in close touch with front line commanders and by 10 A.M. had become convinced that Normandy was indeed the main landing area. Despite feints, and the dropping of dummy paratroopers, there was no real combat activity in the Pas-de-Calais area. Even Allied aircraft activity had declined significantly during the early morning hours, as air assets that would normally have been used to suppress any movement of German forces from northern France to the battle area were diverted to give extra support to the fight against the unexpected strength of German airpower over Normandy. This diversion had at least partially achieved its purpose, however, as many German jets were caught on the ground refueling at the makeshift airfields close to the landing area. For Rommel these air losses were serious, but the development of the air battle had made it easier for him to shift his ground forces to best advantage. And by early afternoon, several additional divisions, especially those of the Panzer reserve, were on their way to Normandy.

By mid-afternoon Rommel had come to the conclusion that the Allied attacks had been contained. To insure the accuracy of the optimistic reports being received from all commands, he had sent trusted staff officers to assess the situation on the ground. Their reports confirmed that the German armed forces had indeed contained the landings. There had been extremely heavy losses to all units committed to the fight and, in some cases, to units moving into the battle zone, but it was clear that the Germans were winning.

A report to the same effect was sent at about 3 P.M. by General Bradley to General Montgomery, commander of the 21st Army Group. Bradley informed the landing force commander that only two regiments were ashore on Omaha, and that the Utah landings were in a shambles. The First Army commander added that the ever-increasing German pressure indicated the necessity to consider the option of withdrawal if something could not be done to alleviate the situation. As an ominous postscript, Bradley added that there was some doubt if the forces ashore at Omaha could be successfully pulled out at all.

Montgomery had received equally serious reports from his British subordinates. The Canadian 3d Division was being chewed up by German armor at Juno Beach, and the British 3d Division on Sword Beach was reporting increasing German pressure and the sounds of many tanks beyond the dunes. Only the British 50th Division on Gold Beach seemed to be doing well by comparison. By 2 P.M. it had moved about 1,000 meters off the beach and had gotten advance units as far inland as the Seulles River. However, the 50th was met along the Seulles by the Panzer Lehr Division, which was soon thereafter reinforced with the lead elements of the 1st SS Panzer Division that had sped to the area from its assembly area east of Caen. The bridges over the Orne, which should have been seized by the British airborne assault force, were now being used by the German tanks.

The night of June 6 only added to the Allied disaster. There was no letup in the German artillery bombardment of the landing areas. German air attacks had all but stopped, but there was no assurance that they would not begin again at dawn. All through the night Allied planners with the forces on the Channel and back in England tried to find alternatives that would lift the pressure on the beaches and allow for more troops to be sent ashore. Allied naval guns fired continuously, forming a curtain of steel and high explosives around the beaches that gave some respite to the men on shore. But it also prevented them from moving inland off the beaches. Every Allied bomber and fighter that could be mustered was sent into the fight, blasting every conceivable gun emplacement and enemy troop assembly area behind the beaches. The numbers of casualties from the Allied air attacks were enormous but—despite Allied air interdiction—fresh Wehrmacht units seemed to arrive by the hour. Could their estimates of German strength have been so far off the mark, the Allied commanders pondered? In fact, they were not. The Germans were simply pouring everything they had left into the fight, and by good planning and good fortune these resources were where they were needed when they were needed. This fact would not be appreciated for some time, however, and it was almost as much of a surprise to the Germans as to the Allies.

Withdrawal

At the moment, however, any conjectures of this type had to be put aside, as more immediate problems were at hand. At 5 A.M. on June 7 Allied Command was informed that casualties were running about 30% across the entire landing zone. Evacuation of wounded was nearly impossible, hardly any artillery had gotten ashore, and intelligence reports indicated at least four more German divisions, though hammered from the air, were approaching the Normandy peninsula from the northeast, east, and south. The weather forecasts were bad; planners, airmen, naval gunners, and especially the troops on the beach, were near exhaustion.

It took almost five hours for everything to be sorted out, and during that time 425 additional American, British, French and Polish soldiers, sailors, airmen and marines lost their lives. This was not anyone's fault. Plans for withdrawal had been worked out as carefully as had the plans for the invasion itself. But the confusion caused by the ferocity of the German response to the landings, and especially the presence of the German jets, had caught the Allies by surprise. At 10 A.M., June 7, 1944, General Eisenhower ordered the withdrawal of forces from the beaches. The invasion had failed.

When the withdrawal order was passed down through the commands it came as a relief to many, and caused even greater confusion among the rest. Most of the forces to be committed to the beaches were still aboard their landing ships. Although for the most part they had been kept informed of what was going on, the simple fact that the landings had failed was almost incomprehensible. The battle-hardened veterans of the landings in Africa and Sicily were the most incredulous.

To the ordinary soldier, it was just another snafu. And so it appeared to the free world when the announcement from Eisenhower was broadcast: "Our landings in the Cherbourg-LeHavre area have failed to gain a satisfactory foothold and I have withdrawn the troops. My decision to attack at this time and place was based upon the best information available. The troops, the air forces, and the Navy did all that bravery and devotion to duty could do. If any blame or fault attends to the attempt it is mine alone."

The world was stunned. Even Rommel, the architect of the plans for the defense of western Europe, could not believe that the Allies had given up. But the elation caused by the stunning victory they had just gained could not dim the realization by many in the German High Command that in dealing such a terrible defeat they had only strengthened the Western resolve. Only Hitler and his trusted acolytes refused to admit the truth. The Allies would try again, and the next time there would be little that could be done to stop them.

Afterword

This story is, of course, pure fiction. Many of the facts are true, however, as the Germans did have the capability of upsetting, and possibly stopping, the Normandy invasion. That they refused to believe the intelligence they received and did not better utilize the forces they had available, was mainly Hitler's responsibility. The Germans did have the Me 262, but in limited numbers, and for some reason they never exploited its use until the very end of the war. They also had the troops available and the communications to use them, but they did not. The Fifteenth Army, principally guarding the Pas-de-Calais, was not even informed of the landings until many hours after they had begun. Rommel went on leave just before the invasion, even though German radio intercept had picked up the warning messages. All in all, the Germans failed to capitalize on what they knew and what they had. The actual landings were less than perfect. The 4th Division did land at the wrong place, and it was many hours after the landings in the American and British sectors had begun before any assurance could be given to General Eisenhower that they were successful. Had the events transpired along the lines of this fictional story—and they could have—there is no question that another attempt would have been made. It is most likely, however, that at least one more year would have passed before the second invasion could have begun. In that interim the Germans and, to some extent the West, would have suffered grievously. And Eisenhower would almost certainly never have become President of the United States.

CHAPTER X

Ardennes, 1944:
Bulge and Fishhook

Conference at the Wolf's Lair

ON THE MORNING of October 22, 1944, two senior general officers passed through the heavily-guarded entrance of the Führer's headquarters in East Prussia—the famed Wolf's Lair—and reported to Colonel General Alfred Jodl, Chief of the Planning Staff of *Oberkommando des Wehrmacht* (OKW), the Supreme Headquarters of the German Armed Forces. The two visitors saluted Jodl, who returned their salutes, then shook their hands.

"Good morning, Westphal, good morning, Krebs," Jodl said. "We have much to talk about. But first, because of the special significance of what we are about to discuss, I must ask both of you to read, and then sign, this statement." He gave each of them duplicate copies of a typed, single-page document.

The two visiting officers were General of Cavalry Siegfried Westphal, Chief of Staff of *Oberbefehlshaber West* (Command West, or OB West), and General of Infantry Hans Krebs, Chief of Staff of Army Group B, one of four groups of armies under OB West. Westphal and Krebs had been summoned to report to Jodl by coded telegram the previous day. Both assumed that they were called to explain why German forces had yielded Aachen to the Americans early on the 21st. They were anticipating the likelihood that they would be berated by Hitler personally. Thus they were surprised to read from the papers in their hands that the purpose of the visit was to discuss Operation *Wacht am Rhein*—Watch on the Rhine—the details of which were so highly secret that if any word of what they learned should leak to the enemy, the person or people responsible would be shot. Both generals quickly read the paper, as quickly signed it, and each returned his signed copy to Jodl, who then gave each of them a carbon copy of the paper they had signed.

"Please take this back to your commanders, when you report to them about this meeting. They, and anyone else who works on this project, will be subject to the penalty indicated should any word of our plans fall into the enemy's hands."

Westphal was representing Field Marshal Gerd von Rundstedt, who had been called from retirement on September 5 to take command of the crumbling German front in the West, following the breakout of Allied forces from Normandy, and the Allied amphibious landings in southern France. During September and October Rundstedt, as C-in-C West, had been able to patch together a continuous front and to halt the Allied offensive as it approached the western frontiers of Germany. His success in this effort had been due only in part to his great military skill and the professionalism of his staff under the direction of General Westphal. The Allies themselves had contributed. In early September they had run out of supplies of fuel and ammunition, and thus were unable to sustain their offensive. But the German defensive success had also been due to the amazing resiliency and professionalism of the entire German Army, and the ability of its officers and soldiers to take advantage of the Allied pause, and of the defensive capabilities of their powerful Westwall.

The defensive success—the "Miracle in the West" some

German journalists were calling it—had also been in large part due to the skill of one of Rundstedt's principal subordinates, Field Marshal Walther Model, commander of Army Group B, of which Krebs was Chief of Staff. Model had been ordered from Russia to the West to take over Army Group B after his predecessor, Field Marshal Erwin Rommel, had been badly wounded by an Allied air attack on July 17. He had also acted briefly as C-in-C West, after the suicide of Field Marshal Guenther von Kluge, in August, as the Allies began their dramatic surge through France. Model had been able to recover more of his battered divisions from that debacle than might reasonably have been expected in the circumstances, thus living up to the reputation as "the Führer's fireman" he had earned in handling a number of difficult situations on the Eastern Front.

In late September and early October the Allies, having gotten their logistical situation in order, and having secured the port of Antwerp to ease their supply problems, began to bring increasing pressure on the Germans in eastern France and Belgium. Skill, professionalism, and grim determination to protect their country from invasion were not enough to enable the outnumbered Germans to stop the equally determined efforts of the Allies, under commanders who were by this time also skilled professionals. Thus the Germans were being slowly driven back to their frontiers. In some areas the Allies were actually on German soil. They had even penetrated the Westwall in several places, in the Eifel region, and just to the north near Aachen. Both Rundstedt and Model had pleaded unsuccessfully for reinforcements, but had been told by OKW that there were none. They were reminded that the approaches to Germany were being battered just as vigorously from the east and the south as they were from the west. So Rundstedt and Model were resigned to doing the best that they could, recognizing that under these circumstances there could be only one conclusion to the war: German defeat and collapse within a few months.

Operation "Wacht am Rhein"

Thus both Westphal and Krebs were amazed to learn that Operation *Wacht am Rhein* was an ambitious plan for a major German counteroffensive in the West, designed to throw the Allies back, and to defeat them so disastrously that they would agree to a negotiated peace. As the two generals soon would learn, the plan had been the brainchild of Hitler himself, first announced to his staff about a month earlier, in late September. Between September 25 and October 22 Jodl and his staff planners had been developing the plan, which was now sufficiently elaborated that it could be presented to the chiefs of staff of OB West and Army Group B.

In brief, the plan provided for a bold German thrust from the Eifel region of western Germany through the Ardennes Forest in Luxembourg and Belgium, to Antwerp. This would deny the Allies their new port, and would split asunder the Allied armies in the West. In the process the Allies would be dealt such a devastating blow as to demoralize them, and make them ready for peace. The offensive was to be carried out by two armies of Army Group B—the Fifth and the Sixth Panzer Armies—with support from the Seventh Army in the south. The total forces available would be approximately 30 divisions—12 panzer or panzergrenadier divisions, and 18 infantry divisions—almost twice the strength then available to Army Group B in the area where the attack would be launched.

This area stretched from Monschau, in the north, to Trier in the south, a distance of about 90 miles along the meandering front.

Westphal and Krebs were told that the main effort would be made by the Sixth Panzer Army on the right, commanded by SS Colonel General Josef "Sepp" Dietrich of the Waffen-SS. Dietrich, a tough beerhall fighter in his youth, owed his high military position solely to favoritism: he had been an early member of the Nazi Party and

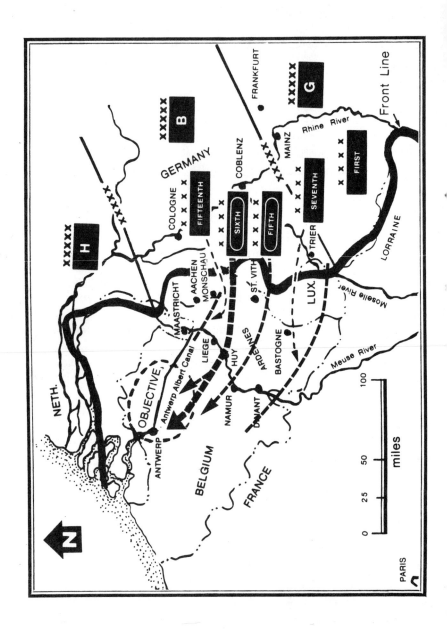

had then been the commander of Hitler's SS bodyguard. He was not stupid; he had learned something about military planning and operational matters in his meteoric rise in the Waffen-SS—the private army of the Nazi Party, which had become a major component of the German Army. But he was totally unsuited for high command, and has rightly been contemptuously dismissed by an eminent historian as a "military ignoramus."

The secondary effort, in the center, was to be made by the Fifth Panzer Army, commanded by a brilliant, relatively young professional, Panzer General Hasso-Eccard von Manteuffel. He had served with distinction under Rommel in North Africa and had then commanded a division in Russia. His bravery and skill had been brought to the attention of Hitler, who promoted the young general from divisional to army command.

A diversionary effort was to be made on the left by the Seventh Army, commanded by Panzer General Erich Brandenberger. A similar diversionary effort was to be made on the right by the left-hand corps of the Fifteenth Army. All of the 30-odd divisions were already being brought up to full strength in manpower and guns, and the panzer divisions would have at least two-thirds of their authorized strength in tanks and assault guns.

After a full day of intense conference with the OKW planning staff, Westphal and Krebs had a brief meeting with Hitler. This was followed by a parting admonition from Field Marshal Wilhelm Keitel, Chief of Staff of OKW. After assuring them on his honor as an officer that adequate stocks of fuel and ammunition would be available, he told them that, regardless of Allied activity in the meantime, they and their commanders must not commit any of the units being groomed and brought up to strength before D-Day. This was tentatively set for November 25. Jodl then promised that they would receive detailed written instructions within a week.

The two chiefs of staff returned to their headquarters that evening, and reported to their respective field marshal commanders. Rundstedt and Model had almost iden-

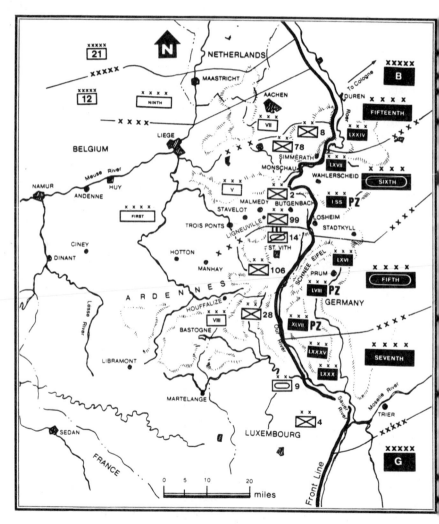

Front Line Situation, December 16

tical reactions. Even if all of the promised divisions should be made available—and both commanders had their doubts—they both felt that there was no possibility that such an attack with such forces could reach Antwerp.

German Planning Begins

However, orders were orders. Rundstedt immediately assembled a tiny planning staff at his headquarters at Ziegenberg, near Coblenz. Because of the penalty for security failure, in addition to Rundstedt and Westphal this planning group included only the Chief of Plans of OB West, Lieutenant General Bodo Zimmermann; the principal supply and administrative officer, Lieutenant General Friedrich John; and Rundstedt's principal aide-de-camp. Working three days and nights without sleep, by the evening of October 26 Rundstedt had a plan for using the forces promised by OKW. This provided for a deep and powerful thrust on a narrow front, northwestward from the vicinity of Prum toward the Meuse, between Huy and Liége. It would have as its objective a bridgehead over the Meuse northeast of Huy.

On the 27th, after some sleep, Rundstedt took his planning group to Model's headquarters at Fichtenhain, near Krefeld. There they met with Model and a similar small planning group of Army Group B, who had been working out a plan not too different from that of OB West. Also present at the conference were the three army commanders: Generals von Manteuffel, Dietrich, and Brandenberger. There was general agreement on the Rundstedt plan, with some modifications, and Rundstedt ordered Model to have the revised plan ready for submission to him the following day, October 28. By that time additional instructions were expected from Jodl.

Although they had no way of knowing it, the professional reactions of Rundstedt, Model, and their senior subordinates were similar to Jodl's when he was first told by Hitler to start planning for *Wacht am Rhein*. In fact, Jodl still hoped he could persuade the Führer to agree to a narrow front, limited penetration, designed to do great damage to the Allies, but without any intention of getting to Antwerp in a single, broad front drive. He therefore postponed sending instructions to Rundstedt, and raised the issue again with Hitler. But the Führer was adamant. The operation would go as he had originally conceived it: converging drives of the Fifth and Sixth Panzer Armies, meeting at Antwerp. So, on November 2 Jodl sent the promised instructions, pointing out that, despite the paucity of resources, the effort must be made as Hitler directed. For the record, Rundstedt protested the decision, then pressed ahead to do his best to make it work.

It soon became obvious to all of the German staff officers that the proposed target date for the operation could not be met. There was too much to be done, too many compromises to be made and adjusted to, as various expedients were taken to scrape together the resources in troops, equipment, and supplies that were needed if the desperate effort was to have any chance of success. While this was being done, it was necessary to revise the plans to adapt them to the real circumstances. In this process the planners made several efforts to reduce the scope of the operation, only to meet with firm rejection by the Führer. It was not until December 9 that the final plan, with scope and concept as he demanded, was approved by Hitler. D-Day was tentatively set for the 12th, then the 15th, and finally for the 16th, when weather unfavorable for Allied air operations was expected.

The troops and supplies for the operation were gathered in the strictest secrecy. An elaborate cover plan had been prepared to make the Allies believe that the activities—which could not be completely concealed— were simply a part of the normal effort of the Germans to assemble defensive forces to cope with the continuing Allied pressure. To the extent that an offensive capability might be detected by the Allies, considerable overt activity was undertaken in the northern portion of the Fifteenth Army's sector, and further south in the First Army's sector in Lorraine, to make it appear that local counterattacks were being planned in those regions.

The Allied Plans

The German deception efforts were completely successful. In fact, the Allies were continuing offensive operations in the northern portion of the US First Army zone, just north of the area where the Germans were planning their offensive. The First Army effort was planned as a preliminary to a major Allied offensive by Field Marshal Bernard L. Montgomery's 21st Army Group, and the left wing of General Omar Bradley's 12th Army Group. This offensive was to sweep across the Cologne Plain to the Rhine and on into the heart of Germany's industrial region. As part of a vast Allied pincers movement, the US Third Army was also beginning the preliminaries of a major offensive in northern Lorraine. The main drive of the Third Army was planned to begin on December 19. It would smash across the border into the Palatinate, advancing south of the Moselle River to the Rhine in the Frankfurt-Mainz area.

The Allies, confident that the Germans had no further major offensive capability, and concentrating on their own plans, paid little attention to activity in the area of German Army Group B. They paid even less attention to the rugged, forested region of the Ardennes and Eifel, lying between the two areas where the major Allied activity was planned. This region was considered to be unsuited for major armor operations, and so was designated an "inactive" sector, to be held with light defensive forces, while the major Allied concentrations were effected to the north and the south. Since the Allies could not be strong everywhere, the Ardennes-Eifel region was thinly manned. As General Dwight D. Eisenhower, the Supreme Allied Commander, explained later at a press conference at Supreme Headquarters, Allied Expeditionary Force (SHAEF), this was "a calculated risk." This area was held by the U.S. VIII Corps, commanded by Major General Troy Middleton.

Although some German activity was detected by Allied intelligence in the zones of the German Fifth and Sixth Panzer Armies during the period beginning about December 12, this was discounted as merely routine redeployment, since it was known that the Germans were preparing themselves to meet the more dangerous Allied thrusts to the north and the south. Bad weather prevented large-scale Allied aerial reconnaissance, and in any case German security measures would have made it difficult for such reconnaissance to see very much. The elements of nature were combining with good planning and an excellent cover plan to prevent the Allies from being aware of what was taking place just to the east of the US V and VIII Corps.

The Keys: St. Vith and Fuel

The road net in the operational area was poor. This was a region of evergreen-crested hills drained by many narrow rivers running between steep banks and through dense woods. The roads were winding and at this time were clogged with snow and ice. Once the Germans had crossed the Belgian-Luxembourg border into the Ardennes, rapid advance westward depended upon the possession of two vital road junctions: Saint-Vith in the north, and Bastogne to the south. Actually, until the high ground immediately north, south, and west of Saint-Vith was gained, westward cross-country deployment of armored vehicles was almost impossible, a situation further complicated by three to five inches of snow.

In effect, then, immediate possession of Saint-Vith was essential—Model tabbed it for the first 24 hours. However, he well realized the difficulties of reaching this intermediate objective in such a short time, under the existing conditions of weather and terrain.

On the other hand, since the Eifel-Ardennes region lay between the axes of Allied invasion—the Aachen gateway to the Cologne Plain and the Moselle corridor to the Rhine—the Germans had been almost certain that it would be lightly held. Now German intelligence confirmed this. The parallel to the situation in this same Ardennes region in 1940, which had also been exploited by Germans under Rundstedt's command, must have been noted, and perhaps dispelled some of the generals' pessimism.

The German operational plans had two unusual features. Peculiarly Hitlerian was Operation *Greif,* to be executed by the 150th Panzer Brigade, under Lieutenant Colonel Otto Skorzeny, a scar-faced Nazi desperado who had come to notoriety by rescuing Mussolini from Italian partisan clutches following his downfall in 1943. This brigade, composed of English-speaking Germans (150 of them spoke English perfectly), was to be clad in American uniforms and use captured or camouflaged US tanks and vehicles. Skorzeny's outfit led Dietrich's Sixth SS Panzer Army. Another element, paratroops, were to be dropped in front of the right of Dietrich's drive, aiming for Eupen.

The other unusual aspect of the German plan was reliance on Allied fuel dumps for maintaining forward momentum. To Model this idea of assuring the success of the operation by feeding the advance at Allied fuel supply points was one of the three key features of the operational plan. The other two keys—more commonplace tactical objectives—were successfully bludgeoning a hole in the Allied lines, and then quickly widening the shoulders of the gap, once the breakthrough was accomplished.

The pre-assault bombardment by the artillery of three German armies began at precisely 5:30 A.M. on the morning of December 16. There were 21 divisions in the eight corps of the assault force.

Disposition of German Forces

The northern, or right wing of Dietrich's Sixth SS Panzer Army, was the LXVII Corps, commanded by General Otto

Hitzfeld. Its two infantry divisions—the 272d Volksgrenadier on the right, and the 326th Volksgrenadier on the left—were deployed between Simmerath, in the north, and Wahlerscheid. Its objective was to establish the right shoulder of the offensive's penetration near Eupen.

On the left, extending down to just southeast of Losheim, was the I SS Panzer Corps of SS Lieutenant General Hermann Preiss. This corps was to make the offensive's main effort. From north to south three infantry divisions were on line: 277th Volksgrenadier, 12th Volksgrenadier, and 3d Parachute. The corps' two armored divisions were further back, ready to exploit the expected breakthrough: the 12th SS Panzer Division in the north, and the 1st SS Panzer, behind the 3d Parachute and 12th Volksgrenadier Divisions, were ready to make a dash through the Losheim Gap.

In the Sixth SS Panzer Army reserve was the II SS Panzer Corps, consisting of the 2d and 9th SS Panzer divisions, and commanded by SS General Willi Bittrich. It was to be a second wave of armor, committed after a clean breakthrough had been achieved. These two divisions were to drive through the hole in the American lines for the Meuse River, between Huy and Liége. By this time the army's five infantry divisions were expected to be holding the northern shoulder from Eupen to Liége.

The Fifth Panzer Army, to the left of the Sixth, also had three corps. The LXVI Corps, on the right, commanded by General Walther Lucht, consisted of two infantry divisions. The 18th Volksgrenadier Division, also on the right, was to carry out a bold double envelopment of the Schnee Eifel ridge, while the 62d Volksgrenadier Division was to advance toward Saint-Vith south of the ridge. In this way the army commander, General von Manteuffel, hoped not only to trap the Americans holding the ridge, but also to open a hole so that Lucht's corps could advance to a blocking position at the crossroads at Saint-Vith, assuring the security of the army's right flank, as well as an open line of communications for the spearheads driving west.

In the center of the Fifth Panzer Army was General Walter Krueger's LVIII Panzer Corps, with its two divisions in column: the 560th Volksgrenadier Division, followed by the 116th Panzer Division.

On the left, General Heinrich von Luettwitz' XLVII Panzer Corps was to make the Fifth Panzer Army's main effort. The 26th Volksgrenadier Division held the center of the corps line, while the 2d Panzer was echeloned behind the infantry's northern (right) wing, and the Panzer Lehr Division was similarly echeloned back to the left rear.

In Fifth Army reserve was the armored Führer Begleit Brigade, which had been built up to approximately divisional strength for this operation. Manteuffel stationed it to the right rear of the LXVI Corps.

The southernmost of Army Group B's four armies was General Erich Brandenberger's Seventh Army. Its mission was first to undertake a holding attack, to facilitate the main offensive, and then to hold the southern shoulder of the penetration that would be made by the two armies to its north, and to establish blocking positions to protect the left rear of the Fifth Panzer Army. To do this General Brandenberger had only four divisions, in two corps. On the right was the LXXXV Corps of General Baptist Kniess, with the 5th Parachute and the 352d Volksgrenadier Divisions abreast. On the left was the LXXX Corps, commanded by General Franz Beyer, with the 276th and 212th Volksgrenadier Divisions on line.

Field Marshal Model had been told by General Jodl that two armored divisions of the OKW Reserve would be released to him at such time as was deemed appropriate by the Führer. These were the 9th Panzer (not to be confused with the 9th SS Panzer Division) and 15th Panzer Grenadier divisions.

North of the Sixth SS Panzer Army, the lefthand corps of the Fifteenth Army, the LXXIV Corps with four infantry divisions, was to initiate a holding attack at the same time as the three armies to its south began their attacks. These divisions were not expected to play a major role and, in fact, as the battle went, they did not.

Thus, without the divisions of the LXXIV Corps, there were committed to the offensive eight panzer divisions, and thirteen infantry divisions, with two panzer divisions (one really a panzer grenadier or mechanized division) probably also available.

The American Dispositions

Opposing the 21 German divisions now poised for their major offensive were two American army corps, approximately nine divisions strong. Since the average strengths of the divisions on both sides were 12,000 to 14,000 men, it will be seen that the Germans had little more than twice the numerical strength of the defenders, a margin of superiority which most modern military planners would consider insufficient for a successful attack. This better than two-to-one advantage in manpower was matched by the ratio in armor. The Fifth and Sixth Panzer Armies had a total of about 1,000 tanks and armored assault guns; the Americans opposing them had about 400 tanks.

However, the Germans had one—and they hoped two— additional advantages on which they were counting. In the first place they had the very great advantage of almost complete surprise, which they rightly counted on to multiply their strength by a factor of two or three. And they were confident that this enhancement would be further augmented by a superiority in professionalism and training. In this, too, they were correct in their assessment, although the margin of combat effectiveness superiority was to prove, on balance, to be less than they had anticipated.

Facing the Sixth Panzer Army on a front of about 30 miles was the U.S. V Corps, commanded by Major General Leonard T. Gerow, consisting of the equivalent of five divisions. On the left was the 8th Infantry Division, and on the right was the 99th Division. In the center, just north of the 99th Division, was the veteran 2d Division, which had begun an attack toward the Roer River Dams on December 13. To its left was the new 78th Division, supporting the attack, while the flank divisions of the corps carried out local holding attacks. In reserve were two armored combat commands.

It is interesting that the V Corps offensive, driving generally to the east and northeast, was directed against the German LXVII Corps, on the right flank of the Sixth Panzer Army, just a few kilometers north of where the I SS Panzer Corps was about to make the main effort of the coming German offensive. The American attack seriously disrupted the plan of General Hitzfeld, as he disposed his divisions in preparation for his own offensive on the 16th. Thus the Germans counterattacked sharply on December 14th and 15th, so that the gains of the 2d and 78th Divisions on those days were negligible.

The 99th Division, directly in the path of the center and right wing of the I SS Panzer Corps, not surprisingly made no progress in its holding attacks on December 13th, 14th, and 15th.

To the right of the V Corps, General Middleton's VIII Corps held a front of about 70 miles with only three divisions plus some armored units. On the extreme left was the 106th Division—which had just arrived in Europe and had been put into the line in its first combat experience on December 12. The 106th had all three of its regiments, plus the attached 14th Cavalry Group, on line, extended along a front of nearly 20 miles. On the left was the 14th Cavalry, holding the Losheim Gap, and linking on its left with the 99th Division of the V Corps. Then from north to south were the 422d, 423d, and 424th Infantry regiments. The 422d and 423d held positions along the Schnee Eifel Ridge, taking advantage of the German Westwall fortifications on the ridge. To the right of the green 106th Division was the battered 28th Division, with its three regiments also in line, holding a front also nearly 20 miles long. South of the 28th Division a combat command of the new and inexperienced 9th Armored Division held a front of about four miles along the Sauer River. And to its right, the tired 4th Division also held a front of about 20 miles, but had the advantage of a water barrier along the entire front: the Sauer River on the left and the Moselle River on the right.

The extreme left of the 106th Division—that part of the front held by the 14th Cavalry Group—was opposite the extreme left of the German I SS Panzer Corps, and in fact lay in the path of the 12th Volksgrenadier and 3d Parachute Divisions. These two divisions—followed closely by the 1st SS Panzer Division—were to make the main effort of the coming German offensive. The remainder of the 106th Division was opposed by the LXVI Panzer Corps of the Fifth Panzer Army.

Two-thirds of the 28th Division (the 112th and 110th Infantry regiments) was opposed by the bulk of two German panzer corps, the LVIII SS Panzer Corps and the XLVII Panzer Corps, consisting of three armored and two infantry divisions. The right-hand regiment of the 28th Division (the 109th Infantry) faced the entire LXXV Corps of the German Seventh Army. Combat Command A of the 9th Armored Division and the 4th Infantry Division, were opposed by the LXXXV and the LXXX Corps of the Seventh Army.

Assault

When the violent German artillery preparation ended at about 7:00 A.M. on December 16, the front line infantry units of the entire Sixth Panzer Army began their planned assault. But only on the extreme southern end of the army front did the attack go as planned. In the north, in the sector of the LXVII Corps, the attacks of the 272d and 326th Volksgrenadier Divisions ran head-on into the continuing attacks of the US 78th and 2d Divisions. On the right wing and center of the I SS Panzer Corps, the 277th Volksgrenadier Division had hardly more success against the 99th Division, although here the Germans began to forge ahead during the afternoon.

But to the left of the I SS Panzer Corps sector, the 12th Volksgrenadier and 3d Parachute Divisions were successful even beyond the pre-assault hopes of the German commanders. Their attack sector was opposite the boundary between the V Corps and the VIII Corps. Actually there was a two-mile gap between the right of the 99th Division and the left of the 106th Division's attached 14th Cavalry Group. This gap, covered by jeep patrols of the 394th Infantry Regiment of the 99th Division, and the 14th Cavalry, was quickly filled with German infantry. On the right the 12th Volksgrenadier Division stormed its way into Bucholz. During the afternoon, however, progress was slower, as the 394th rallied, and the 99th Division commander, Major General Walter E. Lauer, committed his division reserve to bolster his threatened right flank.

Better, from the German standpoint, were the initial results achieved by the 3d Parachute Division. By dark of December 16 it had pushed back the left wing of the 14th Cavalry more than five kilometers.

And still more spectacular were the results that the LXVI Corps was achieving just south of the army boundary. On a relatively narrow front the 194th and 195th Regiments of the 18th Volksgrenadier Division stormed westward into the southern portion of the sector of the 14th Cavalry Group. The third regiment of the German division was some eight miles to the south, opposite the boundary between the 423d and 424th Infantry regiments of the 106th Division. Major General Hoffmann-Schonborn, the division commander, with the approval—indeed encouragement—of his corps and army commanders, Generals Lucht and Manteuffel, had planned a daring double envelopment of a larger American force, counting on the benefits of surprise and of greater combat effectiveness. Boldly, he left only one battalion to hold the front between his two assault forces.

The gamble worked. In the north the two German regiments, which had actually begun their advance while the artillery preparation was being fired, advanced steadily.

By nightfall they were more than five miles inside the American lines and were threatening the left rear of the 422d Infantry. To the south the left-hand regiment of the 18th Volksgrenadiers, advancing beside the 62d Volksgrenadier Division, had blasted its way almost as far into the position of the 424th Infantry, thus threatening the right flank and rear of the 423d Infantry.

During the cold and blustery night the two spearheads of the 18th Volksgrenadier Division pressed forward. In confused fighting in the short day that followed, the spearheads met; the 422d and 423d Infantry regiments, and attached units, some 9,000 troops, were encircled, and for all practical purposes out of the battle.

Breakthrough and Exploitation

Late on December 17th, as it became evident to the German commanders that they were achieving a breakthrough in the Losheim Gap area, the Fifth and Sixth Army commanders ordered their armored units to begin the exploitation phase. In fact their corps commanders had already started some of their armored units forward.

By dawn on the 17th, Task Force Peiper, built around the 1st SS Panzer Regiment of the 1st SS Panzer Division, was headed for Bullingen. The commander of the 1st SS Panzer Regiment, SS Lieutenant Colonel Joachim Peiper, had been directed to reach the Meuse at Huy as rapidly as possible. He was also to capture as much gasoline as possible, to make up for the German shortage of fuel. At dawn the Germans captured considerable gasoline at Bullingen. They filled their fuel tanks and continued westward. During the day a battery from an American field artillery observation battalion was overrun and captured near Ligneuville. The prisoners were herded into a field and gunned down with machine guns—the Malmedy Massacre. The extent to which Peiper himself was responsible for this atrocity has never been truly determined, despite a number of investigations and trials. But that is another story.

By evening Task Force Peiper had reached Stavelot. By this time Peiper, and the commander of the 1st SS Panzer Division, realized that the 12th SS Panzer Division, which was supposed to be advancing on the right, was nowhere around. In fact, the 12th was held up by the continuing resistance of the American 99th and 2d Divisions. The 99th had seriously slowed the advance of the 277th Volksgrenadier Division, and the 2d had completely halted the 326th Volksgrenadier Division, and was actually resuming its own offensive. Peiper decided to wait till dawn before attacking Stavelot. During the night American engineers destroyed the fuel dump in Stavelot.

Thus, by evening of the second day of the offensive, the Sixth Panzer Army had only one of its armored divisions in the exploitation role. By this time Sepp Dietrich had expected to have all four of his panzer divisions on the march.

Things had gone better for the Germans in the Fifth Army sector. But there had also been setbacks. In addition to the breakthrough achieved in the 106th Division sector, the LVIII SS Panzer Corps and the XLVII Panzer Corps had achieved successes only slightly less dramatic against the 28th Division. The Führer Begleit Brigade, held up by the fighting west of the Schnee Eifel, had by the evening of December 17th begun to advance toward Saint-Vith, east of the 62d Volksgrenadier Division. The 116th Panzer Division was making disappointing progress against the 28th Division's 112th Infantry Regiment, but the 2d Panzer and Panzer Lehr Divisions were both driving westward toward Bastogne through the severely battered 110th Infantry Regiment sector.

German Redeployment

That night Manteuffel called Model and reported that he had made two clear breakthroughs. He suggested that the II SS Panzer Corps be released from Dietrich's Sixth SS Panzer Army and given to him, and that the OKW Reserve divisions also be committed in his Fifth Panzer Army sector. He assured Model that with the four additional panzer divisions he could reach, and probably cross, the Meuse by December 20th or 21st at the latest. Model agreed with him, and immediately called Jodl at Rastenberg in East Prussia. After a brief conversation Jodl seemed to be convinced, but said that he would have to consult the Führer.

Half an hour later Jodl called back to the headquarters of Army Group B. Hitler refused to approve the transfer of either the II SS Panzer Corps or the OKW Reserve to the Fifth Panzer Army. "He has promised Sepp Dietrich that Dietrich will be the hero of this offensive and of the war, and he refuses to change his mind," said Jodl.

Model then decided to do something that would have been unthinkable to his superior, Field Marshal von Rundstedt. As a loyal Nazi, and as a fellow favorite of the Führer, he decided to call Dietrich, and enlist his assistance in persuading Hitler to issue the orders to reinforce the Fifth Army.

Model and Dietrich had a long argument. Dietrich insisted that he would soon overrun the US 99th and 2d divisions, and would have his three remaining panzer divisions on the road to Liége within 24 hours. "At most, 36 hours," he insisted.

Patiently, Model told him that the Americans and British were rushing reinforcements to the front. "Thirty-six hours, even twenty-four hours, and it will be too late." The only chance for the offensive to achieve anything like its objectives would be to reinforce the breakthroughs of the Fifth Panzer Army the next morning. Then, before the Allies had a chance to reestablish a line, their troops could be further disrupted, their columns on the road would be destroyed, and victory, at worst a limited victory, could be achieved. "There will be honor for all. Your 1st and 12th SS Panzer Divisions will then link up with Manteuffel's divisons north of the Meuse. You will have your cake and eat it too, because it will be clear from my reports that you, and you alone, made the glorious and

self-sacrificing decision that assured this victory for the
Führer."

Dietrich obviously was shaken by Model's eloquence.
He promised to think about it and said that he would call
Hitler.

Two hours later, just before midnight, Model received
another call from Jodl. "I don't know how you did it,"
said Jodl, "but the Führer has released the OKW Reserve
to you, and has said that he will approve any readjust-
ment of forces you wish to make in the elements of Army
Group B in order to exploit your successes. That means
you can use the II SS Panzer Corps as you see fit. Con-
gratulations!"

Model immediately phoned Rundstedt to tell him of
this latest development. The old field marshal was
slightly annoyed to learn that he had been so blatantly
bypassed, but recognized that Model had accomplished a
virtual miracle. He gave him his blessing and went back
to bed.

Model then called Manteuffel. He told him briefly what
had occurred and asked if Manteuffel was prepared to use
the four new divisions by the next day. Manteuffel assured the field marshal that he had made the necessary
plans and could make good use of the divisions.

"All right, then. I won't tell you what to do, or how to
do it. But Saint-Vith and Bastogne are the keys. Keep me
informed. I may have some suggestions for you by morning."

As the staffs of Army Group B and of the Fifth Panzer
Army worked feverishly through the night, General Bittrich's II SS Panzer Corps began to march south from
Stadtkill to Prum. There, shortly after dawn, it was joined
by the 9th Panzer and 15th Panzer Grenadier Divisions.
General Manteuffel met General Bittrich at Prum at 8:00
A.M.. Quickly Manteuffel sketched his plan on a map. The
two divisions of the OKW Reserve were attached to the II
SS Panzer Corps. Bittrich was to press as rapidly as possible after the 2d Panzer and Panzer Lehr Divisions, with
the objective of occupying Bastogne before dawn on De-

cember 19th. Then the Fifth Panzer Army would turn northwest and, with two panzer corps abreast (the II SS Panzer on the right, the XLVII on the left), would drive for Namur and Huy. A bridgehead would be established across the Meuse, and further instructions would then be given. The right flank might be in some danger from Allied units in the Saint-Vith area, but Manteuffel was confident that these would be taken care of by the LXVI Corps and the Sixth Panzer Army. The rear and left rear of the two spearhead panzer corps would be covered by the Seventh Army and the remainder of the Fifth Army.

It almost worked. Or at least so it seemed at the time. Some historians have asserted that with only a bit of luck Hitler's prompt decision to approve Manteuffel's and Model's plan could have brought success. The employment of four fresh armored divisions to exploit the Fifth Army breakthrough might have changed the course of the war. To this historian, however, it is clear that all of the luck in the world could not have significantly changed the outcome. The German effort was doomed from the moment Hitler conceived the idea in September. To see why this is so, we must look back to see what the Allies had been doing since the beginning of the German offensive.

Allied Reaction

They had been surprised, of course. It is easy, in retrospect, to say that they should not have been surprised. There was plenty of evidence that the Germans were marshalling men, weapons, and supplies behind the front in western Germany. But to the Allied leaders this seemed the natural reaction of a desperate regime making desperate efforts to defend the nation from a mortal threat. That the Germans would risk dissipating their forces in what would appear to be a hopeless offensive effort, thus making later defense more difficult or impossible, seems never to have crossed the minds of Allied commanders, planners, or intelligence analysts. Clearly the logical thing for the Germans to do was to husband resources, and continue to fight the skillful, deadly defensive battle at which they were clearly so good, in hopes that mounting casualties and war-weariness would induce the Allies to agree to a negotiated peace. Since this seemed so logical to the Allied military leadership, they assumed that this must be what the enemy intended to do.

And so, having based their assessment on what they assumed were the enemy's intentions, and not on his capabilities, the Allies lulled themselves into the conclusion that all of the future decisions in the war would be theirs; that the Germans would merely react. And so they were surprised.

On top of this, the deployment of the 106th and 28th Divisions verged on being amateurish. Having been assigned extremely wide fronts, both division commanders had elected to deploy their regiments in line, to try to be sure they covered the entire front as thoroughly as possible. The result was a classic example of a cordon defense, bound to collapse once a breakthrough was made. The very width of the front made a defense in depth even more important than under more ordinary circumstances. The failure of the corps and army commanders to note, and to correct, the faulty deployment of these divisions was as reprehensible as the basic errors of the division commanders.

However, the reactions of the American commands to the German offensive were prompt and professional. Throughout the war the Americans and British were almost always more cautious and pedestrian in their war-waging than were their German opponents, but they were neither stupid nor inept. And in this crisis they reacted promptly, with determination, albeit still with a bit too much caution.

One Allied leader, less cautious than most of his colleagues, saw very clearly what Model and Rundstedt had seen in October; German success in this desperate offensive was impossible, even under the most favorable of circumstances.

The Verdun Conference

Lieutenant General George S. Patton, Jr., commander of the US Third Army, was ordered to attend a high-level conference on December 19th at Verdun—at the command post of the 12th Army Group's commander, General Omar Bradley—to discuss the situation created by the German offensive. Patton attended, after seeing to it that his own offensive, started that morning, was going as planned. General Eisenhower, who had called the conference, was present at the meeting, as was his British deputy, the quiet, pipe-smoking, Air Chief Marshal Sir Arthur W. Tedder of the Royal Air Force. Among the others present, in addition to Bradley and Patton, were Lieutenant General Jacob L. Devers, commander of the 6th Army Group, and Lieutenant General Courtney Hodges, whose US First Army was being ripped by the German drive.

SHAEF G-2, British Major General K. W. D. Strong, who had estimated only ten days previously that German offensive capabilities were practically nil, briefed the group; he told of the disaster to the 106th, the shattering of the 28th. The US 7th Armored Division, he told them, too, was already at Saint-Vith to bolster its defense; SHAEF reserve, the XVIII Airborne Corps, with its 82d and 101st Airborne Divisions, released to Bradley, was already entrucked and rolling east. Com-Z (the rear-area Communications Zone Command) was gathering its service troops to protect the Meuse bridges. The situation was serious, said Strong. It might even be dangerous.

And Patton's voice roared out—at least it was as much of a roar as his squeaky, high-pitched voice would permit—"Hell, let's have the guts to let the bastards go all the way to Paris. Then we'll really cut 'em off and chew 'em up!"

Then Ike announced his plan: counterattack from the south, hold on the north, with Devers side-slipping forces to cover gaps caused by the Third Army's switch northward to counterattack the southern flank of the German salient. Eisenhower knew that the Third Army had just that very morning begun its own offensive northeastward into the Rhineland. How soon could Patton mount a six-division attack?

Within four days—by December 22—a three-division assault would be mounted, Patton promptly responded. To wait longer and assemble a stronger force, he added, would be to lose surprise.

Actually, the amazing Patton, having conferred with Bradley at the first word of commotion on his left, had already alerted his III Corps; its 4th Armored Division was moving north, its infantry divisions standing by, his plan made. It needed but a phone call to his chief of staff to start a seemingly impossible task: shifting to a south-north direction an army already in attack on a west-east axis.

While Patton had been talking, General Bradley was handed a note by a young staff officer. He quickly read it, then pushed it in front of General Eisenhower. Grimly Ike read the message, then summarized the new situation to the officers present.

"Middleton reports that German armor now controls Bastogne. They and leading elements of our 101st Airborne Division both arrived in Bastogne around midnight last night, but there were more Germans there than Americans. The Germans are pushing northwest toward Namur. At least five panzer divisions. There's nothing in front of them except Com Z troops in the Meuse Valley. The 82d and 101st, now part of the VIII Corps, are forming a defensive position west of Bastogne up to Dinant, generally along the Lesse River." Ike paused, then got up and walked over to the situation map. He turned to Bradley as he pointed his finger at Saint-Vith, on the map.

"Brad, you had better get your people out of there. They are about to be cut off. What do you have there now?"

Bradley turned to Hodges, who walked up to the map beside Eisenhower.

"Bob Hasbrouck's 7th Armored Division is there, plus the remnants of the 106th—about a regiment—a regiment of the 28th, and CCB of the 9th Armored."

"That's a pretty mixed bag," said Eisenhower, thoughtfully.

"I was going to put them, along with Gavin's 82d Airborne, all under Ridgway's XVIII Airborne Corps when he and Gavin got there," said Bradley. "But of course the two airborne divisions are now cut off south of the penetration, since the Germans took Bastogne. I could still send Ridgway and his headquarters up there, by way of Namur. They aren't doing anything, now that Middleton has taken over both the 101st and the 82d."

"Why don't you do that?" responded Eisenhower. "Now," he continued, "please send in a stenographer; I want to send a message to Monty."

Thus was drafted the famous "Verdun Message," or "Fishhook Message," that sealed the fate of the German offensive. While consulting with Tedder, Bradley, and Strong, Eisenhower dictated the message. First he informed Montgomery of what had happened at Bastogne, and of the westward extension of the VIII Corps to the Meuse River at Dinant. After consulting Patton he dictated that the Third Army counterattack against the southern flank of the penetration could begin as early as December 21st. Next he told the Field Marshal of his order to Bradley to evacuate Saint-Vith, and of the imminent arrival of the XVIII Airborne Corps headquarters to take control of the withdrawing units. Eisenhower then told the stenographer taking the message to start a new paragraph.

"Twenty-one Army Group will be responsible for the area and all Allied forces north of the line Dinant-Houffalize-Prum; Twelfth Army Group will be similarly responsible for the area south of that line . . ."

"Ike," Bradley broke in. "We can handle our own front."

"I know you can, Brad," responded Eisenhower. "But there are British reserves, particularly Horrocks' XXX

Corps," he pointed to the map northwest of Namur, "that we need to get into the battle on the north flank as quickly as possible. The simplest and easiest way to do this without argument or international debate is to give Monty responsibility for the northern flank of the penetration."

Eisenhower returned to his dictation. He told Montgomery that the V Corps shoulder northeast of Saint Vith should be anchored solidly. He suggested that either the VII Corps or one of the two corps of General William H. Simpson's Ninth Army should be shifted from the present front to take the northern flank front west of the troops now withdrawing from Saint Vith. Other units could be side-slipped to fill the gap.

"Finally," Ike continued, "I suggest that Horrocks be given responsibility for the Meuse Bend between Dinant and Andenne. In this way we should end up with the Germans holding a line that looks like a fishhook, with its point south of the Meuse at Namur."

Eisenhower's prediction proved to be correct.

The Fishhook

Spearheads from the German II SS Panzer Corps approached the Meuse east and south of Namur shortly before noon on December 20. General Bittrich sent back a short message to Manteuffel. "We are on the Meuse. Far bank held by British infantry and armor. We have little fuel."

At about the same time Task Force Peiper was approaching Huy from the south. Suddenly Peiper's exhausted troopers found themselves under intensive artillery and tank fire from the north and east. Hastily they deployed for action, just as they were struck from the east by tanks of the US 2d Armored Division, part of General J. Lawton Collins' VII Corps.

Peiper recognized that he was outnumbered and outgunned. He ordered an immediate withdrawal. The Americans pursued closely, and not until Peiper had rejoined the main body of the 1st SS Panzer Division near

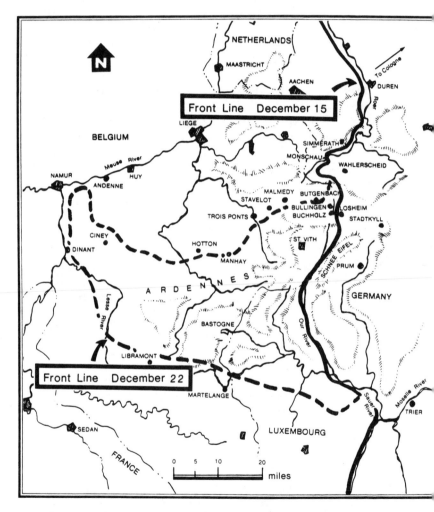

Strategic Situation, December 16, The "Fishhook"

Hotton just at dusk did the German retreat stop. Both sides began to build up their lines just south of Hotton.

About 25 miles to the south, at dawn on the 21st, the III Corps of the US Third Army, commanded by Major General John Millikin, began to attack northward toward Bastogne from the vicinity of Martelange. The troops of the 4th Armored Division, in the lead, soon ran into elements of the LXXXI Corps of the German Seventh Army in hastily prepared positions. The American attack stalled. But during the afternoon General Millikin sent in the 6th Armored Division, on the right of the 4th Armored, and the American attack was renewed. There was little progress during daylight hours and again the American tankers were halted. But Millikin's 35th, 26th, and 90th Infantry divisions arrived at the front by truck during the night. At dawn on December 22 the Americans renewed the attack for the third time, and finally began to forge slowly northward. German resistance was skillful and progress was slow, but it was progress. The southern flank of the penetration was now fixed in place.

At about the same time a continuous front was established by the Allies along the north flank of the penetration. The shoulder of the penetration, near Butgenbach, was still stoutly held by the 99th Division, with the veteran 2d Division anchoring the shoulder to the north of the 99th, and the veteran 1st Division anchoring it to the west.

The northern line then continued southwestward, just south of the towns of Stavelot, Trois Ponts, Manhay, and Hotton. Just west of Hotton the line began to run in a northwesterly direction to Ciney, and then more sharply northward to a point about five miles southeast of Namur. Then the line abruptly turned northeastward, to reach the right flank of the Führer Begleit Brigade, five miles west of Andenne. From here the line then turned westward, following the Meuse to Namur, then south, still on the right bank of the river, to Dinant. The line then went southeastward to Libramont, then generally eastward—a few miles south of Bastogne—to reach the Sauer River, where the American 4th Division continued to hold the southern shoulder of the penetration.

Late on December 22 General Manteuffel looked at the situation map in his command post, just outside of Bastogne. His eye followed the trace of the penetration on the map, while his ears were acutely conscious of heavy firing to the south.

"It looks like a fishhook," he said to his chief of staff. "A fishhook lodged deep in the Allied mouth. But it will do us no good. The jaws are clamping down on us, and I fear they will chew us up, then spit us out."

Manteuffel was right. He and his men were not easily spit out, but as the Allied jaws closed, with most of the pressure coming initially from the south—intensive attacks by the Third Army's III and XII corps—slowly the German tide receded. By January 16, one month after the start of the German offensive, the Fifth and Sixth Panzer Armies were almost back to their starting lines. But in that month they had suffered 200,000 casualties and lost nearly 1,000 tanks. These losses, combined with the consumption of irreplaceable fuel, meant that the German Reich could no longer hope to hold the Western Front once the Allies resumed the offensive.

Afterword

The above account is historically accurate until nearly midnight on December 17, after the German offensive had been raging for two days. In actual fact, Hitler repeatedly refused recommendations from Rundstedt, Model, and Jodl to release the II SS Panzer Corps to Manteuffel's Fifth Panzer Army. That crucial negative decision assured German defeat.

But suppose, the historian asks himself, Hitler had approved the request, and that the fortunes of war had favored the Germans? What would have been the result? There can be little question that the result as described in this chapter would not have been much different. The Germans would have moved somewhat faster. General McAuliffe would not have had the opportunity to say "Nuts!" to the German demand for the surrender of Bastogne. The penetration might well have taken the shape of a fishhook, rather than a bulge. But the Germans would have been stopped, in a fashion not much different from the actual historical events. Allied defensive strength was too great, and the Germans would still have literally and figuratively run out of gas.

From the outset, Rundstedt, Model, and Patton had all been right. A German success had been impossible, under the most favorable of conditions.

Epilogue

THERE ARE SOME useful, as well as interesting, lessons to be drawn from the chapters in this book, which show how the course of events in World War II could have been changed, in some instances dramatically, had a few key men made some different decisions from those that actually were made.

I have prepared a table (See Table 4) to help analyze these lessons. It shows not only some basic facts about the battles, but also the effect upon history if the facts had been altered as suggested.

First, we can see that historically three of the ten battles were actually Axis victories, while seven were Allied successes. The Axis forces were attacking in all three of their successes.

Of the Allied victories, two were gained in the attack posture, and five were achieved on the defensive. Thus, overall, five of the battles were offensive successes, five were defensive victories.

In five of the battles—including all three of those won by the Axis—the historical outcome would not have been expected on the basis of an objective pre-battle assessment of the circumstances and the forces available to each side. In other words, in those five instances, the historical outcome was the result of exceptionally brilliant performance by the winner, or of blunders committed by the loser.

Now, then, how did the changed decisions suggested in the chapters actually affect the outcome?

In six of these battles we have suggested that a different course of action by the attacker would have increased his chances of success (in one case, would have resulted in a greater success), and in four battles we have shown how a different decision would have helped the defenders. For the five battles in which the historical outcomes were unexpected, we showed what would have happened either if the actual winner's brilliance was matched by the historical loser, or if the historical loser did not commit the blunders which had cost him the battle. In all five of these cases the outcome was changed by the changed decision; in other words, in these cases the outcome was changed back to what might have been expected with all other things being equal.

In the other five cases, changed decisions were postulated for the attacker in four cases, but in only one of these instances was the outcome changed. In the one other case (Normandy) where the defender changed his decisions, the outcome was also changed. All in all, different decisions by attacker or defender resulted in different outcomes in seven of the battles, but in three cases the changed decisions were not enough to win battles in which the odds had been against the loser from the beginning.

And how did the changed decisions and the changed battle outcomes affect the course of the war?

We suggest that in only one case—the Ardennes in 1940—would the change in battle outcome have significantly affected the outcome of the war. In six other cases the immediate course of the war would have been slightly affected, but would have been significantly altered in only three of these, and in none of these cases do we believe it likely that the long-term outcome would have been changed.

What conclusions can be drawn from this?

In the first place, it is clear that a crucial decision can change the course of history. But it is also clear that the

TABLE 4
The Results of Changes in Command Options

	The Historical Outcome								Results of Option Change			
	Victor				Outcome Predictable?		Why Not Predictable		Battle Outcome Changed		Course of War Changed?	
	Allies	Axis	Atkr	Dfdr	Y	N	Due to Winner's Brilliance	Due to Loser's Blunder	Y	N	Yes	No
Ardennes 1940		X	X			X	X	[1]	X		X	
Britain	X			X		X		X	X		X	
Barbarossa		X	X			X		X	X		X	
Moscow	X			X	X					X	[2]	
Pearl Harbor		X	X			X	[3]		X		X	
Midway	X			X		X	X	[4]	X			X
Stalingrad	X			X	X					X		X
Rome	X		X		X	[6]				[5]	X	
Normandy	X		X		X				X		X	
Ardennes 1944	X			X	X					X		X [7]

Remarks
(1) Although Allied performance was not outstanding, the win resulted more from German brilliance than Allied blunders.
(2) The implications of a German victory at Moscow must remain a guess because of the effects such a victory might have had on internal Soviet politics, civilian morale, and numerous other considerations affecting both sides.
(3) Japanese performance was brilliant, and luck favored the Japanese; but they could not have succeeded without American blunders.
(4) Japanese performance was mediocre, but American brilliance won the battle.
(5) The course of the battle was changed even though the outcome was not changed and, as a result, the war was significantly shortened, though again the outcome was not altered.
(6) Despite German preparations and fortifications, air and naval superiority assured a decided advantage to Allied forces.
(7) The Allies probably would have persevered to ultimate victory even had they been driven off the Normandy beaches. However, they might have negotiated if Hitler had been overthrown.

course of history is a powerful current that is not easily diverted. Sometimes the forces involved—geographical, numerical, industrial, technological—have so predetermined the outcome that not even the most brilliant or imaginative decisions or actions could change the inevitable outcome. Examples of this are to be found in the chapters on "Moscow," "Stalingrad," and "Ardennes, 1944."

In other cases, historical successes had been achieved by boldness and initiative which brought about success—sometimes spectacular—in battles that the Duke of Wellington might have called "close-run things." In other words, had the victor's boldness and imagination been matched by a stronger reaction on the part of the opponent, the outcome would almost certainly have been substantially different. In these instances the apparently inevitable current of history seems to have been disrupted more abruptly by the shock of the actual event than would have happened in the case of almost any reasonable alternative. Examples of this can be found in the actual historical outcomes of "Ardennes, 1940," "Barbarossa," and "Pearl Harbor." In these cases history was stranger than fiction.

One interesting insight that emerges is that history not only has its long-range currents, but it can also have its short-term tides. The Battle of Midway, for instance, seemingly should have gone one way, but actually went the other. Given the forces involved, and the other circumstances, the Americans should not have won the battle. But, even if the Japanese had made no serious errors—in which case they would almost certainly have prevailed at the time, despite the most inspired American efforts—this would probably not have changed the eventual outcome of the war. The long-term current of history was against the Japanese, even though they might have been able to take advantage of one of its local tides at Midway, just as they had already been able to do at Pearl Harbor.

The course of history's current was also probably inevitably set against Hitler's Third Reich. In this regard the chapters in this book which change a German defeat into victory (Normandy), and some victories into defeats (Ardennes, 1940 and Barbarossa) need to be compared with some German defeats that remained defeats (Moscow, Stalingrad, and Flanders, 1944). These remained defeats either despite different German decisions or because of a different Allied decision (Rome, 1944). Nevertheless, it is not nearly so clear that Germany was as inevitably doomed to defeat as was Japan. German defeats at Stalingrad and Ardennes, 1944 were almost unavoidable, as our chapters show. The Battle of Moscow, however, was more of a fairly "close-run thing," and it does not seem beyond the bounds of credibility that Hitler *could* have overthrown Stalin, or—at the very least—achieved an acceptable stalemate in the East. Furthermore, the circumstances that made defeat at Stalingrad inevitable need not have been allowed to develop, had the Germans adopted a different plan early in 1942. It would seem that Hitler had two opportunities to eke out victory in the East, in 1941 and 1942. Although they were not tremendous opportunities, it would certainly appear that they were as good as the opportunities that *were* seized and exploited in Ardennes, 1940, and in the first few months of Barbarossa. He booted both chances.

Thus, Germany just *might* have been able to change the course of history's current in Europe in World War II more fundamentally than was the actual case. The reason for this slender possibility, of course, was the exceptional capability of Hitler's war machine. But it would not have been easy. The odds were against it. And, fortunately for the Allies and, we think, for humanity, Hitler had a proclivity for contributing to the length of the odds.

We hope you enjoyed our game—and learned as much from it as we did.

Appendix

An Introduction to
Military Historical Analysis

IN THE EPILOGUE we suggest that this book was produced
as a kind of game played with the facts of history. Nevertheless, you, the reader, by joining with the authors in the
game, have also been participating in a more serious by-
product of history: military historical analysis.

The future of our nation just may depend upon real-life
application of the "might-have-been" kind of military historical analysis found in this book to the military problems of our time. Thus you may be interested in seeing
how this kind of analysis can be done. I will use as an
example the 1940 Flanders Campaign, that is the subject
of the first chapter.

The Analytic Methodology of Clausewitz

First, I suggest that we use the methodology proposed
by Carl von Clausewitz in his Law of Numbers:

> "If we . . . strip the engagement of all the variables arising from
> its purpose and circumstances, and disregard [or strip out] the
> fighting value of the troops involved (which is a given quantity),
> we are left with the bare concept of the engagement . . . in which
> the only distinguishing factor is the number of troops on either
> side.

"These numbers, therefore, will determine victory [and are] the most important factor[s] in the outcome of an engagement. . . .

"This . . . would hold true for Greeks and Persians, for Englishmen and Mahrattas, for Frenchmen and Germans."*

This analytical concept of battle outcome can be expressed mathematically as follows:

$$\text{Outcome} = \frac{\{N_r\} \cdot \{V_r\} \cdot \{Q_r\}}{\{N_b\} \cdot \{V_b\} \cdot \{Q_b\}}$$

Where: N = numbers of troops
V = all variable circumstances affecting a force in battle
Q = quality (fighting value) of troops
r = Red force identifier
b = Blue force identifier

Soviet Concept of the Correlation of Forces

To demonstrate that this approach to military historical analysis is not a musty, outdated concept of the 19th Century, quoted below is a recent official definition of the Soviet concept of "Correlation of Forces and Means," which is the heart of the current military doctrine of the Soviet armed forces:

"Correlation of forces and means is an indicator of the fighting power of opposing sides, showing the degree of superiority of one over the other. It is determined by a comparison of existing quantitative and qualitative data of opposing forces.

"An analysis of the correlation of forces permits a deeper investigation into the essence of past battles and engagements.

"It is usually calculated during preparation for battle. An estimate is made of the quantity of forces and means necessary for accomplishing missions.

"A correlation of forces was estimated during the Great Patriotic War based on the combat and numerical strength of our own forces and the enemy's. This method of calculating the correlation of forces is also useful today.

"Where combat capabilities differ significantly, estimated

*Carl von Clausewitz, On War, Book III, Chapter 8.

coefficients of comparability of combat potentials are used. The following are also taken into account: opposing organizations, training, nationality, morale and fighting qualities, armament and equipment, leadership, terrain, etc. Factors are compared with the aid of coefficients.

"Modern computers speed up computation. Changes during combat can be determined by modeling."*

It is evident that the mathematical formula we have derived for Clausewitz's Law of Numbers applies completely to the Soviet doctrine of Correlation of Forces. Where he speaks of the circumstances of the battle, they refer to a variety of factors. Where he speaks of quality of troops, they refer to differing combat capabilities. And when he refers to numbers, they speak of numerical strength.

So, let us apply the Clausewitz-Soviet analytical methodology to the 1940 Ardennes Campaign.

Allied Numerical Strengths

First, the numerical strength of the forces available to the Allies can be summarized in very aggregated figures, as follows:

Manpower:	Anglo-French	2,000,000	
	Dutch	400,000	
	Belgian	600,000	
	Total	3,000,000	
Combat aircraft		1,700	
Tanks		3,600	
Anglo-French field armies:		9	
Anglo-French divisions:			
Infantry		87	(c. 1,740,000 men)
Armored		3	(c. 60,000 men)
Fortress		13	(c. 200,000 men)
Total		103	divisions (plus about 40 Dutch and Belgian division-equivalents)

*Extract from V. I. Belyakov, *Soviet Military Encyclopedia*, 1979.

For purposes of our comparison we may arbitrarily assume that each combat aircraft is the equivalent of 100 soldiers each with his share of supporting weapons (such as mortars and artillery). Thus 1700 aircraft would have been the equivalent of 170,000 men. Similarly we may assume that each Allied tank was worth 50 men and their share of supporting weapons. This means that the 3600 tanks were the equivalent of 180,000 troops.

With the exception of the three armored divisions, the Allies allocated their tanks and planes more-or-less equally among their divisions and armies. The three armored divisions were parcelled out to the army groups.

We can now summarize the numerical strength of the Allied forces, in thousands of manpower equivalents, as follows:

Dutch	400		
Belgian	600		
French fortress troops	200		
Anglo-French field forces		Manpower:	1,800
		Aircraft:	170
		Tanks	180
		Total	2,150
Overall Total	3350		

Since the field forces were divided among nine field armies, the strength of each army was about 240 in thousands of manpower equivalents.

German Numerical Strengths

In similar fashion we can prepare an aggregated summary of the numerical strength of the German forces:

Manpower	2,460,000
Combat aircraft	3,500
Tanks	2,576
Field armies:	8, plus a panzer group (or panzer army)

Divisions:

Infantry	104	(c. 2,080,000 men)
Panzer	10	(c. 200,000 men)
mechanized	9	(c. 180,000 men)
Total	123	divisions

We can assume that each German combat aircraft was roughly the equivalent of the Allied planes, or worth about 100 men and their share of supporting weapons. Thus the Luftwaffe force was the equivalent of 350,000 troops.

The German tanks were, on the average, inferior to those of the Allies. Thus we may assume that each tank was worth about 40 men, plus their share of supporting weapons. This was a manpower equivalent of 103,040 men.

The Germans allocated their tanks exclusively to panzer and mechanized divisions, and then combined these divisions into one panzer group (General von Kleist), and one panzer corps (General Hoth).

A summary of the numerical strength of the German forces, in thousands of manpower equivalents, is as follows:

Field armies	2,080	(or 260 per army)
Panzer group	382	
Panzer corps	101	
Luftwaffe support	350	
Total	2,913	

The breakdown of these forces by Army group is as follows:

Army Group B (2 armies plus panzer corps plus 30% airpower)	766
Army Group A (4 armies plus panzer group plus 60% airpower)	1712
Army Group C (2 armies plus 10% airpower)	595

Variable Factors

Let us next consider the variable factors that significantly affected the outcome of the battle. There were two of principal importance: defensive posture, and terrain.

On the basis of considerable analysis which has been performed by the Historical Evaluation and Research Organization (HERO) it is possible to quantify Clausewitz's dictum that "defense is the stronger form of combat." HERO analyses show that (other things being equal) a force in a hasty defensive situation has its strength multiplied by a factor of 1.3; prepared defense enhances the strength of a defender by a factor of 1.5; fortified defense has a multiplying effect of 1.6.

As to terrain, the multiplying effect (in favor of the defender) of the flat terrain of the Low Countries is about 1.1. The average multiplying effect of the mixed terrain of the Ardennes and northeastern France can be set at about 1.3.

Quality of Troops

Finally, we come to the quantification of the quality of the troops. Again we can make use of extensive analysis by HERO, which shows conclusively that the Germans were better in ground combat than the Allies by a factor of about 1.2. In other words, 100 Germans in combat units were roughly the equivalent of 120 Allies in combat units.

We now have aggregated values for all of the elements of the formula for Clausewitz's Law of Numbers (and the Soviet concept of Correlation of Forces). Let us undertake the analysis.

Overall Comparison

First, a general comparison of the opponents. The deployment is shown diagrammatically in Figure 2. In terms of a total power comparison, without consideration

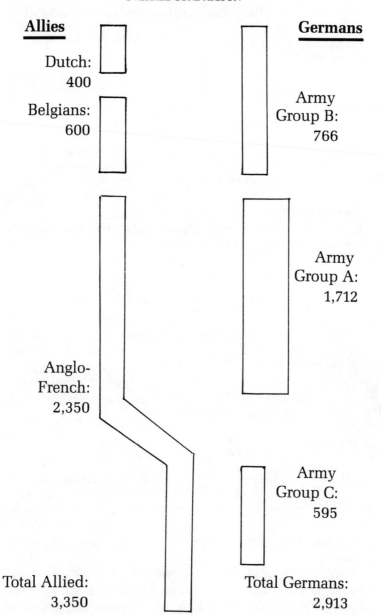

FIGURE 2
OVERALL COMPARISON

of factors, the Allies had a preponderance of 3350 to 2913, or 1.15 to 1.00.

However, when we apply the analytical methodology, that comparison is changed sharply. First let's look at a German attack. Let us assume that the overall average multiplying effect of the terrain for the defender is 1.2, and that the average Allied defense posture factor is 1.4. The formula then is:

$$\text{Outcome} = \frac{\text{German: } (2913)(1.0)(1.2)}{\text{Allies: } (3350)(1.2 \times 1.4)(1.0)} = \frac{3495.6}{5628} = \frac{1.00}{1.61}$$

The German attack is obviously stopped.

If we consider that both sides attack, then the formula gives us a slightly different result:

$$\text{Outcome} = \frac{\text{G: } (2913)(1.0)(1.2)}{\text{A: } (3350)(1.0)(1.0)} = \frac{3495.6}{3350} = \frac{1.04}{1.00}$$

There is a slight German preponderance, but in the light of the crudeness and aggregation of our comparison any preponderance of less than 1.10 must be considered as negligible. This case is clearly a standoff, particularly because whichever side is forced on the defensive will have a combat power preponderance.

The Historical Comparison

But, as we know, the Germans had no intention of making a general attack all along the line. They had massed a powerful striking force in Army Group A, in the center of their line, and planned to make a penetration through the Ardennes. This situation is shown diagrammatically in Figure 3.

The German plan and deployment requires us to analyze the battle in its three major sectors; (1) Low Countries, (2) Ardennes, and (3) Maginot Line. Let's look at each in turn:

FIGURE 3
THE ACTUAL FORCE COMPARISON

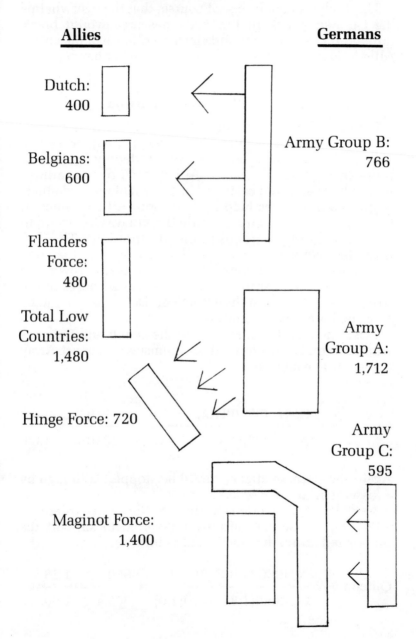

The analysis concludes, of course, that the overwhelming German attack in the Ardennes area would break through the Allied lines and cause a collapse of the entire Allied defensive effort. This is, in fact, what happened.

The Hypothetical Comparison

Figure 4 shows the deployments resulting from the hypothetical De Gaulle plan described in Chapter 1. The principal difference between these deployments and those in Figure 3 is that an Allied force of four armies would have attacked eastward just north of the Ardennes, while the hinge was held by four more Allied armies in the rugged forests. Only one Allied army was to remain to support the fortress troops in the Maginot Line. The German deployments remain unchanged, except that one German army would unexpectedly find itself thrown into a hasty defense posture by the Allied thrust north of the Ardennes. Thus, the hypothetical De Gaulle strategy gives us four areas to analyze.

First, the Low Countries. Here the Dutch and Belgians would, at first, have to fend for themselves against Army Group B. The analysis:

$$\text{Outcome} = \frac{\text{G: } (766)(1.0)(1.2)}{\text{A: } (1{,}000)(1.4 \times 1.1)(1.0)} = \frac{919.2}{1540} = \frac{1.00}{1.68}$$

Again the German attack should be stopped, although by a lesser margin.

Next the Allied offensive in the Northern Ardennes. Allowing for German airpower diverted to support the threatened army, the analysis is as follows:

$$\text{Outcome} = \frac{\text{A: } (960)(1.0)(1.0)}{\text{G: } (300)(1.3 \times 1.3)(1.0)} = \frac{960}{608.4} = \frac{1.58}{1.00}$$

FIGURE 4
HYPOTHETICAL DE GAULLE PLAN

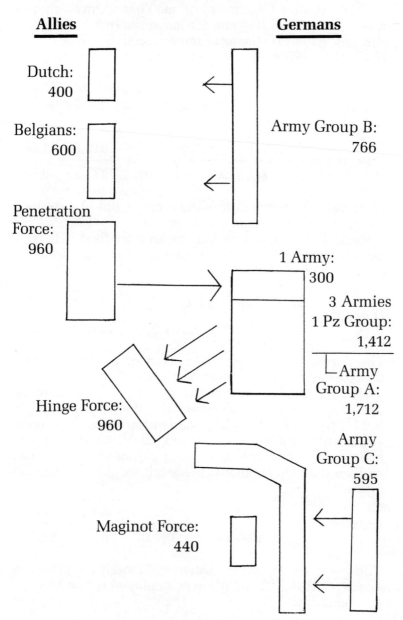

First, the Low Countries region. There Army Group B was to make a holding attack against the Dutch, Belgians, and any Allied forces advancing into Belgium and Holland. Three Allied armies actually moved into Belgium, but only two were very briefly in contact with Army Group B. The Allied posture was a combination of hasty and prepared defense. The analysis (using the Clausewitz formula) is as follows:

$$\text{Outcome} = \frac{\text{G: } (766)(1.0)(1.2)}{\text{A: } (1480)(1.4 \times 1.1)(1.0)} = \frac{919.2}{2279.2} = \frac{1.00}{2.48}$$

Obviously the German holding attack would be stopped under these circumstances.

Next, the Ardennes region. Again the Allied defensive posture would have been between hasty and prepared defense. The analysis:

$$\text{Outcome} = \frac{\text{G: } (1712)(1.0)(1.2)}{\text{A: } (720)(1.4 \times 1.3)(1.0)} = \frac{2054.4}{1310.4} = \frac{1.57}{1.00}$$

The German preponderance of combat power assured a breakthrough, which in fact occurred.

Finally, the Germans never had any intention of attempting a bloody, and essentially doomed, assault on the Maginot Line. All they wanted to do was to demonstrate with sufficient vigor to hold the Allied forces in and behind the fortifications as long as possible. Had they really attempted an attack, the result would have been as follows:

$$\text{Outcome} = \frac{\text{G: } (595)(1.0)(1.2)}{\text{A: } (1400)(1.6 \times 1.3)(1.0)} = \frac{714}{2912} = \frac{1.00}{4.08}$$

This comparison demonstrates most clearly the appalling waste of Allied (French) forces deployed in the Maginot Line area.

This obviously would result in a clearcut Allied break-through.

Next, the German main effort of Army Group A, against four Allied armies holding the Ardennes hinge. The analysis:

$$\text{Outcome} = \frac{\text{G: } (1412)(1.0)(1.2)}{\text{A: } (960)(1.4 \times 1.3)(1.0)} = \frac{1694.4}{1747.2} = \frac{1.00}{1.03}$$

The German attack would clearly have been stopped, despite their preponderance in numbers and combat effectiveness. The Allies, making use of the terrain, and in mixed hasty and prepared defenses, would not have been overrun as they were in fact in 1940.

Finally, although there would still have been no reason for the Germans to try to break through the formidable Maginot Line, the following analysis shows that they could not have done so:

$$\text{Outcome} = \frac{\text{G: } (595)(1.0)(1.2)}{\text{A: } (440)(1.6 \times 1.3)(1.0)} = \frac{714}{915.2} = \frac{1.00}{1.28}$$

Conclusion

The above analysis clearly demonstrates why the proposed De Gaulle plan of Chapter 1 would have been successful.

It may also suggest to the reader how he can do his own military historical analysis. Or you can ask HERO to do it for you.